GIAP

GIAP

THE VICTOR IN VIETNAM

Peter Macdonald

W. W. NORTON & COMPANY

NEW YORK   LONDON

The text of this book is composed in 11/14½ New Caledonia
with the display set in Univers Extra Black Expanded
Composition and Manufacturing by the Haddon Craftsmen Inc.
Book design by Beth Tondreau Design

Library of Congress Cataloging-in-Publication Data
Macdonald, Peter G., 1928–
Giáp:the victor in Vietnam / by Peter Macdonald.
p.   cm.
Includes bibliographical references.
1. Võ, Nguyên Giáp, 1911– . 2. Generals—Vietnam—Biography.
3. Vietnam. Quân đôi nhân dân—Biography. I. Title.
DS560.72.V6M33, 1993
959.704′3′092—dc20
[B]   92-7042

ISBN 0-393-03401-1

W. W. Norton & Company, Inc., 500 Fifth Avenue, New York, N.Y. 10110
W. W. Norton & Company Ltd., 10 Coptic Street, London WC1A 1PU

1   2   3   4   5   6   7   8   9   0

CONTENTS

6 Contents

LIST OF
ILLUSTRATIONS

For a' that and a' that,
It's coming yet for a' that,
That man to man, the warld o'er,
Shall brothers be for a' that.

—ROBERT BURNS
1759–96

CHAZAUD

C H I N A

T O N K I N

Red R.

Day R.

Dien Bien Phu

Hanoi

Haiphong

Gulf of

Tonkin

HAINAN

L A O S

Vientiane

Mekong R.

Vinh

VIETNAM

A N N A M

17th Parallel
Partition Line, July 1954

Hue

Da Nang
(Tourane)

T H A I L A N D

Bangkok

C A M B O D I A

Phnom Penh

Mekong R.

Saigon

Gulf

of

Thailand

COCHINCHINA

S O U T H   C H I N A   S E A

| 0 | 100 | 200 | 300 | 400 km |

| 0 | 100 | 200 | 300 miles |

INDOCHINA

GIAP

CHAPTER ONE

YOUTH

In a process of persistent, heroic, intelligent, and creative struggle to conquer nature, transform society, and defeat foreign aggressors, our nation has developed remarkable strength and has built a civilization with enormous vitality.

—VO NGUYEN GIAP

Vietnam is not a big country. From north to south, along its coastline on the South China Sea, it is about 1,000 miles long. At its widest point—in the north—it is about 350 miles; at its narrowest—in the center—only 30, and in the south about 150. Its total area is just under 130,000 square miles. France is more than twice the size but half its length: inverted on the Atlantic coast of Europe, Vietnam would stretch from the middle of Denmark down to the Spanish border; at its widest, from Amsterdam to Leipzig; in the center, inland only as far as Rouen; in the south from the coast to Toulouse. In the 1950s France had more than twice the population. In the 1960s the United States had seven times as many people as Vietnam; and it is twenty-eight times as big. On its east coast, Vietnam would stretch from New York to Palm Beach, as far inland as Lake Erie in the north, in the center a few miles inland from Wilmington and in the south across Florida to Tampa. Put another way, Vietnam is about as long as California but at the most only half as wide.

Quang Binh province is in the narrowest part of Vietnam, in what used to be known as Annam. Three years before the Great War started, on 28 August 1911, a child was born in An Xa village in that province, near to the 17th Parallel; that is, seventeen degrees north of the Equator. Not many people change the course of history, but that child grew to be someone who did, a man whose name became known throughout the world as the victorious general whose primitive army defeated two great Western powers: Vo Nguyen Giap.

In the mid 1950s Giap's brilliantly fought battle of Dien Bien Phu resulted in French withdrawal from Indochina and greatly hastened the collapse of the pre-World War II European empires: by 1960 dozens of new nations had come into existence in Asia, Africa, and America, completely altering the political alignments of the world. In the 1960s, as commander in chief of the People's Army of the Democratic Republic of Vietnam, Giap brought about the political defeat of the United States in South Vietnam by armed force: the most powerful nation in the world became morally confused, militarily confounded, and financially embarrassed—and withdrew ignominiously from a commitment it had sustained for more than twenty years. In the 1970s as defense minister Giap laid the foundations for the unification of his nation.

That the army of a small, poverty-stricken, industrially backward nation could defeat two world powers was remarkable, but then the man who played such a large part in it is himself remarkable. In his youth he showed great intelligence and enormous vitality; in later years he would demonstrate quite exceptional powers of leadership and organization. In the second half of the twentieth century, he became a man unique in military annals: a general who was in supreme command of a nation's army for thirty years. Starting with thirty-four soldiers, he ended up commanding nearly a million. And at the end of it all he remained undefeated.

Equally remarkably, throughout his life Vo Nguyen Giap (pronounced Vo—with a short "o" as in cot—Nwin Ziap: the Ziap means "armor") has combined politics with soldiering. He was a Communist Party activist long before becoming a soldier: in 1946 he became minister for the interior in Ho Chi Minh's first administration and then, in the 1960s and into the mid 1970s, was deputy prime minister and minister for defense, as well as holding other government and Party appointments. At the age of eighty he was still a deputy chairman of the Council of Ministers. In his own country he is a revered elder statesman and soldier; abroad he is a man who, to many people, has more personal prestige than any other politico/military figure anywhere in the world.

So much has changed since the beginning of the second decade of this century that it is difficult to imagine what An Xa could have been like in 1911. Essentially, though, it had not changed for centuries. Apart from the cities of Hanoi and Saigon, both with populations of around two hundred thousand, and the provincial capitals with their tens of thousands, populated Vietnam consisted of about five thousand small villages, some of them clusters of hamlets, nearly all of them in the irrigated plains on either side of the two great rivers, the Red in the north and the Mekong in the south.

The villages grew around groups of farmhouses built near water—a river, a stream, or a well—with rice paddies radiating out from the center into the countryside. Around the farms lived the people who provided for the landowners and tenant-farmers, and for each other as the population grew. The most powerful person was the mandarin—a spiritual as well as an administrative leader. (In some places the mandarin was of the second class and had less prestige than one in more important places.) There were also artisans, shopkeepers, and laborers who worked the land. Most villagers lived in small houses built of mud and bamboo, with roofs of palm leaves or grass, and slept on thin reed mattresses on the ground.

Every village was surrounded by a thick bamboo fence, the gate of which was barred at sunset, with no one allowed access until daylight. "The emperor's word stops at the fence," it was said, for inside, law was enacted and administered by the elders, an elected body of the most respected men. In each village there was a shrine and a temple. Dogs and cats, water buffalo, cattle, pigs, rats, mice, fleas, ticks, chickens, ducks, and geese shared the site with the human population, and perhaps some caged birds. There was no electricity, so no light after dark except from oil lamps. No running water, only that brought in pails from stream or well. The houses had dirt floors, or wooden floors if they were built on stilts to raise them above possible flood-water level. There were dirt paths between the houses, and along them piles of stinking ordure, human and animal, heaped up ready to be used for fertilizing the fields. There was unending hard work, dismal poverty, and poor food. But also order, organization, welfare for the old and poor, family life, feast days, fun, laughter. And An Xa was a peaceful place; no one then could have dreamed that in the boy's lifetime it would be burned to the ground by the French and later destroyed by American bombs.

Vo Nguyen Giap's father, a *lettré*, a scholar of local distinction, was a mandarin of the second class but poor; as Giap puts it, "I came from a poor family of farmers." His house was better than some, but everyone in the village lived at a basic subsistence level. Today, the average income of a Vietnamese is the equivalent of U.S. $160 a year. Eighty years ago, in buying power, it would have been perhaps about the same. There was not much to buy anyway, then or now. People ate—with chopsticks—rice mostly, flavored with spices, fish sometimes (An Xa was not far from the sea), meat hardly ever—and then usually pork or a fowl. Once a year, at Tet, the time of the lunar new year, there was feasting and revelry that went on for days. Otherwise, apart from weddings, there was a year of looking forward to Tet, for which people hoarded food and beer and rice wine.

Mandarins did not inherit their authority; it was attained by passing written and oral examinations that were held every three
months in the provincial capitals. Following a form of administration
evolved in China centuries before and brought south by their forebears, Vietnamese mandarins were recruited by examining the most
intelligent young men in the towns and villages in the Confucian
classics of religion and history, mathematics and music. Anyone
could become a mandarin, but because the sons of the educated
usually learned more than the sons of illiterate peasants it was they
who passed the tests and consolidated their families' positions in
society. Most of the leaders of Vietnam since 1945 have been men
and women who came from that small educated minority.

Buddhism was the base religion in young Giap's home, but, as in
many Asian countries, people believed whichever aspects of the
three great Eastern religions, Confucianism, Taoism, and Buddhism,
gave them the greatest comfort. So it was that the Confucian ethics
of strict observance of social codes, good manners, respect for age
and experience, and veneration of ancestors were the daily coinage
of life in An Xa.

Giap's father had long been actively involved in nationalist politics, having played a part in uprisings against the French in 1885 and
1888. Unwaveringly maintaining his antipathy to French colonialism, and having already sown the seeds of bitter dissent in his small
son's mind, his life came to an end when he was arrested for subver-
sive activities in 1919 and after a few weeks died in prison.

Vo Nguyen Giap had two sisters and was the elder of two sons.
Soon after his father's death one of his sisters was also arrested.
Though not detained for long, she became ill as a result of the deadly
privations of prison life and died a few weeks after being released.
Two forced family deaths had occurred before he was ten years old.

As a little boy, the young Giap was taught at home by his father
before going to the village school. Then, showing himself to be
precociously intelligent, he went to the district school. His feet on
the ladder, in 1924, when he was thirteen years old, he left home to
attend the provincial school in Hue. Bidding good-bye to his
mother—"with tears in my eyes," he says—he enrolled in the
French-administered school known as the Lycée National. From

then on, French became his second language. (Indeed, it was the official language of the nation until 1954, and anyone aspiring to any position of authority had to speak and write it.) As time passed, despite his intense dislike of colonialism, he grew to admire French culture and learning; French authors are among his favorites.

Hue, an ancient human habitation on the banks of the Song Huong, or Perfumed, River, was the old capital of Vietnam. It was a city of fortresses and government buildings, a thriving center of administration and trade. In 1802 the Emperor Gia Long had built a citadel there, with deep moats and large gates, the focal point of the royal capital. At its center was the Forbidden City. A few decades later an iron bridge designed by Eiffel spanned the river.

The lycée that Giap attended had been founded by a Roman Catholic mandarin by the name of Ngo Dinh Kha, father of someone who, like Giap, was to become world-famous: Ngo Dinh Diem, from 1955 to 1963 the president of South Vietnam. As a youth he had attended his father's school, as had another young man—also the son of a mandarin—then known by his given name of Nguyen Sinh Cung. In 1943 he decided he wanted to be known as Ho Chi Minh, The One Who Enlightens.

During 1924 and 1925, with other youngsters, Giap began to take part in clandestine nationalist activities. He it was who, showing early on his energy and talent for organization, was appointed to coordinate the revolutionary activities of his fellow pupils, in his own and other Hue schools. However, these activities did not go unnoticed, and by the time he was thirteen he was on the files of the Sûreté, the French security service. Aware of the underground anticolonial groups that had existed ever since the French arrived in Vietnam, and had grown in numbers and strength over the years, the Sûreté maintained lists of those who showed themselves publicly during demonstrations, and paid informers to expose those who did not.

Two years later the lycée could no longer tolerate Giap's disruptive activities, and he was banished for taking part in a "quit-school" protest. He went home to An Xa, and while there, undeterred—

indeed having become even more convinced of his commitment to a free Vietnam—and with the encouragement of a local politician, Nguyen Chi Dieu, joined the Tan Viet Cach Meng Dang nationalists, an underground group that had been founded in Annam in 1924.

Though overtly nationalist, the Tan Viet also leaned to communism, and among other pamphlets Giap was given was one entitled "Colonialism on Trial," by someone called Nguyen Ai Quoc, a name he had known from his earliest days in Hue when, aged thirteen, he visited a learned old man, Pham Boi Chau, who was under permanent house arrest for seditious activities. Giap recalls how, wanting solitude in order to concentrate, he climbed into the branches of a tree to read the tracts. The Marxist theories expounded by Quoc changed his life, for they promised a fair, just, and classless society— "the possibility of happiness for all mankind," as he puts it. From being a nationalist, he became a communist.

An Xa, small, sleepy, remote, was no place for him, and soon he persuaded the authorities to allow him to return to school in Hue. There, at a time of great social turmoil, he continued his political activities. This time, though, he overstepped the mark, was arrested for leading student demonstrations, and was sentenced to two years' imprisonment. He was released after only three months because, he says, there was not enough evidence against him.

The next year, despite his reputation as a troublemaker, he was allowed to attend the Lycée Albert Sarraut in Hanoi, named after a former colonial governor. The school ran a special class in philosophy, which he studied for a year. While there, by nature a smiling, courteous person, he was described by one of his teachers as "a charming youth, eagerly searching for truth." And he was determined to succeed: after a year he obtained a baccalaureate, the certificate necessary to obtain entry to university.

To an American or Western European child, passing such an examination or its equivalent is a notable achievement. In those days for a Vietnamese it was a thousand times more so, for in the 1930s about 80 percent of Vietnamese were illiterate. Only 10 percent of children received any schooling—only 4 percent of those beyond the primary grade. Between 1883, when the French arrived, and 1945, in the whole of Indochina (that is, Vietnam plus Laos and Cambodia), only 14,393 children gained the Diploma of Higher Primary Education. A few very exceptional young Vietnamese were allowed to go to one of the three lycées in the country that educated the children of French administrators. Between 1918 and 1939, 827 obtained a baccalaureate. In the twenty-five years to 1945, around 3,000 Vietnamese students attended the only university in the nation, in Hanoi. Of that number 229 doctors, 337 engineers, 160 teachers, and 408 lawyers graduated. Giap was one of the lawyers, and in July 1937 he was awarded a degree in law and political economics. In the same year he joined the Indochinese Communist Party, the ICP, which had just been founded by a representative of the French Communist Party sent to Saigon for that purpose.

While studying at the university, he had taken lodgings with Professor Dang Thai Minh, whose daughter, Nguyen Thi Minh Giang, he had first met at school in Hue, where she was one of the youngsters who took part in revolutionary activities. She too had learned her nationalism from her father, and she too, like Giap, had decided that the right way to pursue it was to promote the communist faith. In June 1938 they were married. Together, though young, they both quickly became established as among the top ten leaders of the Indochinese Communist Party.

By 1938 Giap was writing for the revolutionary newspapers *Tin Tuc* (The News), *Nhan Dan* (The People), *Notre Voix* (Our Voice), and *Les Travail* (The Workers). (In later years it became known to him that several articles that appeared in those papers under the name of P. Lin had been written by Ho Chi Minh.) Also, with a man called Truong Chinh—who was to become another leader of Vietnamese communism—he wrote (under the pseudonym Van Dinh) a short treatise called "The Peasant Problem." But there was a price to pay for all these commitments: Giap failed to pass the examination for the Certificate of Administrative Law. Unable to practice, and needing money to support his family—a daughter, Hong Ahn, had been born in May 1939—he took employment as a teacher of history at the Thang Long Private School in Hanoi.

Giap's sister-in-law was also a revolutionary. In the late 1930s she had gone to Russia to study communism. On her return to Saigon she too was arrested, imprisoned, tried, and sentenced to death—and shot, Giap says, not guillotined, as was the usual French method of execution. Now there had been three forced deaths in the family, all attributable, in Giap's mind, to French colonialism.

An ardent patriot, Giap made a special study of the long wars of resistance against the Chinese, who had repeatedly invaded Vietnam over the centuries. An admirer of heroic deeds, he eloquently described Napoleon's achievements and victories. He had studied his campaigns in great detail and accompanied his rapid-fire dissertations with blackboard diagrams showing the dispositions of Napoleon's armies on the battlefields. In later years many of Giap's students remembered the clarity and fervor of those lectures.

Giap had also diligently studied Lenin, Marx, Engels, and Mao Tse-tung. In the writings of the first three, he found what he believed to be the ideological basis for the new social system that was to replace all the old injustices with a bright new egalitarianism; in Maoist theories he found the military means by which to bring it into existence. In addition, as he was to tell the French general Raoul Salan many years later, he read *The Seven Pillars of Wisdom* by the British Great War soldier T. E. Lawrence, Lawrence of Arabia, learning from it practical examples of how to apply minium military force to maximum tactical and strategic effect. He was also much impressed by Lawrence's belief in the importance of the individual.

Giap's studies had made him fervently idealistic. As with so many young people of the time, East and West, who were concerned to find a cure for the ills of the world, he had turned to communism as the means of salvation. Then, it had a profound appeal: for some because it would end the exploitation of workers that the industrial revolution had created; for some because they preferred it to fascism; for others because the Russian revolution was said to be working miracles. As one visitor to Russia had put it, "I have seen the future, and it works!" Communist theories appealed to man's generous and noble nature, to the best rather than the worst in people. To many people, it seemed there was a new dawn on the horizon for mankind. Giap was one of them.

By the time he is in his late twenties, the picture of Giap that emerges is one of a pleasant, highly intelligent, dynamic, and very articulate young man who by virtue of his personality and quickness of thought tended to dominate the company he kept. These attributes would not change over the years, though as time passed and he gained more authority, he became increasingly verbally aggressive, pressing home any advantage, smothering any opposition. For all that, he was patient—prepared to await developments rather than take precipitate action. He was prepared to listen to another point of view if it was convincingly and logically presented. And he was careful not to push an argument to the point where reaction to it became in itself an obstacle to the achievement of the desired aim. This balancing of forcefulness and caution was to bring him success in war and politics in the years to come.

CHAPTER TWO

GESTATION

Our objective was national independence and socialism—rice fields for the farmers. Before, we had leaders who talked about indepen- dence, but they did not give the rice fields to the farmers and so they could not motivate them. It was my belief that socialism would moti- vate the farmers and the workers.

—VO NGUYEN GIAP TO THE AUTHOR

After the signing of the Nazi/Soviet pact in 1939, the Com- munist Party in France was banned. In Vietnam the ad- ministration followed the lead given by the metropolitan govern- ment and began to round up known members of the Party. Giap was in danger of arrest, and it was decided by the leaders of the ICP that he should leave Vietnam. On 3 May 1940, beside the Ho Hoan Kiem lake in Hanoi, the Lake of the Restored Sword, he said good-bye to his wife, "Comrade Thi," as he called her, and to his infant daughter. Then, with a man four years his senior by the name of Pham Van Dong, another leading member of the Party, he left Hanoi riding in a rickshaw pulled by a trusted friend. A few miles away he and Pham Van Dong boarded a train and went north to Cao Bang province, and thence across the border into China, sometimes hiding in the toilets to avoid the guards who roamed the corridors. (Two broad-gauge steam railways had been built by the French in Indochina, one from Hanoi to Saigon, the other from Haiphong to Kunming, via Hanoi. By 1903 the railroad had traversed the Red River delta, and by 1906 it had reached the Chinese border, but it took another four years and many lives to penetrate the difficult mountainous region beyond it and reach Kunming.) An Annamese like Giap and Ho Chi Minh, Pham Van Dong had been imprisoned for revolutionary activities when he was twenty-four. The destinies of these three men who were to rule Vietnam for three decades were drawing together as two of them rode northward into China, where Ho Chi Minh was working with Mao Tse-tung's communists. Giap's wife went to her family home in Vinh, in Nghe An province in central Vietnam, where she was arrested, tried, sentenced to fifteen years' imprisonment, and transferred to the Hoa Lo Central Prison in Hanoi.

In June 1940, in Kunming in China, Giap, aged twenty-nine, met Ho Chi Minh for the first time. With Pham Van Dong he had waited in a park to meet a man who had made contact with the people with whom they were staying. He recalls that for some reason as soon as he saw him, a person of quiet and modest demeanor, wearing simple clothes, he knew that this must be Nguyen Ai Quoc, whose writings had so influenced him.

There seems to have been no question in his or anyone else's mind, then or later, that this man should be the leader of their independence movement. Ho had spent his whole adult life working for communist ideals. He had been imprisoned for his beliefs by the British in Hong Kong, and by the Chinese several times. His writings had been circulated widely, and his name was known throughout revolutionary movements in the East. But most of all he had a quiet charisma—"a very special humanism," Giap calls it—and a sureness of belief and intention that quickly brought people under his spell. Giap was much impressed by his simplicity of life-style and directness; and, too, by his "concrete and cautious" style of thinking and working, a style he was to adopt as best he could (for by nature he was impetuous) and which was to guide his own conduct, in politics and military matters, throughout the years to come. One of the first principles taught by Ho was that political action was more important than military action; the motivation of the masses must be the first priority: from that would stem all political and military success. It was a principle Giap subscribed to totally.

Because of his lack of formal training, it was Ho Chi Minh's intention that Giap should study at the Institute of Marxism-Leninism in Yenan in China, but two weeks after he set off to go there, in June 1940, the Germans captured Paris. With Indochina left without centralized control from metropolitan France, Ho Chi Minh foresaw the big change that must come in Vietnamese affairs and recalled Giap from Kweilin, which he had reached on his journey. With Pham Van Dong he went to Chingshi in China. There, Giap—whose alias at the time was Duong Huai-nan—learned to speak and write Chinese and also studied the strategy and tactics of the Communist Chinese army, putting what he learned into print in a pamphlet called "Chinese Military Affairs."

After the fall of France to Nazi Germany, under threat from the expansionist policies of the Japanese, on the other side of the world from the motherland, and with only ten thousand soldiers under their command, the French colonial administration in Hanoi allowed the Japanese to occupy the north of the country and during the next year to take over the south.

Japan had entered into an alliance with Germany and Italy, the so-called Axis. With France vanquished by the German army, its colonial possessions went into limbo for a time until the Vichy regime was established. When it took control, pledged to collaborate, it allowed the Japanese to "protect" Indochina. Though in theory the French administration in Hanoi continued to direct affairs, based on edicts emanating from distant Vichy, effectively the Japanese were an occupying power, with significant numbers of troops stationed in the country.

In May 1941 at the Eighth Congress of the Indochinese Communist Party, held at Pac Bo in northern Vietnam, Ho Chi Minh and his associates decided to form an organization of patriots—"peasants, workers, merchants, and soldiers"—which would strive for the independence of Vietnam. Called the Viet Nam Doc Lap Dong Minh, the Vietnam Independence League—its military component was to become known as the Vietminh.

During long hours of conversation, Giap had impressed Ho Chi Minh with his depth of knowledge about military history. That and his eager and dominant personality made him, in Ho's eyes, the man who might take up the sword on behalf of the revolutionary movement. But, as ever cautious, Ho decided that he must prove himself by work among the people. Thus it was that Giap spent much of 1941 establishing an intelligence network and organizing political bases in Cao Bang province, in the most northerly part of Vietnam. By the end of the year two had been established, at Bac Son and Vu Nhai. To keep them informed, and to spread propaganda among the population, a newssheet called *Viet Nam Doc Lap* (shortened to *Viet Lap*) was produced. Giap enthusiastically wrote articles for it, but Ho Chi Minh criticized him for his verbosity, urging him to cut his submissions by half and to phrase them more simply. Giap tried hard, but his natural tendency was to make his point by repeated reiteration, and he never seemed to edit enough to please his mentor. (It seems, too, that he never took the lesson to heart, for repetition is evident in much of his writings, though it has to be said that there were times when he wrote very descriptively, even poetically.)

In 1942 Giap attended a course at Kangta, a political and guerrilla warfare school in Yenan. Then, in Kwangsi and in a complete reversal of what had happened in 1940, under threat from Chinese Nationalists, he was obliged to cross the border and take refuge in Vietnam. By mid 1942 he was in the village of Pac Bo in the Viet Bac region, less than a mile from the Chinese border (a man-made political border, for the people on either side are of the same Nung nationality). There, and in a village called Vu Nhai, near the small town of Cao Bang, almost due north of Hanoi, he and about forty key men, protected by mountain tribesmen, lived in caves. They were the true beginnings of the military army of the Vietnamese independence movement.

The Vietminh formed themselves into Party cells and worked assiduously to convert people in the area to communism. Because few of the local people spoke Vietnamese, it was necessary for Giap and his colleagues to learn local dialects and to draw pictures to explain the meaning of their words. Whenever French security force patrols approached, they temporarily changed their location, sometimes living in a cave under a waterfall, to which access was very difficult, sometimes in the region of the Man Trang people, where they drank water from streams and lived on maize and wild bananas. At one time they moved to Lam Son and lived in a house built on poles on a mountain slope.

At a conference in Liuchow in October 1942, the United Front, the Vietnam Cach Minh Dong Hoi, was founded, the aim being to draw together various nationalist factions that were vying for influence in the north of Vietnam. This was the first example of a tactic that was to be used several times by Ho Chi Minh: where there was opposition he did not waste effort and create enemies by trying to destroy it, he joined it and then took it over from within.

Ho Chi Minh was the guru leader of the movement, the asthete, the saintly man. (It seems that he had some of the attributes of a saint—according to Giap he "set an example of industry, thrift, integrity and compassion." That, to the Vietnamese, was the source of their veneration.) Giap was the action man. Perhaps triggered by having read Mao Tse-tung's belief that "people could do anything," he was convinced that their motivation was the key to success, in political and military matters. In the years to come he was to use people, their muscle and mass momentum, as the chief means by which he achieved his extraordinary successes: in mass attacks that overwhelmed the enemy; in the massive numbers of laborers needed to build roads and move the huge quantities of materiel needed to maintain the mass attacks; in the millions and millions of man- and women-hours of physical effort needed to dig trench systems and tunnels and repair damage.

Giap totally subscribed to the communist principle of proselytizing—brainwashing—people. They were to be turned around, pointed in the right direction, and then, armed in the mind and given weapons in their hands, tasked in their millions to bring down the old order, be it based on ancient national customs, colonialism, or what he was later to call "American imperialism." Everyone must be a soldier—men, women, girls, boys, old people. Everyone had to make their contribution, however insignificant, to the military effort. It was a simple concept, readily understood, that appealed to the intense national patriotism of the Vietnamese. It was not a new idea. It had been used before in the thirteenth century and repeatedly thereafter, but that was all to the good: especially in Vietnam people related to their past, to their roots.

But first things first. The key to the future was to find eager, energetic people who were well motivated. If they were already communists, so much the better. If their motivation was nationalistic and anticolonial, well and good: they could be converted to communism. Once taught, the next step would be to send them, like disciples, into the countryside to convert others. Giap began to gather around him key people, known in communist terminology as *can bo*—cadres: the strong nucleus around whom the rank and file would cluster. Quite deliberately, Ho Chi Minh had made the standards extraordinarily high. Cadres had to have high morals and not indulge in the decadent life of the exploiting classes. They had to be industrious, honest, thrifty, upright, impartial, humble, and simple. They had to have the same standard of living as the peasant.

Giap was thorough and careful in his choice, for these were the people with whom he and Ho Chi Minh and Pham Van Dong were going to have to work for years to come, who would become the leaders of a movement that was to spread throughout the nation, slowly at first, then with gathering momentum.

The theory was that cadres would congregate in a safe area and train recruits, who would form the field operating groups. They in turn would grow into larger groups that would take over territory which, as it grew in size, would become liberated zones. In these zones the people would build up their strength and then strike out at the enemy. As Giap was to write much later: "The struggle must build, however slowly. The way to win is by small defeats, one after another until the coup de grâce." He possessed the inner certainty that enabled him to bide his time and wait for the propitious moment; did not feel the pressure to achieve quick results that so often besets Westerners. It was to be one of his greatest assets in the coming decades: when other people tired of the conflict and thought only of pulling out as quickly as possible, he would remain rock-solid in his determination to achieve his aims. He took his time now, more than a year, in solidly building the foundations of the insurgency.

Under Giap's leadership the cadres studied strategy and tactics and planned their future campaigns. (During this time, when everyone had to contribute to the business of living in a community, Giap was given the task of washing dishes, his attempts at cooking having been declared a disaster. At night, unable to sleep because of the cold, he and the others would rise and warm themselves by a fire until dawn.) Classrooms—lean-to huts of bamboo roofed with leaves—and primitive living quarters were built to cater to the numbers of men who began to rally to the new cause. As well as tapping the local supply, Giap recruited men who had served in the Indochinese regiments formed by the French to help them control the country. By mid 1944 three hundred of them had been trained in Liuchow and Kwangsi in China. In the Viet Bac, fifty or more recruits were being trained at a time, the best of them retained to become instructors in their turn. By the end of 1943 several hundred men and women had joined the National Salvation Army, and at Tet in early 1944 twenty different groups came together.

It was in the summer of 1943 that Giap was told that his wife had died in the Central Prison in Hanoi—a place that many years later was to become notorious in the United States as the Hanoi Hilton, where many American prisoners of war were incarcerated. People who were with Giap at the time said that he took the news of her death impassively, the only overt sign of grief being that he wore a token of mourning for several days, but he himself told a journalist some years later that his "life had been ruined." There is little doubt that the death of his beloved young wife, perhaps more than anything else, resulted in fanaticism replacing the cold calculation that lay deep in his nature. (Their daughter had been taken to An Xa to be brought up by Vo Nguyen Giap's mother. She inherited her parents' intelligence and in course of time studied in Hanoi and became a doctor of mathematics and physics. In 1987 she won the Soviet Union's Kowolenskia Prize for science.)

Many Vietnamese believe in an extraterrestrial, astrological confluence of influences, a tide in the affairs of men known as *Thoi Co:* the right time to act, the opportune moment. As Giap puts it, "At the right time, a pawn can bring victory: at the wrong time, a bad move can lose two knights." In July 1944 Giap stated that "on the basis of the world situation, and of the revolutionary movement in the Cao Bang province, conditions are ripe for starting guerrilla warfare." Ho Chi Minh, still in China, heard of this and, perhaps rather taken aback by this presumptuous announcement, did not agree: in August, he hurriedly journeyed to Cao Bang, to be ceremonially met by Giap.

In September 1944 the first Revolutionary Party Military Conference was held. (It was chaired by Truong Chinh and the four committee members were Vo Nguyen Giap, Van Tien Dung, Le Tranh Nghi, and Tran Dan Ninh.) There it was agreed that Thoi Co had now arrived: now was the time to act. Formally, the formation of the Vietnam Liberation Army was proclaimed, with Giap as its commander. Also, based on an idea that Ho Chi Minh scribbled down on the proverbial back of a cigarette packet, it was decided to form armed propaganda teams. Though their primary task would be to proselytize, in order to defend themselves, they had to be armed. (Years later, in the 1970s, Giap was to show his belief in this mysticism by asserting that it was not, at the time, *Thoi Co* to invade Cambodia. When the time came his army did invade.)

On 22 December 1944, Vo Nguyen Giap formed the first Armed Propaganda Brigade of three teams consisting of a total of thirty-four people—thirty-one men and three women. Named the Tran Hung Doa Platoon in memory of an early Vietnamese hero, it was equipped with two revolvers, seventeen rifles, fourteen breech-loading flintlocks dating from the Russo-Japanese war, and one light machine gun. To mark this very auspicious occasion photographs were taken. One shows Giap, in bare feet, wearing a Western-style suit and a black homburg hat, with a holstered pistol belted around his waist and a map case slung over a shoulder, standing before a band of ruffians who proudly display their banners and weapons. In another he is seated in the middle of them with a guard posted in the background.

It was Ho Chi Minh who selected the people and who guided Giap in how to organize the brigade and judge its effectiveness. Using the name Colonel Nam, Giap was one of the team commanders. Another was Van Tien Dung, who was to be his chief of staff at Dien Bien Phu, and in the mid seventies was to take over from him as defense minister. The third was the mild-mannered Chu Van Tan, one of the minority Nung tribe, who eventually became a senior general in the army. The people chosen to join the "brigade" were platoon commanders, section leaders, and outstanding rank-and-file members of the local guerrilla groups.

Despite having said that their main role was not to fight, Ho Chi Minh next decreed that for propaganda purposes the unit had to win a military victory within a month of being established: on 25 December 1944 Giap led it in successful attacks against French outposts at Khai Phat and Na Ngan. Two French lieutenants were killed; the Vietnamese troops in the posts surrendered. The attacking force, which had disguised itself as French-enrolled Vietnamese levies, suffered no casualties. "We forgot that we were only thirty-four human beings," Giap wrote later. "We imagined ourselves to be an army of steel, not to be defeated by any force. Confidence, eagerness, prevailed." A few weeks later, in early 1945, Vo Nguyen Giap was wounded in the leg when his group attacked a post at Dong Mu.

In April 1945 the Armed Propaganda Brigade absorbed Chu Van Tan's Army of National Salvation, a ragtag outfit composed mostly of Tai tribesmen that had been leaderless since he was asked to join Giap and Van Tien Dung. The tempo of proselytizing increased. Other propaganda teams were formed and spread out among the people, progressively taking over more territory. As the months passed three types of military groups came into existence: main force, district guerrilla groups, and village semi-armed self-defense units. In the years to come these categories were to become the basis for organizing all Vietnamese revolutionary fighters throughout the nation.

As Giap's men moved south toward the Red River delta (he some-times rode a horse) many more units were formed. Three thousand men enrolled at Nuoc Hai alone, and by March 1945 the Vietminh had established guerrilla bases in six provinces: Coa Bang, Lang Son, Bac Thai, Tuyen Quang, Lai Chau, and Ha Giang.

On 9 March the Japanese had taken over control of the country from the Vichy French. In typical fashion they did it sneakily and brutally, arresting the senior French officers of the garrison—includ-ing the commanding officer of the 5 REI (Regiment Etranger d'In-fanterie, the 5th Battalion of the Foreign Legion)—at gunpoint after inviting them to dinner at the Metropole Hotel in Hanoi. They de-manded that all French forces should surrender and when they re-fused, attacked. On 12 March they beheaded Major General Lemonnier, the army commander in Saigon, and Camille Auphalle, the resident, having first forced them to dig their own graves. Hear-ing of this the bulk of the 5th Battalion fought their way out to China after a series of bloody encounters with the Japanese. The rest of the French, including Admiral Decuox, the head of all Vichy French forces in Vietnam, were then put in prison camps. (In doing this the Japanese unwittingly dismantled what remained of the French secu-rity system and unleashed nationalists and communists in the rural areas where the French, through the Sûreté, had maintained some control—which the Japanese had made no attempt to do.)

On 15 April 1945, Giap decided to set up war regions in the six provinces, and on 4 June the various regions were merged into one liberated zone. The numerous military units that existed became a "Liberation Army" under Giap's command, who at that time took the rank of general. By then, the Vietminh had nearly five thousand members. As with cadres, the standards set for the men and women recruited into the Vietminh were high, especially as regards their dealings with the population among whom they moved and worked. They took an oath "to respect the people, to help the people, to defend the people, to win the confidence and affection of the people, and to achieve a perfect understanding between the people and the army." Giap is quite clear about the need for such close integration between soldiers and the community: "Long-term resistance re-quired a whole system of education, a whole ideological struggle,

among the people. Without them we had no information, could neither preserve secrecy nor make surprise movements. The people
suggested strategems and acted as our guides. They found liaison
officers, hid us, protected our activities, fed us and tended our
wounded."

In May, at the Chan Pass, Giap's soldiers attacked a Japanese
post, killing all the soldiers in it. Farther south, the village of Tra
Trao in Tuyen Quang province had been selected as the site of a
new headquarters from which to make plans for the future. It was
there, from May to August 1945, that the "Deer Team," a unit of
American soldiers from the Office of Strategic Services, the precur-
sors of the Central Intelligence Agency, sent to speed the departure
of the Japanese, met Giap, who to them was known as Mr. Nan.
Soon, another unit, led by Major Allison Thomas, parachuted into
the area, to be followed by ammunition and weapons. Three hundred and fifty of Giap's soldiers were assigned to work with the OSS.
(One of them, Lieutenant Colonel Peter Dewey, was to be the first
of nearly sixty thousand Americans to die in Vietnam when his Jeep
was fired on in error by a Vietminh guard several months later.)

By a strange irony, the Americans provided the Vietminh with
their first modern weaponry and trained them to use it. Major Archi-
medes Patti, in charge of the "Deer Team," says, "Giap attacked
several Japanese outposts with our men, after they had been trained
by the Americans in the use of flamethrowers, grenade launchers,
rifles, machine guns and so on. It was combat. It was a very small
operation as far as war is concerned, but nonetheless it is true that
we worked with the Vietminh against the Japanese." In just one
month they trained about two hundred handpicked future leaders of
the Vietminh and in doing so helped to create the predicament they
were to find themselves in in the 1960s: though they gave them only
small quantities of weapons, perhaps they were enough to ensure
the Vietminh's survival at a time when it was living hand-to-mouth.
However, it is not true to say that Giap was trained by the OSS, a
myth that has gained credence in some places.

On 17 July 1945 Giap led about five hundred Vietminh in an attack on a forty-five-man Japanese post at Tam Doa; they killed eight
and captured the rest, men of the Japanese 21st Infantry Division.

On 16 August a Vietminh national congress, attended by more than sixty delegates, was held in the temple at Tan Trao. A provincial government was established, with Ho Chi Minh as president. On the seventeenth Giap's soldiers attacked and liberated the town of Thai Nguyen. His troops were now beginning to act like an organized force rather than a gang of armed men; Giap himself was starting to control them like a commander, rather than a teacher. In mid August, Giap heard that some of his soldiers were in the vicinity of the capital. On the twenty-eighth he led his men into Hanoi.

The first campaign in the struggle for the liberation of Vietnam from colonialism had ended. In their euphoria, no one could possibly have foretold just how long it would be before the war was won. And the one after that. And the one after that.

Just how great a soldier is Giap? Was he, as some think, an officer with a major's knowledge who became a general overnight? Did he find himself in a position of power without the background experience needed to be able to use his authority properly, and before he learned to do so lost thousands of men in stupid attacks? Or was he someone who had studied military matters in depth and, setting out on a new career, quickly applied the theory of warfare with astonishing practical success? Indeed, were the successes primarily his, or was he the figurehead who became famous while the people really responsible for the achievements stayed unknown? Was he a great fighting general or only a brilliant organizer and logistician? How much did he depend on other soldiers' concepts, or was he an original military thinker?

Only a knowledge of the Vietnamese people can help to answer these questions, for no general, however brilliant or fortunate, wins battles by himself. It is the nature of the population from which soldiers are enlisted, and the fervor of their motivation, that determines the success of an army.

Why was it—how was it—that the Vietnamese were to fight with such valor for so long, and to triumph over two great nations?

Understand the people, and the army is understandable. Understand the army, and the victory is explained.

CHAPTER THREE

THE BIRTH OF A NATION

There is nothing else in our history except struggle. Struggle against foreign invaders, always more powerful than ourselves, struggle against nature. Because we have nowhere else to go, we have had to fight things out where we were. After two thousand years of this our people developed a very stable nervous system. We never panic. When a new situation arises, our people say, Ah well, there it goes again!

—PHAM VAN DONG

The peculiar shape of Vietnam as a nation is due to the fact that jungle-clad mountains, largely impassable, mark its western frontiers. In the north they cup the Red River delta and form the frontier with China and Laos. In the center they curve eastward, in a few places sloping right down into the sea. Then they turn west again, tapering away in the south and marking the border with Cambodia. Along these frontiers the steaming hills are full of wild animals—tigers, elephants, deer, panthers, wild boar—and under the thick canopy of tree vegetation that keeps out the light, with swarms of malaria-carrying mosquitos. They and the jungle have kept human beings away, while in the center the mountain barrier has tended to divide people in the north from those in the south.

The source of the Red River is in China, from where it flows about eight hundred miles into the Gulf of Tonkin. Hanoi is on its banks, and Haiphong is the port at its mouth. It carries an average of 140,000 cubic feet of water per second to the ocean, an enormous volume that can increase as much as forty times in the rainy season. Contained between dikes, in places the waters flow several feet above the level of Hanoi; regularly over the centuries breaks in the dikes have brought catastrophic flooding, and the famine that follows when crops are inundated.

In the South China Sea, eons ago, a great shallow bay lay beneath the mountains in the south. As the centuries passed, sediment from the Mekong, which rises in Tibet and now flows twenty-eight hundred miles, filled the bay and created another large, fertile delta full of waterways, three thousand miles of them navigable. (Even today the coastline creeps out fifty meters a year.) On its journey the Mekong forms the border between Thailand and Laos, passes through Cambodia, then splits into two major and several minor branches before reaching the sea. Because its waters are absorbed by a great lake in Cambodia during the rainy season and because they are dispersed in Vietnam, the Mekong is much more benign than the Red River: in the south, flooding and famine are rare.

Lying on the eastern side of Asia, Vietnam's climate is controlled by the great seasonal movements of cloud-bearing wind, the monsoons, dry months alternating with times of heavy rainfall interspersed with typhoons that rage along the coast. In summer, temperatures in the north and the south are much the same—Hanoi has an average of 85°F (30°C), Saigon 86°F—but in winter Hanoi averages only 62 (16) degrees compared to 80 (27) in Saigon. In the highest altitudes, in the north, freezing temperatures are frequent in winter, but because it is the dry season it is rare for snow to lie even on the slopes of the Fanispan Peak, at 10,308 feet Vietnam's highest mountain. During the rainy summer months the average rainfall in Saigon and Hanoi is seventy inches, almost three times that in Paris in a whole year, and twice that in New York.

In 208 B.C. people of Mongolian origin from Nam Viet in China migrated into the Red River delta. The south remained populated by people of Australo-Asiatic origins who had moved North into empty lands; today, the descendants of similar people live in Indonesia and the Philippines. The Chinese called those they encountered "black, ugly, and almost naked," but they had writing and books, which the Chinese thought they alone possessed.

A state called Funan, which covered the whole of the Mekong delta and most of present-day Cambodia, had already existed for about a hundred years. Then in the second century A.D. a highly developed civilization called Champa evolved in the territory between Funan and the Viets. Funan faded away during the sixth Century, absorbed by people from the northwest, the Mon-Khmer. In the tenth century the Viets made themselves independent of China and then, creeping slowly southward century by century, five hundred years later, when Shakespeare was a boy, destroyed the Champa nation.

Before the Viets became independent, their earliest social organization was a form of feudalism: hereditary tribal lords had absolute power over all civil, military, and religious institutions, owned the land and kept the peasants in serfdom. Above the aristocracy was a king, usually the man who had proved himself in battle to be the most powerful of the lords. He exercised control through military districts headed by Chinese governors, whose policy of noninterference with local customs made Vietnam a leniently governed Chinese protectorate.

The first revolt by people who had come to regard themselves as different and separate from the Chinese was the rebellion of the Trung sisters in A.D. 39. Trung Trac was a high-born woman whose husband had been executed by the Chinese for rebellion; her sister,

Trung Nhi, led some of the lords and their armed men in attacks on the Chinese. After defeating them—riding on elephants at the head of hordes of shrieking Vietnamese—the sisters proclaimed themselves queens of an independent Vietnam, but their kingdom lasted only three years: an army sent by the Han emperor re-established Chinese rule. They committed suicide by drowning themselves in a lake in Hanoi, where today there is a shrine to their memory.

A series of uprisings early in the tenth century ended in a decisive defeat of the Chinese in A.D. 939, the year from which the Vietnamese date their national independence. But sovereignty in the north had to be paid for with blood. The Chinese came again in 1057, and it took four years of bitter fighting to get them out. The Cambodians and the Champa invaded eight times between 1128 and 1216, and each time departed grudgingly. In 1257 a Mongolian army sacked Hanoi, but was forced to withdraw. Another swarmed into the Red River delta in 1284, and another three years later, but as their fathers had done before them, the invaders succumbed to armies of Vietnamese and legions of mosquitos.

In the twentieth century Vo Nguyen Giap was to write: "The fighting coordination between the main army and the regional forces, which gave rise to the strategic conjuncture of attacking the enemy both in his front and his rear, appeared in ancient times. The Tho Binh were the main force, the Huong Binh were village troops, organized by the feudal authorities to ensure feudal order." This meshing of organized troops and local militia was one of the basic themes around which he was to formulate his concepts of operations in the wars against the French and the Americans.

The general who led the rebellion during these frightful medieval times was Tran Hung Dao, the man after whom the first Armed Propaganda Brigade was named. Giap wrote of him: "He was a national hero who preached 'unity of the whole people,' and: 'when the enemy comes to your house even the women should fight.' That is an impressive practice but also a very familiar one in our nation's life and struggles. National uprisings and wars in our history have long been people's uprisings and people's wars."

In 1407, Chinese of the Ming dynasty reconquered Vietnam. Besides ruthlessly exploiting the resources of the country, the new rulers took stern measures to eliminate its nationhood: in order to tighten control an identity card was issued to every citizen; schools were permitted to teach only in Chinese; local cults were suppressed; Vietnamese authors were not allowed to write and most of what was already in print was sent to China or burned; women were forced to wear Chinese dress and men to have long hair. Such punitive measures only strengthened nationalist feelings and made the Vietnamese determined to regain their national independence. Eventually the Ming also withdrew, leaving behind a detestation of the Chinese that is long in dying. But peace was to be but an interval between wars: the nation entered into periods of internal strife between strong tribal chiefs. As time passed they founded dynasties in the two deltas and in the middle link.

In the seventeenth century, European nations seriously began their colonial expansion. Southeast Asia was a desirable prize, but it proved difficult to do business with Vietnam, where there were three dominant tribes, the Tay Son, the Trinh, and the Nguyen. They all wanted modern weapons with which to fight each other and in order to get them traded, allowing Christian missionaries to come with the traders. But when in 1672 the wars between them temporarily came to an end all that changed.

Contacts with the West were strongly discouraged, and in consequence, in 1700, a trading center set up by the Dutch in Hanoi in 1637 foundered and closed; the British, who arrived in 1672, shut up shop after twenty-five years; the French trade center, which opened in 1680, also failed. After 1700 only the Portuguese managed to keep a foot in the door. The mandarins saw that their authority was being undermined by Christian teachings and began to persecute the missionaries and native Catholics, who by then were some 10 percent of the population. For about a hundred years outside influence in Vietnam was minimal.

To Vo Nguyen Giap, "Vietnam was one of the cradles of mankind. Viet tribes had their own language, set up an economy with a sociopolitical system, created their own cultural and moral traditions, and so developed a national feeling and consciousness." Certainly, the Vietnamese were remarkably unified, mainly for two reasons. First, whereas in many nations there are thousands of family names, evolved over the centuries and added to by migrants, in the whole of Vietnam there are less than a hundred, based on tribal groupings such as the Ngo and the Nguyen: people are part of a big family of clan ties. Second, they have Confucian traditions going back over twenty-five hundred years; an unbroken chain of response to higher authority and responsibility for personal conduct. Power emanated from the tribal leaders at the center, who delegated their power to the mandarins, who in turn delegated to the village council, and they in their turn to the head of the family, submission to whose authority was the highest moral obligation of every person.

There were thousands of villages in the nation, some of them consisting of several hamlets grouped together. The village council, consisting of the most prominent citizens, such as landowners and retired mandarins, dealt with all purely local affairs, including law enforcement, the assessment and levying of taxes, and the provision of labor on a communal basis. Nearly every village had a mutual-aid society (*hoi tu cap*), which people paid into to cover the expense of funerals. There were also guilds (*hoi bach nghe*), of metal workers, carpenters, stonemasons—which monitored standards of craftsmanship—and the elderly women's Buddhist association (*ho chu ba*), open to women over fifty and sometimes to widows in their forties.

Also, every village had an emergency relief organization (*nghia tuong*), a concept that began in the Red River delta. Farmers gave an agreed amount of their rice, depending on how much land they had, to create a stockpile. Any surplus was sold off and the profit shared by the poor. In the event of a crop failure the rice was distributed equally to everyone in the village. There were also associations for people interested in leisure activities such as cockfighting, wrestling, and fishing. Economically and socially the village was a self-contained entity.

The most important institution, the basic political unit, was the household (the *nha*). It, and not the individual, was the tax base (*nong ho*). It, and not the people in it, was counted in the census.

The *nha* was a collective work group, forming a single economic unit—"one fire, one lamp." It was a place of worship. It was the arbiter of conduct. It abided by village laws. (It was seldom that national laws intruded into its affairs, though certain aspects of the code of filial piety could be enforced; for example, a prisoner might be paroled on the grounds that he was needed at home to support his aged parents.)

Historically, Vietnamese were tolerant of each other's beliefs. Their social system was based on ethics, not religion; they concerned themselves with the here and now, with proper conduct and trying to attain happiness in their present existence, not with what happened in the hereafter. Not exclusively Buddhist, Confucianist, or Taoist, they regarded those three religions, which share the doctrines of the original goodness of man and the possibility of salvation through the recognition of one's essential nature, as being harmonious, as being "three roads to the same destination." There was no ordained priestly caste or ecclesiastical body: they revered the spirits of their ancestors through rituals conducted by the village elders. In the country districts, when people died they were buried on the edge of the rice paddies so that the spirits of the departed could enter the bodies of their descendants through the food they ate. In addition to a Buddhist pagoda, every village had a *dinh*, the shrine of the guardian spirit, which was also the center of village community life.

Because Vietnamese people believe that society is subject to many conflicting social forces that can only be controlled by keeping them separate, there is a tradition of secrecy: unless an organization has good reason to be publicized it should be covert; not only should it be clandestine, its membership should be too, and very few people should know who really runs it.

It is quite usual for Vietnamese to use more than one name during their lifetime. Normally they are given three at birth. The first is the family—in many cases the original, tribal—name, as, for example, Nguyen. The second can indicate the sex of a person; for instance Van means male, Ba means a married woman, Co is an unmarried woman. The third is the name that identifies the individual: Yen, Dong, Giap, Thuc. Thus a female may change her second name on marriage but will always be addressed as, for example, Thuc, which means "virginal," or "tall." Add to this flexibility of name-taking a tradition among males of sometimes wanting anonymity, and the confusion of Vietnamese names can be better understood. (Ho Chi Minh, with as many as twenty-three aliases, took this to extremes.)

Mystery and secrecy are admired. Power is not easily gained but is easily lost, so keep your own council. The less you give away the more likely you are to succeed. The world should never know precisely where you stand. No commitment is ever truly final. (In Vietnam there is no criticism for changing sides, provided a decent interval has elapsed.) The most admired leader is sly, duplicitous, the master of the deceptive move . . .

In 1788 China tried to exploit another internal crisis but was defeated by the Tay Son in the northern part of the country, known to the Vietnamese as Bac Bo. However, while they concentrated on keeping Vietnam independent from the Chinese, farther south the Nguyens succeeded, with French help, in making themselves masters of Saigon and the Mekong delta, Nam Bo: sailors and administrators from the French Navy and French overseas possessions were privately recruited by a Catholic bishop who had become principal advisor to the ruler, Nguyen Anh. Crowned emperor at Hue in 1802 he took the name Gia Long and united North, center, and South in the old name of Vietnam. His descendants would rule until 1954, when Bao Dai stepped down and became another last emperor.

At the beginning of the nineteenth century, the French were concentrating on Napoleon's European wars, and it was not until 1858 that they decided to do something about finding a colonial outlet in the East for their rapidly growing industrial capacity. In the summer of 1858 twenty-five hundred of them arrived in fourteen little ships and captured the village port of Tourane, in central Vietnam—Da Nang. However, strong resistance prevented them from getting any farther.

In order to apply the force needed to make the emperor accept a French base at Tourane, it would be necessary to capture Hue, but to reach it overland was out of the question. Lacking the shallow draft ships needed to sail up the Perfumed River, the French were stalled. Soon tropical diseases started to decimate the force, and sick people began to outnumber battle casualties: a way out had to be found. Leaving a small garrison behind, in February 1859 they sailed south and captured Saigon. But again consolidation proved impossible, and a year later they had to leave. The next year they retook the city, and by June 1861 reinforcements from China enabled them to control three adjacent provinces.

The mandarins' traditional conservatism had left the country without the modern weapons needed to repel invaders. In June 1862 military expediency obliged the emperor to sign away Saigon and the three provinces. A year later the French imposed a protectorate status on Cambodia and created what they called the Indochinese Union, headed by a governor general resident in Saigon. Four years later the entire south of Vietnam, called Cochinchina by them, was theirs, and was granted colonial status.

In April 1882 Saigon sent a military force to Hanoi, and sixteen months after that a treaty was signed that extended French authority to the whole of Vietnam and made what they called Tonkin in the north and Annam in the center protectorates of France. On paper Vietnam was conquered, though it would be another fourteen years before the French could claim that they controlled the whole country.

In 1893 they annexed Laos and added it to the Union. (They took Cambodia and Laos under the pretext that they had once been under Vietnamese control—which they had, tenuously, in the middle ages—though at the time Laos was actually under Siamese suzerainty.)

Now the French had an Eastern empire.

CHAPTER FOUR

THE TWENTIETH CENTURY

We fight and win not because we are endowed with steel skin or copper bones but because we are Vietnamese; because we are moral, loyal, patient, strong, indomitable, filled with compassion.

—LE DUAN

Colonial conquest had been relatively easy, the key factor being that 80 percent of what was then a very small population lived in scattered, isolated villages from which they seldom if ever moved. Travel was difficult, since roads were unpaved (and often impassable in the monsoon), and anyway why go anywhere when everything needed for life was in the village? If central government was remote, the villages were equally remote to the administrators, so once the three big cities had been taken, the colonizers could impose themselves on the governed without their knowing, for months perhaps, that a change had taken place. And when they learned of it, what could they do? Life went on largely as it had before, with change slow and imperceptible.

But change there was. Even salt, a product everyone needed, was taxed, and people could be imprisoned for its unauthorized production: as a result there were shortages and the price rose to more than ten times what it had been in precolonial Vietnam. Peasants were encouraged to grow poppies in order that opium could be extracted from the crop and cynically sold by the state to users in Vietnam and in other parts of the world.

The French settlers in Cochinchina, who for a generation now had done well in the rich south, vigorously opposed any centralized economic policy, but in 1897 a new governor general changed things radically. With the aim of making Vietnam a tariff-protected market for French goods and a source of valuable rice, coal, and rubber, Paul Doumer disregarded the protectorate status of Tonkin and Annam, established direct French rule over the whole country, and insisted on imposing his policies on his obdurate fellow countrymen in Cochinchina. He also instigated the construction of railways, harbors, roads, canals, bridges, and other public works, modernizing the whole infrastructure of the country. He recruited thousands of Frenchmen to run his administration—but paid the few Vietnamese who were employed only a fraction of what Frenchmen got for doing the same job.

During the nine hundred years of independence prior to French rule, Vietnam's economy had been almost exclusively agricultural. There were artisans and fishermen, and a few coal miners, but the majority of people were peasants who grew rice to feed their own families. Internal and external trade was insignificant, since most villages and the country as a whole—except in times of famine—were economically self-sufficient. No property-owning class had developed to compete with the mandarins for power, and when the French brought new ways of using Vietnam's resources that made the rise of such a class possible, successive emperors and mandarins, aware that all economic innovation was a threat to their power, clung to the old order.

For their part, the French were content to avoid any unsettling changes in society, a laudable motive, but in consequence the economy in the countryside continued as it had for centuries, with few trading contacts. Those who organized trade maintained the worker on the level of the rural economy but sold the product on the level of the city economy: the difference went into their own pockets. Little was done to industrialize the nation, though hundreds of Vietnamese were taken to France to work in mines. (And several tens of thousands were to go there as laborers during the Great War.)

For the majority of the Vietnamese, life was harder than it had been before the French arrived. Though in the half century between 1880 and 1930 the acreage of cultivated rice-growing land increased fourfold, and the annual yield of polished rice rose from 284 tons to nearly a million and a half, the individual peasant's rice consumption decreased during the same period without being compensated for by the availability of other food. Vast irrigation works, chiefly in the Mekong delta, reclaimed huge tracts of land, but this was not distributed to peasants who had too little, or to the landless: it ended up in the hands of French speculators, who sold it to the highest bidder among themselves or to the few Vietnamese who could afford to buy. This resulted in enlarging the number of Vietnamese landowners who needed landless tenant-farmers to work their fields.

Such farmers sometimes had to pay as much as 60 percent of their crop in rent, leaving them without enough to feed their family and obliging them to work even harder in order to fill the food bowls: in the process, of course, they increased the owner's share. Hardly better off were the small-holding peasants, who gave 40 percent of their crop to their landlord and after paying Chinese middlemen and French exporters their share ended up with 15 percent of the market price; they continually ran into debt, and if they were unable to repay their debts, as was often the case, lost their land. More and more small land holdings were wiped out, and toward the end of the colonial regime the large landowners of Cochinchina, a mere 2.5 percent of the people, owned more than 45 percent of the land.

Considering that colonization was supposedly being done for the benefit of France, the irony of all this was that only private French businesses and a very small number of Vietnamese landowners benefited from the work of the colonial regime: neither the French state nor the French people shared in the profits.

Although between 1920 and 1939 most of the imports (62 percent) into Indochina came from France, the colony never became an important market for French industry simply because the peasant masses remained too poor to become consumers of French goods. The rewards of colonial rule were available to only a few people, less than half of 1 percent of the population: only the six or seven thousand Vietnamese who owned sizable plots of land, a few thousand Vietnamese officials and the colonists themselves—the *colons*—could afford to pay for goods imported from France.

By the first decade of the twentieth century, Tonkin was again a direct protectorate, with a French resident superieur in Hanoi acting as viceroy for the Vietnamese emperor; Annam was an indirect protectorate, its capital Hue the seat of the emperor but with power vested in the French; Cochinchina was a French possession, with a colonial administrator.

There, the population were more dependent on French administrators rather than the established corps of mandarins, and were therefore more influenced by them. In addition, as the years passed they became much wealthier than people in the north: in Annam and Tonkin those who owned less than 1.5 acres amounted to 68.5 percent of the population, in the south those with less than 2.5 only 33.6 percent; in 1930, out of 6,530 landowners in the whole of Indochina who had more than 125 acres of land, 6,300 of them were in the south; of the 244 with more than 1,500 acres, all were in the south; of the 8,600 wealthy persons (defined as earning more than $5,500 per annum) 8,200 of them were southerners. France was pursuing a policy of assimilation, education, and eventual dual-citizenship, but though the south had only 20 percent of the whole population, it had more than half the naturalized citizens.

However, the barrier between the south and the north was an artificial one, for in their customs and attitudes to life people in the south are much the same as those in the north. Though southerners might voice superficial, childish animosity toward northerners, calling them aggressive and warlike, wily and overly political, at root they remained first and foremost patriotic Vietnamese, aware of their common ancestry and inheritance. And, too, they were united by a common language and mutual detestation of foreign interference and domination. Ignorance of these important facts was to be the cause of death and anguish for millions in the future.

Like the other colonial powers the French brought new ideas about religion, culture, and administration to the people they colonized. To the Vietnamese who were offered these gifts the religion was generally offensive and much of the culture was superfluous—they had their own, going back even farther than that of France—but the knowledge was priceless: of medicine, law, finance, business systems, and industrial technology.

The French built a neo-Gothic cathedral in Hanoi and also an opera house—a scaled-down replica of the one in Paris—in which to play Berlioz and Bizet. They built a theater in Saigon in which to present Racine and Moliere. They turned the two cities into wide-avenued miniature copies of Paris, brought wine and electric light, sewage systems and vaccination, libraries, haute cuisine, rat traps, motor cars, and newspapers. And employment for thousands and thousands of Vietnamese as the builders, carpenters, cooks, gardeners, waiters, children's nurses, dishwashers needed to create, maintain and staff their villas.

Unfortunately, they also brought with them a feeling of arrogant superiority over the "natives" and, conscious of their benevolence in enlightening them in European ways, regarded what they took from them as fair payment without bothering to draw up a balance sheet. If they had, they would have seen that they, and not the colonized, were in debt; if they had, they might have averted what was to come.

It is easy now, in a different age with other values, to condemn the colons, but in fairness to them they showed great enterprise in leaving France to start a new life far from home in an alien place. Many of them worked hard. They had to adapt to an enervating and difficult climate. They took the risk of succumbing to all manner of tropical diseases. And they faced years of separation from their families, for in those days it took weeks to reach Vietnam by sea.

For all that, they could have done a lot more. For example, because nobody thought it necessary to train professional people, colonial Vietnam had only two physicians for every hundred thousand people, compared with twenty-five in the Philippines and seventy-six in Japan. And, too, the metropolitan government was stingy in providing funds for the administration of the country, with the result that progress was slow or nonexistent. The colons enjoyed a good life in the sun while the natives still lived as they had in medieval times.

All the failings of the French colonial administration were apparent to the population, for though they might have been illiterate and poverty-stricken, they were anything but stupid. Inevitably, there was a reaction.

In 1908, after a jailbreak by agitators, the socialist Vietnamese Restoration Association was formed, an anarchist blood brotherhood that was too inward-looking to make any long-term impact. In 1927 the Vietnamese nationalist party, the Viet Nam Quoc Dan Dang, the VNQDD, led by Nguyen Thai Hoc, a twenty-three-year old teacher, was founded in Tonkin. The party organized terrorist action with the aim of ousting the French through a military uprising in its garrisons, but on the planned day, 9 February 1930, only the garrison at Yen Bay responded. Its native troops assassinated their French officers but were stormed by French troops a day later and themselves summarily executed. In a wave of repression that took hundreds of lives and sent thousands to prison, Nguyen Thai Hoc and twelve other leaders of his party were arrested and beheaded. Almost destroyed in Vietnam, the VNQDD existed during the next fifteen years chiefly as a group of exiles in China, supported by the Nationalist Chinese Kuomintang.

By 1929 there were three communist parties in Vietnam. One, founded by Tran Van Cung, was the Communist Union. Another was the Revolutionary Youth Association, the Thanh Yien, which had been founded in 1925 and soon absorbed a small group in

Annam. Exploiting conditions of near starvation in Annam, in May 1930 the communists staged a general peasant uprising. "Soviet" administrations were set up in several provinces, and many landowners and Vietnamese officials in the service of the French were killed. Full French control over Annam was not re-established until the spring of 1931. During 1930 and 1931, 699 Vietnamese were executed without trial, 83 sentenced to death, 546 imprisoned for life, and about 3,000 others arrested and put into concentration camps.

A jubilant governor general told his countrymen that "as a force capable of acting against public order, communism has disappeared from Vietnam." By the end of the year, the Party was in ruins, not least because they had been attacking the wrong enemy: their actions were directed primarily against their own people rather than the colons. Though the Nationalist movement too was wrecked, the communists had the advantage because they were more cohesive and better organized to make a comeback.

In Hong Kong in 1930 Nguyen Ai Quoc (Ho Chi Minh) was jailed for two years by the British after a tip-off from the Sûreté, but it was too late, for in January he had held a conference in which he unified the three existing groups and then integrated the newly named Indochinese Communist Party, the ICP, into the Commintern, on an equal footing with Siam and Malaya. He also arranged for the creation of a party newspaper called *Tien Len* (Forward), a phrase that was to become the battle cry of Vietnamese soldiers. The ICP's structure was territorial, functional, and external: it was split territorially into three regions—Bac Bo, Trung Bo, Nam Bo—and into zones, provinces, and districts; it was functional in that it drew together people of common interests—farmers, workers, students, youths, women, old people; it was externally bound to the Eastern Commintern in Shanghai. With doctrinal purity and dedication to unity, with tight discipline and blood oaths to hold it together, it was a model of its kind and was to stand the test of time without major alteration.

By the end of 1931, there were an estimated fifteen hundred Communist Party members in Vietnam, but there were tens of thousands of sympathizers. The French regarded the nationalists as the greater threat because they were more overtly anti-French, but the communists had a better cadre corps and stronger discipline and appealed to the people by promising specific action to correct grievances. In 1932, trying belatedly to defuse the situation, the French allowed the first organized political party to be formed in Saigon: the Constitutionalist Party later came under the influence of a small and peculiar religious organization called the Cao Dai—and in doing so alienated itself from the mainstream of politics and came to nothing. In the years leading up to the outbreak of World War II, the ICP, alone of all revolutionary groups in Vietnam, was in command of a well-indoctrinated and -disciplined following and was by far the strongest faction in the independence movement.

By 1936, when the government of the Popular Front in France granted some civil rights to the people of the French colonies, the ICP apparatus, fully reconstituted, was able to extend its influence over intellectuals, workers, and peasants by creating legal "front" organizations. In Tonkin, for example, the Party operated under the cover of an Indochinese Democratic Front, led by two as-yet unknowns, the future prime minister Phan Van Dong and the future general Vo Nguyen Giap.

What had emerged in Vietnam out of the wars and mixing of races was an industrious, clever, and hardy people, though small in stature: the average male is only five feet, two inches high and weighs between 120 and 130 pounds; the women are slender, perhaps four feet, ten inches high, and usually weigh not more than 100 pounds.

Ninety percent of the population are ethnic Vietnamese: Mongoloid, like the Chinese from southern China. The other 10 percent are the descendants of the people who were gradually pushed out of the deltas and into the jungles by the Viets. Smaller even than the Vietnamese, known as Montagnards—from the French word meaning "mountain people"—in the 1930s there were more than a million of them in some thirty-three tribes, among them the Rhada, the Jarai, the Nung, the Meo, the Tai. (There were black Tais and white Tais, identified in times past by the color of the blouses worn by the women.)

In the south there were 12 or 13 million people, of whom 1 million were Chinese, 350,000 Cambodian, and between 500,000 and 700,000 Montagnard. In total, there were about the same number in the north, with fewer Chinese and more Montagnards.

The hill tribes lived primitively and were considered by the Vietnamese to be stone-age people. In the north they spoke a dialect of Chinese origin, whereas the Vietnamese language is basically Mon-Khmer from the southwest, though mixed with many Chinese terms. They were animists, attributing a soul to inanimate objects and worshipping them.

Originally, the Vietnamese tongue—strange to Western ears, a sort of twittering bird song, with many throat and nasal grunts and whines—was written, like the Chinese, in characters, thousands of them. Then in 1627 a Jesuit priest by the name of Alexander of Rhodes came to the Cochinchina Mission of Faith in a place called Faifo, which was the Portuguese trading post. Within months he had learned the language and within a year or two had transcribed its Chinese ideographs into a simplified script—*quoc ngu*—in the Roman alphabet, a truly amazing achievement. Today, the shape of Vietnamese words is instantly recognizable to Westerners even if the pronunciation is not. Some words have up to seven different meanings, depending on the context in which they are used and the tones of their utterance. Not surprisingly, to the millions of foreigners who were to come to Vietnam in the 1950s, '60s, and '70s, the language was totally incomprehensible, however educated they were.

In Vietnam as a whole there were endemic problems that would take a lot of resolving: 90 percent of the labor force was engaged in feeding themselves and the remainder of the population; geographically, two-thirds of the nation was mountainous and only 5 percent arable, so there was less cultivated land per inhabitant than anywhere on earth. The Red River delta had 75 percent of the population and 75 percent of the arable land in the North; under the French it also had the highest individual land ownership anywhere in Asia—98 percent of the farmers owned the land they used, but 60 percent of these had less than one acre. Reform of this unfair situation was to cause the death and torture of many thousands in the middle of the twentieth century.

Religion, in the 1930s, was a significant factor in the life of Vietnamese people. Though, because it was an imported creed, people had always tended to be biased against Roman Catholicism (in the mid-1850s in the north converts were branded on their left cheek with the words *ta dao*, meaning "disbeliever"), about 10 percent of the population were of that faith, most of them living in the north. With the elevation of Ngo Dinh Diem to the presidency of South Vietnam, in the 1950s Catholicism was to have an influence out of all proportion to its share of the population.

Buddhism contains the contradiction that on the one hand nothing is significant, and therefore politics is not, and on the other that the condition of man is important, and therefore politics is. In the years to come, Buddhism was to play its part too in politics in South Vietnam, primarily because of the policies of the president.

This, then, was the background against which the young Vo Nguyen Giap grew up.

On the surface people were going about their business in the traditional way—obedient, orderly, self-sufficient, family-oriented, smiling, and polite—but inside they were hiding a seething discontent that was waiting to erupt in violence as the only means of achieving what they were absolutely convinced was their rightful independence.

To the Vietnamese, history is not a nightmare from which they have awakened; it is a gift, a present, from their ancestors: the "present" of their ancestors. If they fought for independence, then their children's children must too, if they were not to betray their trust.

This conviction, together with patriotism, astonishing determination, and an ingrained martial spirit were to prove an unquenchable combination.

CHAPTER FIVE

THE FRENCH RETURN

*If insurrection is an art, its main content is to know how to give the
struggle the form appropriate to the political situation.*
                                                    —VO NGUYEN GIAP

Turbulence is the word that encapsulates Vietnam's history.
Armies marching back and forth. Waves of blood-stained
soldiers surging around village fences, splashing over the rocklike
peasantry, here one dawn, gone the next, leaving dead bodies and
animal carcasses and empty rice bowls, fading like a dream only to

reappear in the next generation, an unpreventable recurring nightmare that would come again in a long night, unbidden. Through the ages the people had known spears, swords, flintlocks, rifles, machine guns, grenades: in the next three decades they were to be killed or maimed by jumping mines, fleshettes, cluster bombs, napalm, rockets, and laser-guided missiles, and by mountain-removing land mines dropped on them from seven miles above out of a clear blue silent sky.

During much of the last three hundred years Vietnam has been divided in half or into thirds: in half after about 1600, in thirds during the reign of the Tay Son brothers (1788–1802); then united in the early nineteenth century, only to be divided into thirds again by the French. They had first established themselves in Cochinchina and as the years passed had given that rich province different status from Annam and Tonkin, so that when the future of Indochina was discussed by the wartime Allies it was decided that after the war Vietnam would be partitioned at the 16th Parallel, pending decisions as to its future. The thought in the minds of some of the leaders who met at Potsdam in July 1945 was that perhaps the northern protectorates would attain independence quickly while the South would revert to colonial status in the first instance but eventually also become independent.

The main reason for the Potsdam decision was President Roosevelt's antipathy to colonialism, a conviction that was due not to a clever appreciation of the realities of the situation around the world in the mid 1940s but to the fact that such a sentiment had become part of American overseas policy ever since their rebellion against the British more than a hundred and fifty years before: then, they had cast off their imperialist bonds; now, they felt they must help others to find their freedom. But, no doubt without realizing the irony of what he was doing, Roosevelt had first offered Vietnam to Chiang Kai-shek, leader of the Chinese nationalists. The gift had been courteously refused: the Vietnamese were not Chinese, Chiang had said; they would always be different, would always harbor a historical grudge, would never assimilate into China, would always be ungovernable. No, thanks.

For his part, General Charles de Gaulle, who had established a provisional government in Paris when the Germans retreated in 1944, had reluctantly accepted the idea of partition but without any doubts as to the future of Indochina: when the Japanese were vanquished the French would return. With metropolitan France overwhelmed by the Nazis, its distant possessions in the Far East had been easy prey for the Japanese. While battles raged around the Pacific, the fortunate Japanese garrison had idled the years away. Now, war in Europe was coming to an end, and the Japanese would soon bear the full force of a concerted Allied attack. (The impending use of nuclear weapons had not been divulged to the French.) When they were beaten and their troops expelled, France would reclaim its prewar possessions. Certain that the Chinese would be less likely to create difficulties about a continuing French presence in Indochina than the Americans would, de Gaulle agreed that, to supervise the departure of the Japanese, Chiang's troops should go into Tonkin and Annam and British troops into Cochinchina.

Meanwhile, on 28 August 1945, when Vo Nguyen Giap and his soldiers crossed the Doumer Bridge over the brown waters of the Red River and marched into Hanoi—without hindrance from the thirty thousand Japanese troops stationed in and around the city— they found the place in chaos, made worse because almost within hours their arrival let loose a general uprising directed at all foreigners: the Japanese occupiers and the demoralized remnants of the French administration. Above all, the people wanted to be their own masters.

Thousands of them surged through the streets and stormed the iron fence of the Bac Bo Palace, formerly the governor of Tonkin's office. According to Giap:

> The uprising spread rapidly and in a space of ten days the colonial rule and its feudal predecessors ceased to exist. The armed forces consisted of units of the liberation army, self-defense forces, and a multitude of guerilla groups. Revolution broke out like a whirlwind. Within only a few days, much of the shame and suffering caused by slavery was swept away. The revolution's power of revival was extraordinary. One day before, the city had been paralyzed by famine, epidemics, and terror. Now, life was seething in every street and

lane. Thousands upon thousands of people marched through the streets with the force of surging waves. The people's revolutionary power had been established. Robbery and stealing virtually disappeared. Beggars were nowhere to be seen. The atmosphere was one of purity and excitement. Golden-starred red flags appeared evermore numerous and splendid, coloring scarlet the houses and streets. The revolution was really a festive day for the oppressed. It was the first victory of Marxist/Leninism in a colonial, semifeudal country.

This turmoil was caused not only by the release of pent-up frustrations due to the apathy of the French administration and the ineptness of the Japanese, but also in part by panic, for the north was in the grip of a terrible famine. The Japanese decision to imprison French administrators, including those responsible for irrigation, in particular around the banks of the Day River south of Hanoi, left the control of the water level in the hands of Vietnamese workers who did not have the necessary expertise. When the rains came they opened the floodgates too much, and oceans of water swept out over the neglected dikes and across the rice paddies, inundating eight out of the fourteen provinces in the north and destroying the growing crops.

The resulting starvation was to cause the death of between half a million and six hundred thousand people. The price of rice went through the roof, especially in Hanoi, and the population, never well fed anyway, began to die in the streets. "The water had risen in every river," wrote Giap: "The flood had destroyed the dikes left uncared for by the colonial rulers and six of the delta provinces, the granary of north Vietnam, were inundated."

The chaos turned out to be all to the good: many of the French administration were still dying quietly in their detention camps; the Japanese who were supposed to be running the country were in limbo, receiving no direction from Tokyo because the government there had foundered after the explosion of two atomic bombs on 6 and 9 August. The important thing to do now was to fill the vacuum and establish the Vietminh as the legitimate government before the Japanese or the Allies had time to react.

On arrival, after seeing to the disposition of his troops Giap was taken to the home of a sympathizer in Hang Ngang Street, where he learned that Ho Chi Minh was on his way, escorted by a platoon of the Quang Trung detachment of the Liberation Army but carried in a litter because of his poor health. Not long before, Giap had sat up all night beside Ho's bamboo bed in a small hut in Tran Trao, nursing him. Now he was coming back to Hanoi. As Giap describes it:

> Ho had wandered alone in various regions of the globe and it had taken him more than thirty-five years to reach Hanoi from the small thatched house in Kim Lien village three hundred kilometers away. A few days before he arrived, Hanoi was feverish with black-market activities and life was precarious. There were not enough dust carts to carry those who had died from starvation to the outskirts of the city, where they were thrown into common graves. At the city gates large numbers of starving people were pouring in from the countryside. They staggered about as lifeless as withered leaves in winter. A light push from a policeman might send someone down never to rise again.

The next day, on 29 August 1945, while Japanese officers strutted around the Hotel Metropole slapping their leather boots with riding crops and waiting in vain for orders from Tokyo, and their soldiers sat around in their barracks next to the Citadel—the one-time headquarters of the French army in Hanoi—smoking and waiting to be told what to do, Ho Chi Minh took over Vietnam and formed his first administration.

In the hope that the French would accept a fait accompli, and that he could draw together the various nationalist groups and bring them under his control, Ho's government included non-Marxists, Independents, and Roman Catholics. Vo Nguyen Giap was named minister for the interior, the most important job in the cabinet, responsible for sorting out the chaos and starting to reform society on communist principles: it seemed that now that the fighting was over Ho was steering Giap back into politics. Chu Van Tan, the Montagnard leader of the National Salvation Army and section commander of the original Armed Propaganda Brigade, was named minister for defense.

On 2 September, before a chattering, cheering crowd of about one hundred thousand people, almost half the population of the city, who had crammed into Ba Dinh Square outside the opera house, Ho Chi Minh proclaimed the independence of Vietnam, in doing so paraphrasing America's Declaration of Independence: quoting the words "each man has an inalienable right to life, liberty and the pursuit of happiness," which he had asked one of the soldiers of the OSS to write down for him on a scrap of paper. Vo Nguyen Giap then made a long speech about political, economic, and other matters, and also spoke about foreign affairs, emphasizing that in the future Vietnamese relationships with China and the United States would be close, and saying that America was "a good friend of the Vietnamese." As he described the scene later:

Hanoi was bedecked with red bunting, a world of flags, lanterns and flowers. Fluttering red flags adorned the roofs, the trees, the lakes. Streamers were hung across the roads, bearing slogans in French, English, Chinese, and Russian. "Viet Nam for the Vietnamese," "Independence or death," "Support President Ho Chi Minh." Factories and shops were closed. Markets were deserted. The whole city, old and young, men and women, took to the streets. This is how President Ho Chi Minh appeared for the first time before his people as a great leader: a thin old man with a broad forehead, bright eyes, and a sparse beard, wearing an old hat, a high-collared khaki jacket, and white rubber sandals. During the next twenty-four years as president he always appeared in this simple unchanging attire—a plain suit, without any decorations—as on that occasion when he first appeared before his people.

On 7 September, implementing the results of long discussions with Giap over campfires, Ho renamed the Liberation Army the National Defense Army—Quan Doi Nhan Dan—and announced the setting up of a general staff, a core of elite officers who would control the army. It was to be "unified, secret, responsive, accurate and prompt, so as to defeat all enemies," and was to have three separate staffs:

• A central political office, which would exercise strict Party control over all aspects of army life, overseeing joint political/military control at all command levels down to platoons;
• A political general staff, divided into intelligence, operations, communications;
• A rear services department, divided into transportation (i.e., primarily the coordination of the labor force; they had hardly any vehicles at this stage), supply—of food, ammunition, and weapons (and their repair), and medical services.

On 8 September, as the second priority and with the aim of preparing people for their new life, a national mass education service was begun. As well as providing general education, it would, of course, become a nationwide outlet for proselytizing. So far, the main task of agitative propaganda had been to mobilize the masses in preparation for the general uprising; now it would harness them to the creation of a communist state. The base theory had been chillingly set out by Mao Tse-tung: "A neutral population is slowly convinced by a combination of selective terrorism, intimidation, persuasion, and massive agitation. Leadership is never more important than in the first stages." The Vietnamese were to get all those ingredients, and were certainly to get strong leadership, in the years to come.

There were so many things to think about, so many urgent matters needing attention, that those first weeks were ones of frenetic activity. But in a way this helped Ho Chi Minh, for the Japanese were only too willing to let him get on with it. "Japanese commanders lost the will to use their troops in countering insurgency," says Giap, and were incapable of stepping into the void left by their removal of the French. Grabbing their chances, in the next few months, Ho Chi Minh's administration began to enact laws, set about creating a police force, started to enforce justice, and laid the basis for the expansion of the army. Also, wanting to integrate all parts of society, Ho gave the Montagnards representation in the National Assembly; and in the months to come brought nearly ten thousand of them to Hanoi to train as teachers, doctors, political agents.

On 9 September 1945, implementing the decisions made at Potsdam, 152,500 men of the Nationalist Chinese Army under General Lu Han, consisting of the 53rd, 60th, 62nd, and 93rd Armies and the 23rd, 39th, and 93rd Independent Divisions, marched over the border and spread southward, eventually concentrating around Hanoi. There were a lot of Chinese, and their locust presence, pillaging the countryside, made food shortages even worse. They had wasted no time, and in the south too the British were moving quickly, for on the twelfth part of the 20th Indian Division, under Major General Douglas Gracey, arrived in Saigon. (Formations in the British Indian army were composed of a mixture of British and Indian units, the latter led by British officers.)

It was unfortunate that the British chose to send a general of the Indian army, however capable he was and however well he was regarded by Admiral Lord Louis Mountbatten, supreme commander of all British forces in Southeast Asia, into a delicate political situation that required great tact. All his background experience lay in dealing with colonized people, with all that meant in terms of attitudes; his sympathies were bound to be with the French wish to re-establish their empire. Had he been open-minded and objective, events might have turned out differently. As it was, when a delegation of Vietnamese who said they represented the administration in Hanoi came to see him, he disdainfully showed them the door, remarking later that he had found his short meeting with them most distasteful and had "promptly kicked them out."

Mountbatten's orders had been that Gracey was to disarm the Japanese, maintain order, and remain neutral; that he was "not to re-establish French sovereignty." But under pressure from Colonel Cedile, the French commissioner for Cochinchina, he failed to carry out those orders. Imposing martial law and then finding himself without enough troops to enforce it, he armed the French troops the Japanese had interned and used them, and Japanese soldiers, to try to bring the unruly population under control. Giap:

The Allied Powers had decided to divide Indochina into two zones for the disarming of Japanese troops after Japan surrendered. Under American pressure the French were left out of the operation, which was to be done by the British army south of the 16th Parallel and by Chiang Kai-shek's army north of it. Of course, our people were not consulted on this important matter.

In the first half of September nearly two hundred thousand Chiang troops swept over the north like a plague and the British mission under Major General Gracey came to Saigon, the first English and Indian units of the 20th Division landing from the sea one after another. They ordered the Japanese to police the city and demanded that our forces should hand in their weapons: from the very beginning the British betrayed themselves as interventionists.

On the twentieth, General Gracey issued his first communiqué. He affirmed the British right to maintain order and imposed martial law. He prohibited the carrying of arms and declared that offenders would be severely punished, even shot. His troops seized the prison and released fifteen hundred soldiers of the 11th Colonial Infantry regiment, who were re-armed. Then, early on the morning of the twenty-third, they, supported by British and Japanese troops, came out on to the streets to attack our police posts. Soldiers and colonialists who had meekly surrendered to the Japanese only a few months earlier showed the utmost savagery in massacring and ill-treating unarmed civilians. In an atmosphere of seething anger, self-defense units and the ordinary people of Saigon rushed to their combat positions, determined to fight back.

Two weeks later, in early October, two battalions of French infantry, a commando unit, and an armored car regiment arrived in Saigon under the command of General Leclerc. A few days after that the British government decided that a French administration should take over as soon as possible: in London and Delhi it had become clear that Gracey's small force was quite incapable of handling the situation. In any case the problem was clearly one for the French to resolve and the sooner British troops withdrew the better. With relief Gracey began to hand over to Leclerc. Then in early November Admiral d'Argenleau arrived in Saigon as high commissioner for Indochina.

A few months later, in February 1946, the 2nd Battalion of Foreign Legion Infantry (2nd REI) arrived in Saigon and was immediately sent to Annam, where it lost 230 dead and wounded in three months of bloody operations against Vietminh insurgents. Then in April the remnants of the 5th REI, the unit that had fought its way out when the Japanese imprisoned the French administrators of Vietnam, returned from China and regrouped in Saigon. In the same month the last of the British officers and their sepoys departed, replaced by French troops armed and clothed by the British and driving around Saigon with equipment marked "Lend-Lease. Provided by the Government of the United States of America."

Jacques Phillipe Leclerc was an aristocrat—Jean de Hautecloque—who had changed his name in 1940 on joining the Free French under de Gaulle in order to avoid reprisals by the Nazis on his relatives who remained in France. He had raised an army for the Free French in Chad, had been an exceptional commander in the North African campaign, and had spearheaded the Free French Army's part in the liberation of Paris. Georges d'Argenleau had served in the French navy in the Great War and in World War II but had spent most of the intervening years in a Carmelite monastery— Giap referred to him as "an unfrocked priest." He was a dry, humorless, bigoted man with a rigid outlook on life who was sardonically described by one of his aides as having "one of the most brilliant minds of the twelfth century." In the months to come his appointment was to prove a terrible mistake.

Meanwhile, he and Leclerc, reinforced by more French troops, and by administrators quickly brought in from French possessions elsewhere, set about re-establishing the prewar situation in Cochinchina. During the next four months, the French army fought several battles with the ragged and badly armed insurgents. They beat them, stabilized the Saigon area and parts of the Mekong delta, and in February 1946 d'Argenleau officially declared the south "pacified." Tran Van Giau, the Vietnamese who had led the insurgents in the south, took his ten thousand or so men north to join forces with Giap's troops, leaving a hard core of cadres in the villages to become the nucleus for dissent in the future.

Taking his men north was no straightforward task: travel in Vietnam then was much the same as it is today. Now, it takes two and a half days in a vehicle, lurching along rutted roads, threading a way between lumbering water buffalo and oxen led by children, weaving past slim, bare-footed women carrying slung loads on poles draped across their shoulders, honking past bicycles and carts and battered lorries, to get from Hanoi to Dien Bien Phu, one hundred and seventy-eight miles distant: in 1945 moving several thousand troops five hundred miles to the North took weeks. Nevertheless, Giau's men eventually were integrated into Giap's expanding army.

In October Giap, accompanied by a French diplomat by the name of Jean Sainteney, who had arrived from France to be the commissioner for Tonkin, went to Saigon to meet Leclerc. The two men did not get on at all well, for during their meetings Leclerc snubbed Giap, looking down his nose at him and making little attempt to hide the fact that he thought it preposterous that he should be expected to do business with this intense but comical-looking little man with baggy trousers and an oversized hat. It was a big misjudgment, which was to have long-term consequences: though Leclerc would not stay in Indochina for long, the damage had been done in terms of mutual regard between the number-three man in Ho's administration and the French.

CHAPTER SIX

THE WAR BEGINS

This is not a fight against an army, it is a fight against a whole nation.
—GENERAL JACQUES PHILIPPE LECLERC

Effectively, Vietnam was now divided in two, not just as an interim measure pending resolution of its long-term future by negotiation, as had been intended at Potsdam, but because the precipitate departure of the British before such negotiations had even begun had enabled the French to move back into Cochinchina and reassert their former status. Whatever happened in the north, the south was now to remain separate for nearly thirty years.

In the north, though Ho Chi Minh's administration regarded themselves, (and were regarded by the population) as being in control, to the French they had no authority. As far as they were concerned the Potsdam decree had been made on the assumption that after the war the future of Vietnam would be determined by mutual agreement; it had not been envisaged that the colonized peoples would create a fait accompli by usurping authority in this way. In Paris the government chafed at being balked by Ho Chi Minh. In Hanoi the colonial administrators, freed from internment, found it galling to have to stand by and see the Vietnamese ineptly trying to exercise administrative functions for which they had never been trained and in which they had no experience. The Vietnamese for their part were suspicious of French intentions and, not strong enough militarily to see them off, began covertly to build up the strength of their army by smuggling weapons through the ports and manufacturing them locally.

In November 1946 Ho Chi Minh, still clinging naively to the belief that his administration would be recognized by the French as the long-term government of Tonkin and Annam, and trying to placate all the factions in Vietnam—especially the nationalists, who were supported by Chiang's representatives—dissolved the Indochinese Communist Party, saying that his country was his party. He abolished the detested salt and poll taxes, banned the use of opium, and ended the state monopoly on the production of alcohol. He even wooed the Roman Catholic clergy and, wanting to demonstrate that democracy could exist in Vietnam, called for an election to be held.

On 6 January 1946 about 90 percent of the people turned out to elect a huge majority of Vietminh candidates. Giap himself got more than 90 percent of the votes in his consituency, his old home area. Ho had guaranteed the nationalists seventy seats in the Assembly; in the event, they won only forty-eight, but he kept his word. And to show that he was unbiased, when he formed his new cabinet, out of the twelve members only three had been members of the now-defunct ICP. Giap, considered far too hardline and difficult to deal with by the Chinese, lost his post as minister for the interior and was appointed chairman of the Military Council.

It was no sinecure. In March 1945 the Vietminh had had only a thousand or so armed men, who for all that had exercised control over more than eight hundred thousand people in the liberated zone—and thirty thousand square kilometers of territory, a third of Tonkin; in June, Giap had formed the first battalion-sized unit; by August he had five thousand men under command to lead into Hanoi; by the end of 1945 more than fifty thousand had been recruited.

One of Giap's first tasks was to equip these new soldiers with weapons. He arranged to buy thirty thousand rifles and two thousand machine guns from the Chinese communists, to be paid for out of part of the proceeds of a "Gold Week," which Ho had instigated within days of arriving in Hanoi. (Ho had appealed to the people to give money and valuables to the government, which was desperately short of funds. The bulk of the money raised—20 million piastres—he gave to General Lu Han to buy Chinese noninterference in Vietnamese affairs, and thus give him a free hand.) Giap also sent his agents, Nguyen Van Cam and Tran Van Giau—lately commander in the south—to Hong Kong and Bangkok to barter gold, opium, and rice shipments—sent covertly from small ports in the south—for weapons.

Also, Giap set about organizing arms production in primitive "factories" and workshops. At Thai Nguyen fifteen hundred Vietminh soldiers worked with several hundred Japanese ex-POW technicians, some of the three thousand or so deserters from the Imperial Army who had opted to side with the Vietminh: perhaps the disgrace of surrender, an unforgivable sin in the Japanese chivalric code of Bushido, which governed the conduct of fighting men, was something they could not face in their home country. At Thai Nguyen the output was fifty rifles and ten pistols a day, and three or four machine guns a month, meticulous copies of weapons already in their arsenal.

The second most important factory was at Quang Ngai, where three hundred men and women worked under the direction of

Major Saito, another Japanese deserter. Another workshop was at
Phu Tho, and yet another at Thap Muoi, where five hundred workers relied on direction from more Japanese, and even a few Germans
who had deserted from the French Foreign Legion. For the benefit
of the cadres who were recruiting in the center and south, there was
a production line of sorts in Annam, and another in Cochinchina.
There were even a few Chinese workers making rifles at Tra Linh
on the Chinese border. Also, there were numerous crude village
workshops, some of which made bullets, though mass production
was difficult to achieve. Every facility, however small, that could be
pressed into production by Giap was used. It was another example
of the extraordinary ability he had to organize, to administer by
delegation, and to motivate his subordinates.

In the provinces, cadres recruited young men to form regional
troops. Neither they nor the soldiers of the regular units were paid.
(Indeed, until 1958 nobody in the army was paid, and then, to begin
with, only officers.) Unsure of what the future would bring, despite
Ho Chi Minh's attempts to create a government acceptable to the
French, Giap's aim was to "mobilize, organize, and arm the people
for a people's war." Nevertheless, on 26 March he made a speech
praising the French army: it seemed that even Giap the intractable
could be diplomatic on occasion.

In early 1946, deciding to take the initiative away from Ho Chi
Minh, French diplomats, representatives of the metropolitan government, signed away French prewar rights in China in exchange
for the Chinese withdrawal of their troops from Tonkin and Annam:
with their departure the way would be clear for the return of French
troops to the North. At the same time in Hanoi Sainteny negotiated
an agreement with Ho Chi Minh, signed on 6 March, which would
allow the French to station, for five years only, twenty-five thousand
troops in the North. In exchange, Vietnam was to become a free
state—part of an "Indochina Federation" in a French Union—with
its own government, treasury, and army. In order quickly to establish a greater French presence in Indochina, just two weeks after
that the 13th Demi-Brigade of the Foreign Legion, famous for its

World War II exploits, arrived in the south, soon to be followed in
the north by the 3rd REI and significant numbers of French army
reinforcements from garrisons in France and North Africa.

The legion had been in Indochina since 1883 and prided itself on
knowing and working with the Vietnamese. Now, in the north, it
began a program of community development aid. But seeing the
dangers of this the Vietminh carried out reprisals against villagers
who accepted it. The legionnaires too received harsh treatment at
the hands of the Vietminh: castration, disembowelment, even cruci-
fixion were words that went into the official histories of the force.

The strategy adopted by General Valluy, now the military commander in Vietnam, was to hold the cities and towns with garrison
troops and dominate the countryside from outposts. As the French
army spread into the countryside, the demand for men grew daily, a
demand that was met by recruiting Vietnamese and Montagnards.
In the Legion they were not given full legionnaire status but wore a
white beret instead of a kepi blanc; in North African units they were
mixed into companies to dilute their presence and ensure loyalty. To
increase tactical flexibility, the Legion began to train Vietnamese
parachutists. In November the 1st Battalion of Foreign Legion Parachutists (1st BEP) arrived from North Africa, to be followed in February 1947 by the 2nd BEP.

To Ho, the agreement of 6 March was a step forward. He had told
the nationalists, who preferred the Chinese to the French, that the
last time the Chinese had come to Vietnam they had stayed a thousand years, and this was not the time to give them another chance.
But for all that the presence of French troops was a threat to future
independence, and when the news got around there was a swift
reaction from the population. The next day, outside the opera house,
the city's traditional central meeting place, before another great
crowd of about a hundred thousand people, Ho tried to explain this
apparent sellout. "I swear I have not betrayed you," he told them:
"The only way to avoid war is to negotiate." Giap, who thought the
use of force was the only way to gain independence, nevertheless
was loyal to Ho and also tried to mollify the crowds. In an emotional

speech he said that the agreement had the same purpose as Lenin had in asking the Germans to stop the invasion of Russia during the Great War: then, it had enabled the communists to consolidate their power; now, though the French had been allowed to stay temporarily, the Vietminh would strengthen its position. The alternative, he said, was armed resistance, for which the Vietminh were not ready. Eventually, the crowds dispersed, unconvinced.

And they were right, for with the departure of the Chinese and the British, Vietnam became to the international community an internal French matter that was none of their business. In effect, the French had a free hand, though the Americans, ever mindful of the increasing threat of world communism as the Russians took a tighter grip on postwar Eastern Europe, kept a watchful eye on things.

On 18 April a conference, at which Giap led the Vietminh delegation, was held at Dalat—a mountain resort with many fine villas and much favored as a holiday center during the hot months by the prewar French administrators—to iron out details of the 6 March agreement. It ended without any consensus because, contrary to what the Vietnamese had assumed to be the spirit of the agreement, the French announced that there would be important restrictions on Vietnamese control over their own internal affairs: it seemed they were not, after all, to have authority over such things as justice, economic planning, and communications. Convinced of French perfidy, Giap returned empty-handed to Hanoi. Then in May, with the Chinese starting to withdraw, he was appointed minister of defense.

During the Dalat conference, according to a French officer who was present, Giap had "let himself go. Bent forward, with his inscrutable smile he told us what his youth had been like. How his wife had been imprisoned and had died. How his life had been destroyed. And yet, he said, he could forget all this and could still hold out his hand in loyalty; swallow his suffering and reserve his hatred for those he considered responsible, and whom he did not identify with France." For in Giap's mind, France was greater than its minions; French history and culture transcended the actions of the country's petty officials.

Ho Chi Minh hoped for a more reasonable attitude at another conference scheduled to take place in France and on 31 May departed by sea from Haiphong with Pham Van Dong. The very next day, d'Argenleau proclaimed the creation of the "autonomous republic of Cochinchina," but in effect retained power in the hands of the French commissioner in the South. By dividing the country now he hoped eventually to be able to impose French rule over all of it.

In Cochinchina the French, in the face of continued unrest and the killing by insurgents of more than 350 village leaders, had continued their buildup of troops, and the recruitment of Vietnamese into their forces. Now, they had thirty-three thousand soldiers of the French army there, plus six thousand of the locally recruited levies, some of whom had served with the Free French Army in Europe.

On 12 September at Fontainebleau some minor concessions were made to the Vietnamese, so trivial that they were almost worse than nothing at all. On the thirteenth, most of Ho Chi Minh's delegation sailed for Haiphong, but he refused to leave emptyhanded: on the fourteenth he met the French prime minister and begged him to give him something to show his people. He got promises of a referendum in Cochinchina and more negotiations next year.

Back in Hanoi, Giap had not been idle. In front of a great crowd of Vietnamese and representatives of the French, he made a speech on the first anniversary of the founding of the Democratic Republic of Vietnam, but though on the surface things might appear normal and calm, behind the scenes there was much turbulence.

With the imminent departure of the Chinese, the nationalists, fighting the French and the Vietminh at the same time, were becoming very vulnerable. Now, desperately trying to gain the upper hand, they stepped up military action and began to vilify Giap in the newspapers and discredit him by word of mouth. Giap lost his temper, closed all newspapers, and deployed Vietminh units against nationalist troops in the suburbs, sometimes with the support and participation of the French Army, who regarded them as more militant and a greater threat than the communists. In Hanoi, on Giap's instructions, most of the leaders were arrested and killed or imprisoned and the VNQDD was disbanded. Coldly, Giap wrote them off: "The liquidation of the VNQDD was crowned with success and we were able to liberate all the areas which had fallen into their hands"—a short statement that hides turmoil and tragedy and hundreds of deaths. It was an episode that down the years was to give Giap the reputation of being a ruthless killer.

In among all this activity he had found time to form an association with a beautiful and famous dancer, Thuong Huyen. An extrovert, always flambouyant by nature and these days given to wearing bow ties and dressing snappily, frequenting nightclubs with his glamorous paramour, Giap came in for much criticism. Eyebrows were raised high by some of the communist hierarchy and their followers: this was no way for a senior member of the government to behave. Moving quickly to protect him, Ho Chi Minh introduced him to a woman he thought much more suitable, Ba Hanh, a highly intelligent graduate who came from a well-known family. Encouraged by Ho, and drawing back from possible disaster, in August Giap married her. They were to have four children, two boys and two girls. But before that came to pass there were to be many years of separation.

On 10 October 1946 d'Argenleau, convinced that the only way to stop the arms smuggling was to cut off the main supply route through the customs house in Haiphong, decided that he had had enough and ordered the French commissioner in Tonkin to take over control of the Customs Authority. On the fifteenth, when they announced their decision without any explanation, the reaction was instant. In Haiphong people came out on the streets in protest; in Hanoi, Giap saw red. It was not so much the fact that Customs were to be taken out of their control, it was the French acting as if they and not the Vietnamese were the government that rankled.

On the twentieth a junk carrying contraband was siezed by a French patrol boat. Vietnamese soldiers on shore fired on the French sailors, who fired back. Troops on both sides started to move into position facing each other, and then to exchange shots. On the twenty-third, d'Argenleau ordered the naval commander in charge at Haiphong to take drastic action to implement his orders. As a result the French cruiser *Suffren,* backed by marine artillery and aircraft, bombarded Haiphong. Most of the shells and bombs fell on the Chinese quarter of the town. Something like six thousand people died, and another fourteen thousand were wounded. Again, as was to be so often the case in Vietnam, nobody knew with any certainty how many casualties there had been.

Now things were at fever pitch. Giap, acting as de facto president in the absence of Ho Chi Minh—at the time on his way back to Vietnam by sea—intervened to try to take the heat out of the situation but got no change. When Ho arrived back in Vietnam at the beginning of November, both sides were moving to a war footing and it was not long before shooting started in Hanoi. The next days are best described in Giap's own words:

The French army began to intensify its provocative actions in Hanoi. Bands of red-capped foreign legionnaires roamed Trang Tien Street, looting shops, tearing up press publications displayed in the information center and even on one occasion snatching a Vietnamese flag off the wall. French motorcycle patrols rode recklessly through crowded streets. They deliberately caused road accidents and needled our traffic police. French soldiers even fired from the upper storeys of their houses at passing trams. French armored cars rumbled through the streets day and night.

On 7 December the French army in Haiphong launched a new offensive. They met with a stiff counterattack and had to pull back. On the ninth, eight hundred legionnaires illegally landed in Da Nang and on the thirteenth a big French cruiser called there. On the fourteenth, four hundred more legionnaires were sent to Haiphong from the south as reinforcements.

All this gave rise to a movement of protest throughout the country. On behalf of its 9 million members, the Viet Minh National Committee sent an open letter to President Ho and the government urging them to defend national sovereignty resolutely and expressing their readiness to sacrifice their lives to safeguard every inch of the fatherland. Mass organizations of youth, women, and teachers issued appeals calling for active contributions to the efforts of the entire people to smash the French army's schemes.

Our Party assumed exclusive leadership of the armed forces and directly led the army. Militia and guerrilla forces were consolidated. These had grown considerably and now numbered nearly 1 million members. The building of fortified villages was pushed forward. The army and militia were drilling day and night to improve their combat skills and prepare for war.

Many former French factories and workshops were transformed into arms-manufacturing plants. The workers, together with the technicians, mostly from French schools of practical technology, set out energetically to repair damaged rifles and artillery pieces. We also began to manufacture a quantity of weapons needed for the infantry: ammunition, grenades, mines, antitank bombs.

One Day Uncle Ho asked me how long Hanoi could be held if the enemy widened the war in the north. I told him, "Possibly for a month." He then asked, "What about the other towns?" I replied, "We can hold them more easily." "And the countryside?" I said immediately, "We can surely hold the countryside." He pondered for a while and then said, "We shall return to the Viet Bac" [the northern border of Vietnam].

A detailed combat plan for the defense of Hanoi was made. Every day, crowds of people thronged the city, members of district committees asking to be enlisted into guard squads, first-aid teams, and logistic services. Women put away their graceful *au dai* long dresses, cut their hair short, wore military uniforms, carried firearms and swords, and shared in patrol and sentry duty. Workers got trams and railway carriages ready for overturning when necessary to complete the blocking of streets still left open for French force movements. The big trees lining the streets had holes drilled in them ready for dynamite, so that they too could be brought down to complete the isolation of the French detachments.

From mid December the French forces increased their provocative actions in Hanoi. On the fifteenth they opened fire in several parts of the city. They shot at our policemen in Precinct VIII, they threw grenades, wounding two National Defense guards in Ham Long Street. All day on the twenty-seventh aircraft flew reconaissance flights over Hanoi. Then at ten in the morning they sent armored cars, for the first time, to demolish our fieldworks in Lo Duc Street. Legionnaires fired on people in Hang Bun Street. On the morning of the eighteenth fully loaded troop carriers, escorted by tanks and armored cars, charged into the streets around the Citadel area. On the same day Uncle Ho said that we had made concessions but the more we made the more the enemy pressed forward. "Our people will not go back to another life of slavery. The resistance war will be long and hard but it is bound to be victorious."

On the afternoon of the nineteenth I visited the army. In the suburbs many houses were securely closed. Some old persons and children continued to leave Hanoi on rickshaws hemmed in amid bundles of clothes and bedding. Carts full of earth were being pushed along the alleys by enthusiastic men and women, accompanied by cheerful shouts to people to keep clear. Earth walls were being heightened. Wooden pillars were being driven into the ground to strengthen the ramparts. A service team was singing to cheer them on. Young people were making energetic preparations for a fierce battle. They knew little about war, but talking to them I could see that they were confident and optimistic. Their appearance told me they would overcome all trials.

Since the night of the nineteenth the war had spread all over the country: Hue, Da Nang, Nam Dinh rose up to destroy the enemy. On 20 December Uncle Ho's call for a resistance war was broadcast by the Voice of Viet Nam Radio from a place not far from Hanoi. "We would rather sacrifice all than lose our country. Never shall we be enslaved! Compatriots, rise up!"

That winter, fifty-six years old, carrying a bamboo walking stick and wearing a pair of rubber sandals, he set out for the resistance war. "If we endure this cold winter, we shall see spring," he told me. He was a great patriot. His immense love for his country and his profound solicitude for his toiling and poor people knew no bounds. He devoted his whole life to the cause of national salvation and of liberating his people.

Reading these words it is possible to understand the depth of feeling of those days, and the determination in the hearts of the people to fight on for independence.

CHAPTER SEVEN

THE FIRST BATTLES

The decisive factor of victory on the battlefield is the readiness of the revolutionary masses to go forward, shed their blood, make all the sacrifices required of them, and fight for their fundamental class interests and for the nation's right to life.

—VO NGUYEN GIAP

T he Vietminh withdrew from Hanoi on 27 November 1946 and retreated to the Viet Bac, specifically to the area around Bac Can, eighty miles north of Hanoi. There, they re-created the liberated zone, a nebulous frontier that the French army could not pinch out from the Chinese border and that was too big to cordon. On 19 December the Vietminh officially declared war on France.

Giap had much to do, and he set about it with a will, tirelessly full of ideas, energy, and spirit. The first need was to recruit more soldiers, the second to arm them, the third to train them.

Recruiting was not difficult. The fervor of revolution that had been stirred up two years before in the Viet Bac was still smoldering; some of the cadres were still in place and had been continuing their work: men soon outnumbered weapons. The catchment area was, of course, hill country, Montagnard country, so they recruited first from the tribes. Men who spoke the dialects were sent to appropriate places to establish themselves in the community, perhaps marry local girls, and then search out recruits in their own and surrounding villages.

As to weapons, the production from "home-made" sources had given the Vietminh about a third of the eighty-three thousand or so weapons with which they would fight until 1949. Another third had come from the Japanese on their surrender or from the OSS, and a third had been bought from Thailand and from British sources in Hong Kong: six thousand rifles, four hundred machine guns, five small-caliber anti-aircraft guns, two hundred mines, and a thousand grenades. In the years to come, Giap would add to this arsenal with captured French weapons. Also, in September 1946 he had arranged to buy 12 million piastres' worth of communications equipment from Mao's army: at last he would have proper, though limited, means of command and control.

As to training, in 1946 the Vietminh had established officer and NCO training schools at Tong, on the site of a former French base northwest of Hanoi, and at Quang Ngai in central Vietnam. At both, they had Japanese instructors, men who were part of renegade Lieutenant Colonel Mukaiyama's Organization for Collaboration and Aid for the Independence of Vietnam. By the end of 1946 these schools had produced fifteen hundred NCOs but only a few hundred of the several thousand officers needed. Surprisingly, in view of the Party's strong commitment to communist principles, officers were not elected, they were selected from the keenest and ablest, in that order: a keen, competent man was preferred to a less well-motivated, more competent man.

After withdrawal to the jungle, other officer and NCO training schools were created—like the original one in Pac Bo consisting of palm leaf–roofed teaching and sleeping huts with supporting cooking facilities and an "office"—the products from which went to recruit training centers and to the ever-expanding number of units. And as weapons production began to match recruitment, some of the Japanese left their factories and accompanied the Vietminh into combat, especially as experts in the use of the heavier weapons—mortars and machine guns and the few artillery pieces that had been left in Vietnam by the Japanese occupation force when it surrendered.

There were, of course, basic communist theories and guidelines that were taught in the schools in addition to weapon handling and tactics. Easily grasped and easily remembered slogans were a favorite means of getting basic principles into the heads of unsophisticated people:

> The war of liberation is a protracted war and a hard war in which we must rely mainly on ourselves—for we are strong politically but weak materially, while the enemy is very weak politically but stronger materially.

> Guerrilla warfare is a means of fighting a revolutionary war that relies on the heroic spirit to triumph over modern weapons. It is the means whereby the people of a weak, badly equipped country can stand up against an aggressive army possessing better equipment and techniques.

> The correct tactics for a protracted revolutionary war are to wage guerilla warfare, to advance from guerilla warfare to regular warfare and then closely combine these two forms of war; to develop from guerilla to mobile and then to siege warfare.

> Accumulate a thousand small victories to turn into one great success.

So wrote Vo Nguyen Giap, great reader of communist theories, great developer of them. In the communist world there had to be a theoretical solution to everything; or everything had to be made to fit a theory. Revolution and Regeneration were the themes of most of them: how to bring down the old order and create a new and better one. But Giap did not just repeat ideas, he gilded them with thoughts of his own and invented new ones, adding to the burgeoning literature of an already overburdened, stodgy book list and becoming one of the pantheon of communist ideologues read by believers and students all over the world. In years to come people would search his writings for the guiding beacon that would lead them to Utopia, like him, putting their faith in theories. Some of them worked and brought down the old order: the problem was creating a better one.

Mao Tse-tung, following the ideas put forth in the Marx and Engels Communist Manifesto and improving on them, had spent years in the wilderness thinking deep thoughts, puzzling over problems, finding solutions, and then consigning them to print and posterity. Over the years he was to write many tracts and pamphlets, and some larger works: in 1928 he wrote: "Struggle in the Chi Kan Shan Mountains," in 1937, "Guerrilla Warfare," in 1938, "Strategic Problems of the Anti-Japanese war." He also figured out the prerequisites for guerrilla warfare. There had to be:

• Deep water for the fish to swim in: in other words, insurgents should be able to remain hidden in amongst the population they were subverting.
• Discontented people who would respond to subversion—made discontented if they were not already discontented.
• Rough terrain in which the subversives could hide if threatened by the security forces.
• Crops on which to be fed by sympathizers.
• A frontier with a sympathetic neighbor . . .

After China became communist in 1949, Vietnam would have them all.

Mao's seven steps to ensure the success of guerrilla warfare were:

• Arouse and organize the people.
• Achieve internal unification.
• Establish bases.

- Expand the bases.
- Recover national strength.
- Destroy the enemy's national strength.
- Regain lost territories.

Ho Chi Minh and Vo Nguyen Giap were, step by step and in the laid-down order, to achieve them all.

Giap added his own fighting principles to Mao's seven steps:

- If the enemy advances, we retreat.
- If he halts, we harass.
- If he avoids battle, we attack.
- If he retreats, we follow.

There, in those words, is the pushing, punchy Giap: direct, deliberate, determined, patient.

Ho Chi Minh, Giap, and Pham Van Dong laid down organizational laws for the Vietminh:

- Fragment the opposition's (either foreign or anticommunist) leadership, if necessary using assassination and torture.
- Do not destroy the opposition, take it over.
- Do not smash the existing social system entirely.
- Do not try for too much.
- Appear outwardly reasonable while working secretly against the opposition.
- Use overt and covert groups, with little contact between them.
- Do not antagonize if it can be helped, for doing so creates rival groupings.
- Work from small to large, from the specific to the general.
- Win small gains by communism, large gains by nationalism.

There is much food for thought there—especially the acceptance of the use of assassination and torture. The last rule is, perhaps, the most surprising, though in fact logical.

Mao had laid down that there were three different types of political activities: those toward the enemy (proselytizing); those toward the people (agitprop); those toward the guerrilla forces and their supporters (organizational and indoctrinational). Giap thought of two more, preceding those three chronologically: creating a psychological base among the people; small-scale organizational activity (finding reliable contacts, setting up courier networks) including the formation of armed propoganda teams. He gave names to the various proselytizing activities of his cadres: *dan van* was action among people controlled by communism; *binh van* was action among the enemy's military forces; *dich van* was action among enemy people. Armed with all this theory, his soldiers would be prepared for war.

In 1946 d'Argenleau had mistimed his actions in the North. In Hanoi the communists were concentrating on removing the threat from the nationalist groups (especially the VNQDD) and on consolidating their government. They were not actively resisting the French; indeed they were trying hard to accommodate them. Had d'Argenleau worked to find a means of increasing French influence and waited until French military strength had grown in Cochinchina, he might have been better placed to take on the Vietminh in decisive, snuffing-out action before they retreated into the jungle. Though anticolonialism was a wind of change that would undoubtedly have blown the French away in the end, they might have postponed their departure and, when the time came, gone with dignity.

With the departure of Ho Chi Minh and his army, the North was wide open to the French, who immediately consolidated their position in Hanoi by increasing the number of troops in Tonkin and Annam. The scene was set for military action to eliminate the Vietminh, but unfortunately for the French generals in Indochina in 1947, France was in dire economic straits and in political confusion.

America was pouring astonishingly generous financial aid into Europe to help nations recover from the war, and France, regarded at the time as probably the key nation to support because it was thought to be teetering on the brink of communism, got more than its fair share. But instead of using the money to regain strength and stability, the French spent almost the whole of their Marshall Aid on financing the war in Indochina, thus postponing their economic recovery. Public discontent brought political instability, which resulted in frequent changes of government. Prime ministers came and went, and so did the military commanders in Indochina appointed by them. Consequently, in Saigon there was little long-term strategic thinking and planning: instead, there was always pressure to get quick results, to get the war over in order that bad news from Indochina did not precipitate yet another political crisis at home and yet another change of government. And the arrival of yet another commander in chief . . .

Giap, in two paragraphs of great perspicacity, saw it thus:

> French governments held that all efforts had to be concentrated to find an "honourable way out," that is to say a "victorious" one. To reach this goal they had to do their utmost immediately to intensify the war, and win relatively great success, but because French imperialism had been weakened after World War II, their manpower and material resources were limited. Also, the colonial war was opposed by many French people at home. Hence the impossibility of mobilizing a colossal material strength against us, which they tried to overcome by using more and more puppet troops. [Giap and the other communists had begun referring to those who worked and fought for the French—and those who would later work for the Americans—as puppets; people not in control of their actions but responding to the directions of their masters. The French had recruited men from their colonies into their army during the nineteenth century and went on doing it into the twentieth.]
>
> The main cause of their difficulties lay in the very nature of the unjust war of aggression. The ultimate goal of the French colonialists was to grab our land; faced with our opposition, they had to scatter their forces and set up thousands of military posts, big and small, to protect what they had siezed . . . a constant scattering of their army. The more it was scattered the better were the opportunities we had to destroy it bit by bit; the bigger the proportion of puppet troops, the lower the morale of the enemy.

The first months of 1947 were spent by both sides in preparing for confrontation, the French building up their military resources and taking control of the main cities and towns throughout Vietnam, Giap creating the required three tiers of insurgency: the regular army (main force, *chuc loc*), regional forces, local self-defense forces.

At the lower level everyone in a village, male or female, young and old, had a part to play in assisting the higher level troops—directly, if required to take part in guerrilla attacks or defensive action, or indirectly by making booby-trap spikes or digging tunnels or providing labor or giving food—and also by being capable of defending the village. Regional units, less organized and less well-equipped than main force units, training together only two or three times a year and based mostly in their home villages, were capable of concerted action, with a limited degree of mobility, in support of the main force. According to Mao, second-tier regional units could cooperate best strategically, by harassing the enemy's rear, tactically, by creating diversions, and in battle by fighting alongside the regulars. Self-defense units could provide information, labor, sentries, casualty evacuation (generally known in military circles as casevac).

Giap's main force itself grew in size and complexity as time passed, based on a tripod organization of three platoons in each company, three companies in a battalion, three battalions in a regiment, three regiments in a division. Self-defense troops became guerrillas as they gained experience, and guerrillas became *chuc loc* if they were good enough. It was a scheme whereby the manpower resources of the nation were tapped at the lowest level, trained, and then directed upward to the cutting edge of rebellion.

In early October 1947, after much planning and preparation the French launched a large-scale military attack employing seventeen battalions in an attempt to wipe out the Vietminh main force and its leadership. During Operation "Lea," in which in total twelve thousand soldiers were deployed, Ho Chi Minh and Giap narrowly escaped capture by hiding in a hole while French paratroopers, who had been dropped on top of and around their headquarters, scoured the ground above them. When the paras went, they came out of hiding and vanished into the jungle: the jungle "where everything rots, and your flesh is the first to rot." To some extent Vietnamese were geneticially inured to such a life, but the French troops were not; they rotted and caught fevers and died when the Vietminh filtered through the jungle and shot them dead in the night.

On 16 October Giap's guerrillas destroyed bridges behind the paratroops that had to be rebuilt before they could be extricated. Farther south, in the Red River delta, two battalions of Tai Montagnard paratroop levies, led by French officers, swept the Vietminh out of the area between the Red and Black rivers. (Vietnamese who served as paratroopers in the French army were exceptionally tough and effective, as they were to prove many times in the years to come.) Other paras carried out successful operations on the banks of the Day River, and for a time things seemed to be going reasonably well, but by the time the rainy season came the French command realized that they were overstretched at the front and vulnerable in the base areas. Orders were given for the troops to withdraw back to barracks.

In future years both sides would largely suspend operations during the rainy season because of the restrictions on movement that wet weather brought, but not this time. Giap was not content to let them go: "By dispersing part of the main force into independent companies and battalion-sized groups I was able to give strong support to the militia and guerilla forces in the enemy's rear. At the same time I endeavored to build up mobile units and to push forward with mobile warfare. The people's armed forces, with their three categories, had taken shape."

In a masterly short analysis of the Operation Lea episode and the subsequent guerrilla operations, he writes:

> In the winter of 1947 the enemy threw over ten thousand seasoned men into a great offensive against Viet Bac with the purpose of smashing our organs of direction and regular forces so that they could secure a decisive victory and speed up the formation of a puppet government for the whole country.

General Revers's policy [he was the latest commander in chief] was to increase the number of troops on the Bac Bo front, expand the occupied areas in the delta and the midlands—to strengthen the defense of the quadrangle Lang Son/Tien Yen/Haiphong-Hanoi—and close the Sino-Vietnamese border. Other facets of Revers's plan comprised:

1. The development of the puppet army (to be used as occupation forces).
2. The re-groupment of European and African troops into mobile units.
3. The intensification of mopping-up operations with a view to suppressing our guerilla movement.

As for us, we advocated the launching of guerilla warfare on a large scale in all occupied areas. The tactic of using independent companies was brought into practice and crowned with success: part of our regular force was split into independent companies that went deep into the enemy's rear and there combined fighting with political work among the population; they coordinated armed struggle with the political struggle—destroying the enemy while setting up and consolidating bases among the population—and led the local armed and paramilitary forces in fighting the enemy in collaboration with the population. Propaganda work among the enemy troops, especially among the puppet soldiers, was considered as a strategic task and received particular attention.

Between 1948 and early 1950 the Vietminh began a number of small-size campaigns that retained certain characteristics of guerilla warfare, fielding from three to nine battalions. By 1950 the French had spread their troops over large areas of Vietnam, but thinly. Furthermore, the French command had not formed a strategic mobile force with which to take on enemy troops when they struck at the forts or ambushed the relief and logistic columns going back and forth along the roads.

Progressively, Giap's troops stormed their way through the northern provinces. Cao Bang, Lang Son, Lao Cai on the Chinese-Vietnamese frontier, Hoa Binh on the road south from the Viet Bac, and the greater part of the northwest, stretching from the Red River to the Laos-Vietnam frontier, all had to be successively abandoned by the French. In the south, they were recruiting still more Vietnamese into their own colonial forces: by the end of 1947 they amounted to two-thirds of the French troops there. Being more privileged, the officers and NCOs were more committed to the French cause than the rank-and-file.

The French army had now taken the shape it was to fight the Indochina war with: some French elite units, notably "Les Paras" (the red-bereted toughies of the army); other French units with conscripted short-term soldiers; colonial troops from North Africa, some of them paras, led by French officers (Algerians, Senegalese, Moroccans); and lastly, but of great importance, the highly elite international Foreign Legion, which had been the first to go into the ring. About a third of them were Germans, some of whom had left the chaos of postwar Europe to find another life where the only thing they knew, fighting, was valued. The Wehrmacht had finally made it to the Far East . . .

In March 1948, in order to create a command structure and so be better able to exercise control over his dispersed forces, Giap formed six interzones: (1) the Red River delta; (2) Northwest Tonkin; (3) Northeast Tonkin; (4) North Annam; (5) South Annam; (6) Cochinchina. Each zone had its own Party and military structure, each zone reported upward to the Party hierarchy and through it to him, the commander in chief. The Indochina war was to be fought mostly in zones 1 to 5, but with some activity in zone 6 around Hue and along Route 1 on the coastal strip, named by French soldiers "The Street Without Joy," a road that wound through wooded defiles from which French army convoys were incessantly ambushed.

But winning the people was the top priority that year, and the next: winning their commitment to the liberation of their country. In this Ho Chi Minh and his lieutenants were to be highly successful, building on the resentments that had lain dormant for decades. This is how one man, retired Lieutenant Colonel La Van Cao, now living in Hanoi, remembers his induction into the Vietminh, as told to the author:

My mother was from the Tai minority in the border area near China and my father was from the Nung minority. I was born in 1932 in the village of Nah Twan near Ding Phong in Cao Bang province, a very beautiful place on a river that starts in China, flows through Vietnam, and then returns to China. Many special products come from that area, including particular fish that taste very good because they eat a powerful herb that grows in the river.

I lived there until I was three years old, but then my father was unable to pay his taxes, was beaten by the French colonialists, and finally he died. They said I was too young to keep the property so my mother went back to her native village. It was not until after the revolution that I was given back my land. I now have rice fields in that place, nearly one hectare, irrigated by a wheel that takes water from the river to the fields.

My mother was very young when my father died, and many people told her she should marry again, which she did. Then I lived in Dung Diem with my second father, who was also of the Tai minority. We lived in what the Chinese regarded as slave country, and one day in 1943 bandits came, stole our buffalo and oxen and everything belonging to the family. As a result of the fighting during the robbery my second father died.

In December 1946 we started the resistance against the French colonialists. I was among many children who had an ardent wish to take part in the fighting, but I was very sick and very weak because I was affected by malaria. The only thing left in my body was my feelings toward the revolution. Every day I heard the bombs dropping on Cao Bang, and on 20 October 1948 I decided to join the army. I engaged in the 671st battalion of the 316th regiment, a local unit of the Cao Bang province that had many minority people in it—Tai, Nung, and Zao. The officers were the people who in normal times were the village leaders of the minority groups.

On the way to the training center, which was in the jungle, I and some friends who were also joining the army had to go through a district occupied by the French. We were intercepted, and some of my friends were shot, but that made the rest of us even more determined to go on. Then on the night of 25 October we came to a village that had been damaged by the French. The houses were still burning, which made us very angry.

At that time people were still very poor, so we had serious shortages of medicines, food, and weapons. I had only two sets of clothing,
prepared by my mother before I left, and because we could not dry it
in the sunshine in case it was seen by enemy planes, it was never
really dry. In consequence, because of our weak state and poor hygiene, we all suffered from bad skin diseases—and also from malaria.
When we could, we used traditional medical plants we found in the
forest. Sometimes we used leaves that were similar to antibiotics and
tasted like them, but most of the time the only thing we could do was
to use our own energy to suppress the disease: we worked very hard
and tried to sweat, because the heat of sweating killed the disease.
When the fever had died we started again.

I trained for three months, learning to march and fire a rifle and use
grenades, and to give first aid to the wounded. All the time we were
very optimistic. During the day we trained, and at night we sat
around a fire singing patriotic songs. We dreamed that one day we
would have tanks, guns, and an air force. We lived together as if we
were in the same family, even though the soldiers and the officers
were from different minority nationalities.

CHAPTER EIGHT

TOO MUCH TOO SOON

Confuse the enemy. Keep him in the dark about your intentions. Sometimes what seems a victory isn't really a victory, and sometimes a defeat isn't really a defeat.

—VO NGUYEN GIAP

In 1948 there was a stalemate, both sides building up their strength. The Vietminh raided French posts to capture weapons, then built tunnel mazes and hidden storerooms in villages in which to hide them, using camouflage in such a way that they could be found only if you knew exactly where to look, as many frustrated and harassed French and American infantrymen were to testify in the years to come.

In December 1949 the Chinese communists, after years of fighting, took over control of the country from Chiang Kai-shek as the remnants of his army took ship to Taiwan. (Some of his soldiers fled across the border into Vietnam, were disarmed by the French, and eventually were sent to join him in Taiwan.) The change of regime in China instantly altered the situation for the Vietminh, for now they really had sympathetic neighbors across the border, who early in 1950 formally recognized the Ho Chi Minh regime. The only problem was, they were Chinese! Despite their distrust of them, the Vietnamese begging bowl was thrust out, though they stayed cool and kept their eyes open for treachery. It was to stay thus for years, friendship waxing and waning, and has not changed even now.

Reacting to the situation, Ho Chi Minh and Giap visited Peking in December 1950 and Nanking the next month, leaving a handsome man by the name of Nguyen Chi Thanh temporarily in charge of military affairs as head of the Central Political Bureau of the army; his was a name that Americans would come to know. Ho and Giap did not return empty-handed, having signed an agreement whereby the Chinese would supply munitions, machine tools, and medicines. They also undertook to train the Vietminh in China and to send soldiers and administrators to Vietnam as advisers.

Recognition of the Democratic Republic of Vietnam by China was quickly followed by its recognition by Russia and the Soviet bloc in Europe, a political development of tremendous importance to Ho Chi Minh's campaign for independence. Now, whether the French liked it or not, they were fighting not an illegitimate band of rebels but an administration recognized by governments who were members of the United Nations Organization.

By April 1949 Giap had 32 regular battalions and 137 regional battalions. In May 1950 Ho Chi Minh announced that all Vietnamese males between the ages of sixteen and fifty-five living in Tonkin and Annam would be conscripted. (This was an edict easily applied within the liberated zone, though at first less easily outside it, where the French were ostensibly in charge. However, as time passed the Vietminh took control of two thirds of the country by day and three quarters of it by night—French troops retreated into their barracks after dark—and were able to enforce the rule. In mid 1952 they were to apply conscription to Cochinchina as well.) By June 1951 Giap had 117 regular battalions, which had been progressively formed into regiments, and 37 regional battalions.

Next, the regiments were formed into divisions of about ten thousand men each: the 304th, 308th (the Iron Division), 312th and 316th; and the 320th in the Mekong delta. Another, General Vu Hien's 351st Heavy Division, consisting of twelve artillery regiments and eight engineer regiments, capable of giving strong support to the infantry divisions, took shape as heavier weapons became available and was ready for war by mid 1952. (The concept of such a division had come from the Red Army, where massive use of concentrated firepower repeatedly achieved success against the Wehrmacht. In Vietnam, where there were not many well-trained artillerymen, and engineer equipment had to be carefully husbanded, centralized coordination of firepower and engineer resources made good sense.)

Each division needed fifty thousand porters, called *dan cong*, to provide its logistic support, each man (or woman) carrying specified loads. (Giap and his staff, after trial and error, had worked out what logistic norms were: a man could carry 55 pounds of rice or 40 pounds of other stores (because rice bags molded themselves to the body and made for easier carrying) over fifteen miles by day or twelve miles by night, and half as much half as far over mountainous country; a buffalo cart could lift 770 pounds over seven and a half miles in a day; a horse-drawn cart could move 470 pounds twelve miles in a day.)

In October 1951 the Chinese completed the rail link between Liuchow and Chen-nan-kuan via Nanning, using two hundred engineers and something like thirty thousand laborers. Over this, Vietminh soldiers were able to travel to military-training centers in China, among them Yulin, Liuchow, Tungsing, Haikow on Hainan Island, and Kwangyan. Between that date and the end of 1952, around forty thousand soldiers and ten thousand officers, including engineers and technicians, were phased through the schools. They even trained some paratroopers, though Giap never had the aircraft needed to enable him to use them as such. The Chinese arsenal at Kunming in particular was assigned exclusively to supply the Vietminh.

In the early days Giap relied heavily on Chinese expertise, seeking professional help where there were voids of knowledge. General Lo Kuei-po had been appointed chief Chinese military adviser, and in August 1950 two more generals, Chiang Yun-i and Ch'en Keng, came to the Pac Bo to confer and plan. Of the leaders of the Vietminh, at least five of them had had experience in China, either having been trained at the Whampoa Military Academy or having served with Chinese communist guerrilla units. One, Nguyen Son, had been appointed in charge of the central Vietminh operational and training command at Quang Ngai, and his deputy, Le Thiet Hung, was also Chinese-trained. Of the six who were given command of divisions by Giap in 1949, two had a Chinese military background, two were of Tho minority origin—as was Giap himself, distantly—and one was a former NCO in the French army. Only the sixth had made his way entirely within the Vietminh.

During 1951 the Chinese gave Giap four thousand tons of weapons, including 75-mm cannons of Russian and Chinese make, hundreds of Skoda rifles, and several German-made guns. They also sent one hundred thousand hand grenades, ten thousand rounds of 75-mm ammunition, and 10 million rifle bullets. Now, he was a military commander in the true sense, and not a guerrilla leader; with such military hardware available he could expand his forces and create the proper organization for the conduct of conventional war.

And as he expanded his forces, so the Chinese gave more material support: in 1952 they sent another forty thousand rifles, four thousand machine guns, some 120-mm recoilless rifles, thirty-five field guns, four hundred and fifty mortars, and, with a consequence no one could have foreseen at the time, fifty light anti-aircraft guns. Though it was bountiful aid, given to support a fraternal neighboring communist regime, at the time they were fighting in Korea and could not afford to give more. Interoperability of calibers was good because the French used American lend-lease weapons, the Vietminh had some American OSS-given weapons, and the Chinese and the Vietnamese made copies of them.

It was natural for Giap to rely on men with military training, and natural that most of those that had such training had received it in China, but after having open-mindedly and carefully studied both the Russian and the Chinese military systems, Giap opted for the Chinese. In his view it was a "complete system of military thought in which was embodied strategy and tactics suitable for colonial and semicolonial countries." The Vietminh became modeled on the People's Army of China.

The French too were building up their forces. At the end of 1947 they had more than fifty thousand soldiers in Vietnam; by 1948 the figure had doubled, though only 42 percent of them were Frenchmen; the rest were North African troops or members of the Foreign Legion. In 1949 there were one hundred and fifty thousand there, most of them in scattered barbed-wire-enclosed forts, in theory dominating the countryside, as medieval castles had dominated feudal lands and as they had dominated the Vietnamese when they first "pacified" them, but in practice besieged by Vietminh units who moved around them almost with impunity and harassed them constantly.

Almost always tied to the roads, the French army was hostage to ambushes and hit-and-run attacks: by the time the soldiers got out of their vehicles and formed up ready to counterattack, the Vietminh had disappeared into the jungle, pursued by volleys of rifle bullets that vanished, like the enemy, into the trees. "If the enemy attacks, we retreat . . ."

The French buildup continued with the expansion of the locally recruited Vietnamese into a force of over a quarter of a million, headed up by a cadre of only four hundred or so European officers. It was a situation that was to be repeated in the 1960s: young Vietnamese men were recruited by both camps, the side they served on often being a matter of chance—though given the option young men joined the one they thought was going to win. Often they had no option, and sometimes brothers found themselves in opposition. In many ways the Vietnam conflicts became civil wars, each side using available manpower for its own ends. Propaganda played a big part, as did psychological warfare, though the latter was predominantly used by the Vietminh. By 1954 they had more soldiers than the French.

That, then, is the background against which the fierce battles waged by the French against the insurgents took place. And there were hundreds of them, small and large, with extraordinary bravery and fortitude being shown by both sides, as is shown in this continuing account by the Tai soldier La Van Cao:

> When we had finished training we started fighting. We took part in more than thirty battles between 1948 and 1950. It was unusual not to fight every day. I myself killed twenty-five enemy soldiers but my comrades killed hundreds. I seized seven rifles, but together we captured hundreds. It was precious for us to have one more rifle or one more bullet.
>
> Most of the time we were fighting legionnaires, including Germans, British, and Americans who had taken part in the fascist war. We liked to fight with them. They were very highly qualified soldiers, mercenaries who were very stubborn, and when we beat them we felt that we were growing up. They had no families, but the French conscript soldiers had parents and wives and so did not fight as well as the Legionnaires. Many of them surrendered and changed sides, working with us to convince the new ones to surrender. Our officers highly valued their contribution, which is why one of our regulations was that if they surrendered we must treat them well. Even when we were short of food we shared it with them.

The battle of Dong Khe, which began on 16 September, was one of the crucial battles of the border province campaign, so crucial that Ho Chi Minh himself appeared there at Giap's side. His presence ensured that the Vietminh units fought especially hard. La Van Cao continues his story:

> To guarantee victory our battalion set up a special group of twenty-five people divided into five teams. We all carried large boxes of explosive. You see, we did not have enough artillery, so the explosives had to be delivered to the target by men. The French called us the

"man guns." Though it was very dangerous work we were ready to sacrifice ourselves. Before the battle we wrote a letter expressing our determination. First, we pledged that we would fight to the last man, to the last drop of our blood. Second, we had to unite with each other to fulfill our duty. Third, we had to implement very strictly the regulations for the battle, including not to seize the property of the enemy and not to shoot them when they surrendered.

We deployed our force about one kilometer from the enemy position. Three hundred of them were in a post on top of a small hill overlooking the Dong Khe plateau. The battle began at six in the morning with the explosion of one of our bombs as the signal. Very soon we were able to see that our artillery, using their 75-mm Japanese guns, had done their job well, because with the first round they knocked down the flagpole on top of the enemy position. We were so happy to see that the enemy had been beaten in the first few minutes!

At six-thirty in the evening, by which time it was dark, La Van Cao and his comrades started running toward the French position. He was hit in his right arm by a burst of machine-gun fire and fell forward into barbed wire, catching the wounded arm on it and fainting from the pain.

When I woke again I realized that I was going to die but had not done my duty, so I decided to ask my friend to cut the arm off, since it was impeding me. He refused, saying that I was an only son and that my family needed my arm, but I told him that I was going to die anyway so please cut it off. After a few minutes he agreed, and held my arm out over a piece of wood and cut it off with a bayonet. Then he tied the bit that was left tightly with a piece of string.

I then went forward up the slope to the enemy position and with my good arm and the shoulder of my bad arm pushed my box of explosives into the slit from which the enemy were firing. Then I retreated and detonated the explosive. The blast knocked me over, and when I came round again I realized that my blood was flowing into the ground. However, for some time I had been trying to become a Party member, and had been told that if I did well in the battle it would help me, so I decided to try to get to the first-aid post, which I knew was in the jungle behind me.

I was very tired and felt like lying down, but I knew that if I did I would die, so I went from tree to tree, leaning up against each one until I regained enough strength to go on to the next one. Eventually, I saw a light and knew it was the first-aid post. When I reached it I fell to the ground. The doctor looked at my arm and said that he would have to cut it off properly. He said that he would give me an injection and that after I had counted to seven or eight I would know no more, but I counted to twenty before I went to sleep . . .

For my action there at Dong Khe I was made a Hero of the Democratic Republic of Vietnam, and after I had recovered I was sent from place to place to urge people to join in the battle against the colonialists.

It was not easy to become a Party member. Aspirants were required to show consistent zeal and determination, had to be recommended by two Party members, screened by two inspectors, and then pass an oral test. Those who qualified were an elite, which, of course, was the whole idea. They were the kernel of communism in the nation, the totally loyal and fervent disciples of Marxism on whom the Party hierarchy relied to implement its decisions among the population. In return, they were given privileges and promotion. Not surprisingly, after the battle La Van Cao became a Party member.

The battle of Dong Khe was part of the struggle for Route Coloniale 4, which ran between limestone cliffs along the border with China, and the string of forts it connected. Employing classic picketing tactics, the French tried to secure the defiles and hillsides in advance of their convoys going to the key forts of Cao Bang, Lang Son, and Dong Khe, but they were ambushed nonetheless. The French thought that if they could control this road, they would be able to cut Giap's supply routes out of China: in response, the Vietminh hacked out parallel footpaths through the jungle, closer to or over the border, and manpacked their supplies.

When the monsoon came to Dong Khe in May, so did five battalions of the Vietminh, the first to have been trained in China. Low cloud cover and teeming rain made air support impossible, and forty-eight hours after La Van Cao and his fellow soldiers in the "death volunteer" unit attacked, the outpost surrendered. Within days the French recaptured it. They held it for a few months, but then it was overrun again. This time none of the garrison escaped; two legionnaire battalions virtually ceased to exist.

One after another the chain of forts were evacuated until the whole frontier area was in Vietminh hands. Then, in October, Lang Son, the provincial capital, and its fort with all its military equipment, was abandoned without a fight. Giap told a cabinet meeting that more than six thousand enemy troops had been wiped out and that the French had lost 13 guns, 125 mortars, 940 machine guns, 450 trucks, 1,200 submachine guns, and more than 8,000 rifles. And five provincial capitals! He was awarded the Ho Chi Minh Medal, Third Class, the first of countless honors.

About this devastating success he wrote:

> The victory won in the battle for the frontier zone in 1950 was a mark of the great progress of the three categories of the armed forces, especially the regular army. Organized on a larger scale, with improved equipment and armaments, our army, for the first time, launched a major offensive, annihilating a major part of the enemy's crack mobile forces, breaking their frontier defense line, and liberating a vast territory. The people's war had evolved from guerrilla warfare into conventional warfare. With the founding of the People's Republic of China, our victory in the battle of the frontier zone put an end to the imperialist encirclement of the Vietnamese revolution. Our communication lines with the socialist countries were open.

According to Mao's theory of revolutionary warfare, there were three stages, explained by Giap thus:

> During the first, localized guerrilla warfare is primary and war of movement secondary, but the latter becomes increasingly important. During the second, war of movement occupies the main role, at first only on the battlefield of local counterattack, but then over larger and larger areas. Guerrilla warfare is then intensified but plays a role

second to that of movement. [In its early phases] . . . the second stage is a combination of armed and political struggle, during which there is no active pursuit of hostile forces but rather a consolidation of position. Then, as enemy troops become more defensive, so revolutionaries go on to the offensive in mobile warfare, tactically a series of widely scattered guerrilla-band attacks on outposts, convoys, and patrols. The third stage is the General Uprising.

It is very difficult to say at what date we switched from guerrilla to mobile warfare, since there is actually no mechanical demarcation between the two. During the time we were using guerrilla warfare, we were also using independent companies and marshalled battalions. Subsequently, we fought battles involving first one, then several regiments, and in 1950 I launched our first major campaign involving brigades. The frontier-liberation campaign of 1950 may be regarded as the turning point in the development of the mobile warfare phase.

Giap had done stages one and two successfully—now, he thought, was the time to go for all-out attack, to deliver the coup de grâce.

He was wrong, the main reason for his error being the arrival in Hanoi in December 1950 of General Jean de Lattre de Tasigny, a man of enormous personality and presence, and great personal courage, as high commissioner and commander in chief. De Lattre had been a company commander at the beginning of World War II, had quickly been appointed to the command of a division, and had ended up in command of the Free French army. He immediately canceled the planned withdrawal of French women and children from Hanoi, saying that as long as they stayed his soldiers would not dare to leave Vietnam, and he brought his own wife there. Then he quickly set about building up morale and preparing to meet Giap's next onslaught.

He did not have long to wait. Between 11 and 17 January 1951, in Operation Hoang Hoa Tam, twenty-two thousand troops of Giap's 308th and 312th divisions attacked the fortified town of Vinh Yen, the last major French position northwest of Hanoi. They were bloodily repulsed and lost between six and nine thousand dead. The French, who had dropped napalm bombs from aircraft for the first time a month before, used it again: the panic-stricken Vietminh soldiers thought they were being attacked with atomic weapons.

Between 23 and 28 March, the 316th Division attacked Mon Khe near the coast in a lunge for Haiphong. They too were defeated, lost several hundred men and pulled back.

Between 28 May and 18 June, the 304th, 308th, and 320th divisions carried out a series of attacks along the Day River. They lost direction and cohesion, and they too had to withdraw, leaving several thousand dead on the battlefield.

Giap had overreached himself and had to retire hurt, but in doing so again left cadres in among the population to sow the seeds of rebellion. He had not made a good showing, keeping nothing in reserve to exploit sudden opportunities or retrieve adverse situations and having great difficulty in disengaging his troops in the last battle. But he had used large formations in wide pincer movements intended to open the western road to Hanoi; take de Lattre's forces in the rear, on the other side of the capital; draw troops away to the South while the first, Vinh Yen, assault pressed on to Hanoi and the second, Mon Khe, attack cut the city off from its port. Had it succeeded, his 1951 campaign would have been hailed as a masterpiece of coordinated strategy; as it was, his clever plan did not work because he did not have appropriate command and control equipment or procedures—or previous experience of directing such a complex operation, even at a lower level. And because his adversaries fought with a desperation never seen before, their lives, and those of the French families in Indochina, their pride, their empire—all were at stake.

De Lattre began the creation of a fortified chain of positions that would protect the Red River delta from the Vietminh surrounding it in the hills. Fifteen million tons of concrete went into the making of them, and eventually twenty infantry battalions were permanently rooted in them. Unfortunately for France, he soon became terminally ill, had to be sent home, and died of cancer in Paris in January 1952. He was replaced by General Raoul Salan.

A minor incident, but typical of the fierce intensity with which the Vietminh fought their battles, and of the way the Vietcong were to fight theirs in the 1960s, was the night attack on a small fort held by North African troops on the Street Without Joy.[*]

Defended by two Moroccan rifle companies and a tank platoon, organized as two separate but mutually supporting strongpoints, and able to call on the fire of distant artillery, the position was also covered by an outpost line that would give warning of an attack. Between the two strongpoints ran a small stream.

After twenty minutes' intensive general preparatory bombardment, the Vietminh 120-mm mortars concentrated their fire on the southern strongpoint, and at ten minutes past ten shrill screams of *"Tien-Len"* ("Forward") were heard as the enemy infantry threw themselves onto the barbed wire. One human wave after another was smashed into bloody pulp by the intense fire of dozens of automatic weapons. In an attempt to stop the assault, shells from the French batteries were directed closer and closer to the position until they were landing on the Moroccan barbed wire, but by midnight it was obvious that the southern strongpoint could no longer be held; the barbed-wire entanglements, covered with a carpet of enemy bodies, were no longer a hindrance, most of the foxholes had been shattered by enemy mortar bombs, the survivors were running out of ammunition. Soon after one o'clock the order was given to cross the narrow bridge and join up with the men in the northern strongpoint.

But it too was given no respite. At three in the morning five Vietminh battalions made a mass attack against the two hundred men who were left. Inside the enclosure, the light tanks of the armored platoon, their guns depressed as far as they would go, fired unceasingly into the screaming human clusters who came crawling over the parapets. Their treads crushed heads, legs, arms, and chests as they slowly lumbered about in the small open space, but soon they too were submerged by the seemingly neverending waves of men. With scores of hands clawing at the turret hatches trying to pry them open, stuffing incendiary grenades into their cannon, and firing machine gun bursts into their driving slits, they were finally destroyed

[*]Here the author is indebted to the description given by Bernard Fall in his book *Street Without Joy* (see Bibliography).

by pointblank bazooka fire that lit up the hulls with sizzling patches of white-hot metal.

The smell of roasting flesh hung in the air as all five tank crews died to the last man, to be followed soon after by the remnants of the infantry.

The buildup of the Vietminh continued unabated despite the setbacks, and by 1952 Giap had more than a quarter of a million regular soldiers and a militia estimated to be around 2 million strong.

CHAPTER NINE

THE SWORD IS POISED

Rapidity of decision making was vital. Rapidity of decision making meant readiness to fight the enemy at any time when he was not reinforced or was withdrawing; readiness to fight in the mountains or the delta; readiness to fight with the enemy in position or on the march; readiness to engage in mobile warfare, seige warfare, or guerrilla warfare provided we could wipe out enemy effectives, the basic goal of all ideas.

—VO NGUYEN GIAP

In Korea, in killing zones lashed with artillery and mortar fire, and sometimes pounded by ground-attack aircraft, the Americans had been able to stop Chinese human-wave attacks. During the next three years, one after the other, French commanders in chief would try to draw Giap into a set-piece battle where their superior ground and air firepower would give them a big advantage. But Giap had made his mistake in the Red River delta and would not make it again; in future battles he would sacrifice units that were hopelessly trapped rather then get drawn into "meat-grinder" situations; if he could see that continued effort was worthless and would result in long-term weakness, he would withdraw, even if it meant short-term losses: if units already committed to battle had to be sacrificed, so be it. Out of his belief in this principle grew a reputation for the ruthless squandering of lives, a charge that is made by his main adversaries, such as Generals Bigeard and Westmoreland, as well as many military writers.

After the debacles of the spring of 1951, the Vietminh nursed its wounds, but continued to enlarge and train. And fight—the best way to train, providing the basic lessons are known. Giap, a pragmatic man, admitted publicly that he had made a mistake in going over to the General Counter Offensive too soon, but there was nothing to be gained from bewailing errors or lost opportunities. As he had done before, and as he was to go on doing, he turned away from the past and got on with the future.

There was, inevitably, some criticism from within the Party for Giap's failures, but it seems that, generally, people understood the difficulties under which the army was operating, and there was no movement to replace him. Everyone had to learn while fighting the war, and though there were other tried and tested soldiers who might have been chosen to replace him, thanks to being one of the original leaders of the Party and having already achieved so much, he survived.

As always, he took his orders from the Party (of which, of course, he was a senior member, and in which he had a strong voice), whose Central Committee, under the chairmanship of Ho Chi Minh, now clearly set out, in an iron grip of doctrine, the principles for the strategic direction of the war: "The general guiding principle is to conduct a long war of resistance. We must not underestimate the enemy, take hasty steps, or indulge in recklessness. We must strike surely, advance cautiously, strike only when success is certain: if it is not, then we will not strike. Fighting with victory is allowed; fighting without victory is not allowed."

In the limestone caves of the Vietminh headquarters at Thai Nguyen, fifty miles north of Hanoi, Giap and his Military Committee evaluated the choices open to the Vietminh and the French: "The delta, [the Red River delta] with its transport and supply facilities, offered many possibilities for our troops to launch a big offensive, hence its defense would be most carefully organized [by the French]. In the mountains, the French were vulnerable—their forces were scattered, artillery and air support was restricted because of the jungle canopy, re-supply was difficult, and the topographic conditions were not favorable to them. But though we had advantages, we assessed that we too could not ensure re-supply and reinforcement on a large scale, and therefore could only use a limited force for relatively short offensives." The committee decided that "mobile warfare would become the main form of war on the chief battlefield—north Vietnam—while, on the other fronts, the main role would still be played by guerilla warfare."

The People's Army also had other advantages. Seven carefully thought-out rules had been laid down for the soldiers when dealing with the civilian population:

> Be polite.
> Be fair.
> Return everything borrowed.
> Cause no damage if it can be helped; if you do cause damage, then pay for it.
> Do not bully people.
> Do not fraternize with women.

These common-sense rules, taken seriously by the soldiers, ensured that they worked harmoniously with the people among whom they lived—in contrast to the French troops, who, whatever they did, were sure to alienate them: that is one of the facts of life in an insurgency situation. The rules also gave them a moral ascendancy over their enemies: ethics were a part of being in the People's Army; ethics gave them an edge over those who fought without them, who did not even think about such things. It was a factor unfortunately not noted—or if it was, not given much credence—by their opponents, then or in the 1960s and '70s.

The Vietminh had, too, a clearly defined aim and real faith in their chances of achieving it: a burning zeal to fight and win, which the French colons and the motley army of conscripts, North Africans, mercenaries, and not totally convinced Vietnamese did not have. Indicative of this was the case of a French battalion commander who, after several years of war, knowing that there was nothing to show for the tens of thousands of battle casualties—dead, wounded, missing, and captured—had asked his superior to give him a moral reason for their presence in Vietnam, "if only, mon general, so that I can say something to my soldiers." Like Pontius Pilate, he did not get an answer.

Another advantage was that discipline was maintained by social pressures rather than by punitive restrictions. There was no way in which offenders could be "detained" in the jungle. Certainly there was no question of applying forfeiture of money as a sanction, since nobody was paid. (Soldiers were given their uniforms, weapons, food, a mosquito net, and medicines, if there were any, when they became sick; the *dan cong* got food only—sometimes: mostly they fed on the food willingly given by the people in the countryside.) Sanctions were based on the fear of loss of face: loss of self-esteem caused by invoking the contempt of one's peer group.

To this end, units held self-criticism sessions during which men owned up to their errors and omissions. Once their "sins" were admitted, as with the confessions of a Roman Catholic, there was forgiveness and time for amendment of life, though serious faults or an accumulation of them resulted in ostracism within the unit or, worse still—the ultimate sanction—banishment from any contact with the Party or the army: to return to one's village in disgrace, unwanted and untrustworthy, took a lot of living down; the contempt of society, and its effect on one's family, were far worse than any short-term punishment. In contrast, the French had to resort to penal detention for serious crimes, which meant that a lot of the time offenders got what they wanted if they misbehaved—removal from danger.

Abiding by the principle of striking whenever possible, in the winter of 1951 and the spring of 1952, the Vietminh began many hit-

and-run campaigns: for example, in 1951 in the Red River delta; in 1952 in the northwest, where they obliged General Salan's troops to withdraw from a key position not far from Hanoi. But there were limitations, as Giap noted:

"In the Midlands, Highway 18 and Ha Nam Ninh campaigns on the delta front, with our armed forces mustered to a certain degree, we could gain absolute superiority only for short periods of time. As soon as the enemy, taking advantage of his capability for rapid reinforcement, brought in more mobile forces, we then met with many difficulties in continuing the development of our offensives." But all the same, such attacks obliged the French to dilute their forces: like a man swatting at a swarm of attacking wasps, they flailed about in all directions.

In 1953, wanting to draw the French away from the delta and extend their supply lines, Giap turned west, toward Laos, where for years his men had taught, and fought minor battles with, the Pathet Lao, the Laotian communist insurgents. (Language was not a great problem, since the two nationalities could understand each other.) Thousands of conscripted Vietnamese found themselves not directly fighting the French but passing the war years in the jungle as part of the Pathet Lao. (As an example, Bui Cong Ai, an Annamese who eventually became a *dai uy loc quan*—a brigadier general—in the People's Army, was married in 1950 at the age of eighteen but soon had to leave his wife to go to Laos, where he lived for four years. He had no contact at all with his home during that time; his wife did not know if he was still alive, and even when his father died he did not hear of it.) In April, Giap sent Vietminh soldiers into Laos, where, after skirting the French fortifications on the Plain of Jars, they reached the outskirts of the capital, Luang Prabang—whose inhabitants had allegedly been told of their imminent arrival by a blind soothsayer. Having made his point to the French high command in Saigon that no part of Indochina was out of reach of his troops, before the rains came to bog him down, Giap pulled his troops back part of the way:

"In the early summer of 1953, in a joint effort, Pathet Lao Liberation troops and Vietnamese Volunteers made a surprise attack against the township of Sam Neua and the major part of the enemy's troops in that region. The whole province of Sam Neua and vast areas of upper Laos were liberated." It was then, in May 1953, that General Henri Navarre replaced Salan as commander in chief.

Navarre was an introvert. Not cast in the typical military mold, he had been described by a French official as "physically and morally feline." In World War II he had commanded an armored-car regiment. After that, over the years consistently good staff work had resulted in his eventually becoming chief of staff of NATO's Allied Forces Central Europe before he was sent to Indochina. He was a clever man and in the fast lane of promotion but in the opinion of many combat "sharp-end" soldiers had spent too much time in military intelligence and lacked real battle experience. It was the sort of in-house army bigotry to which infantry in general and paratroops (and, in France, Legionnaires) in particular are prone, and which is hard to refute: however charismatic and efficient a soldier may be, he either belongs in the fighting club or he does not. Giap thinks that "Though not having de Lattre's fame and rank, Navarre was among the young generals of the French army, a cultured man having a sense of strategy."

As the conflict dragged on, the French had come to depend more and more on American aid: in 1951 financially it had amounted to 12 percent of the cost of the war, and by 1953 it had risen to 71 percent; in material terms, by 1953 it amounted to between twenty thousand and forty thousand tons of military equipment per month. And they were giving advice as well; Navarre arrived in time to implement a plan thought up by French and American generals in the Pentagon in Washington earlier in the year: the Vietnamese-manned units that had been created would be given greater responsibility—in particular, would take on the pacification of the countryside and the guarding of installations, thus freeing French combat troops for more important tasks; at the same time, increased French forces would be concentrated so as to provide a mobile force to seek out and, as Navarre put it, "harry and destroy the enemy." (It was a concept—then to be called "Vietnamization"—that was to be mirrored fifteen years later, by the Americans, with equal lack of success.) Giap:

Navarre decided—despite his slogan of "always keep the initiative, always be on the offensive"—that in the autumn-winter of 1953 and the spring of 1954 he would stay on the strategic defensive in the north, develop the puppet army, and build up a strong mobile force. Then, early in 1954, he would avail himself of the forced rest of our troops [due to monsoon conditions] and transfer the greater part of his mobile force to the south. If an offensive there worked well, in the autumn of 1954 he would transfer back to the north a greatly increased mobile force and move to a strategic offensive. If he could achieve great military successes in the north, he could force us to negotiate in conditions unfavorable to us; if we did not accept his conditions he would destroy our regular forces.

In his mobile force he wanted seven divisions (six infantry and one paratroop), comprising twenty-seven mobile brigades in all. For this purpose he ordered the regroupment of picked European and African units and at the same time asked the French government to send him two more divisions. He received only twelve battalions, from France, North Africa, and Korea. [In fact, he asked for fourteen battalions and got nine.]

In Saigon Navarre assessed the situation and came to the conclusion that during what remained of 1953 he would increase the size of the Vietnamese component to fifty-four mobile battalions, and double that strength in 1954. If this came about he would then have nearly three hundred thousand soldiers in addition to his own French Expeditionary Corps. In fact, he succeeded in creating 107 new levy battalions, ninety-five thousand men. However, this expedient was only a quantitative increase at the expense of quality. Giap:

> The situation of the two sides in the summer of 1953 can be summarized as follows: On our side, all our regular divisions and regiments had been organizationally strengthened and re-equipped with new weapons. The People's Army comprised many regular divisions and regiments, besides a great number of local regiments and battalions. Guerrilla forces had also developed quickly. As a result of political remolding classes, our soldiers had a clearer view of the goal of their fight; their hatred for the enemy and their fighting spirit had heightened.

On the enemy's side, they had about 450,000 soldiers in the whole of Indochina, comprising 120,000 Europeans, Africans, and legionnaires, the rest puppet troops. Although those effectives showed a big increase in comparison with the beginning of the war, the balance of forces between the two sides had already tipped visibly in our favor. Politically, the unjust nature of the war had aroused mounting opposition from the French people, and French and African mercenaries became more and more fed up with it. As a result of many successive defeats the morale of the French army had sunk. Many of the puppet troops had enlisted not because of conviction but because they could find no work.

In July 1953 Navarre dropped paratroops deep into our rear, attacking Lang Son, and boasted that we had suffered heavy losses, though in fact our losses were insignificant. In August, he withdrew the whole of his armed forces from Na San to the delta, claiming that this withdrawal was a great success, and that Na San had lost all military significance—even though earlier he had said it was a "Second Verdun" blocking the road to the southward advance of communism!

The one really successful tactic that French commanders developed was the use of Groupement des Commandos Mixtes Aeroportes, GCMAs—Composite Airborne Commando Groups—and, from December 1953, Groupement Mixtes Intervention, GMIs. These were guerrilla forces modeled on Wingate's Chindits and Merrill's Marauders in Burma but bigger. One of the seminal units was a French battalion that had fought bravely in Korea with the U.S. Army's 2nd Division and then, augmented with Vietnamese and other colonial troops, had been formed into Groupement 100, with a strength of thirty-five hundred men. By mid 1954 there were fifteen thousand such soldiers, needing three hundred tons of airborne supplies a month. They operated deep in the jungle, sometimes with Montagnard tribesmen, sometimes with Vietnamese peasants not yet brainwashed by the proselytizers. Sometimes, taking a leaf out of the Vietminh handbook, they married the daughters of tribal chiefs in order to cement relationships (and, no doubt, to alleviate the pangs brought on by many months without female company). They were so successful that ten Vietminh battalions were tied down on anti-GCMA operations and a whole battalion, the 421st, was responsible for gathering intelligence information about them for Giap's head-quarters.

The main reason for the success of these special units was that, for once, they put the Vietminh on the defensive. Until now it had been the French who were obliged to respond to the enemy's initiatives, who were always waiting for the ambush on the road or the night attack on the defended position. By going deep into the jungle and turning the tables, they gained the high ground of morale and having done that achieved successes out of proportion to their numbers. They proved the point that the only way successfully to take on and beat the Vietminh was to use the same tactics: accept extreme priva-tion, fight fiercely, strike and fade, strike again, for as long as it took.

With Western man too sophisticated to accept crude brainwash-ing and highly materialistic in his values, the only way to create the necessary spirit and endurance would be to give him other incen-tives—make such a force outstandingly elitist and pay its members many times as much as ordinary soldiers. If in a year or two they could save a really significant amount of money, that, and the self-respect—even fame—generated by having fought with such units, would compensate for the hard life and danger. Unfortunately, de-spite the obvious successes of the Groupements it seems that such a concept was never seriously considered, then or in the 1960s.

(To show the dedication that the GCMAs and GMIs fostered, for three years after the war had ended, until 1957, remnants of them fought on, the last report to come out of the jungle being picked up by People's Army signalers in September of that year. One wonders what happened to those solitary men. Did they rot and die, all of them, or did some eventually bury their weapons and identities and stay in the jungle with Vietnamese wives? Are there today, scattered around the northern provinces of Vietnam, half-castes who don't quite fit in to the life they lead?)

In 1953, though, Giap was figuring out the next step:

> The Party Central Committee had decided that the strategy for the winter 1953/spring 1954 campaign would be:

To liberate Lai Chau and the whole Northwest;
To launch an offensive into Laos;
To conceal an important part of our regular forces and keep them
  ready for action;
In the delta, to increase guerrilla warfare;
In the south, in the Fifth Zone, to launch an offensive in the
  Western High Plateau to defend our free zones there.

To carry out our strategic plan we had scattered our stores [the
main supply depot was at Yen Bai], transferred our offices and
schools deeper in our territory and, during October, mobilized thousands of *dan cong.*

In mid November, as part of the plan, we moved some of our forces
in the direction of Lai Chau. With this move the military situation
changed radically, for the enemy detected the transfer. Were we
going to attack toward the northwest or toward the delta? If we attacked toward the northwest, how would he protect his soldiers in Lai
Chau and stop us from going into upper Laos? On 20 November 1953,
he dropped six picked parachute battalions on the Muong Thanh
plain and occupied Dien Bien Phu.

Major Marcelle (Bruno) Bigeard was the first man to land there. As
a sergeant he had been taken prisoner by the Germans after the
capitulation of France in 1941, had escaped and then joined a unit of
French colonial troops in North Africa as a sous-lieutenant. Next, he
was trained by the British as a parachutist before being dropped in
France to fight with Les Maquis, the underground liberation organization—for which battles he was awarded the British Distinguished
Service Order, a rare honor indeed for a junior officer. He had already done two tours of duty in Indochina—in 1945 as a captain, in
1948 as a company commander in a battalion of Tai Vietnamese
soldiers—before returning in 1952 as commander of the thousand
men of the 6th Parachute Battalion.

Bigeard had been told that there would be no opposition, but, he
says, "there were two companies exactly where we jumped. Some of
my men were killed before they even touched the ground, others
were stabbed to death where they landed. The combat lasted all
day, with forty men killed on our side and two Vietminh companies

almost totally destroyed. It was a hard day—but Dien Bien Phu had been taken." A week later Navarre himself arrived on a fact-finding visit; with ten thousand men there by then and another five thousand in reserve, he decided that the situation was "excellent." Giap, again:

> Navarre's intention was to link up with Lai Chau and then extend the radius of his action so as to ensure the defense of upper Laos. Then in late November the enemy found new signs: many of our regular units, including the most seasoned ones, were marching toward the northwest. Now he was faced with a decision; should he withdraw from Dien Bien Phu or reinforce the garrison there? On 3 December, Navarre chose the second solution and ordered that Dien Bien Phu would be defended at all costs. It was a decision of great strategic importance.

So, indeed, it was, but not one entered into without much thought.

Throughout history Dien Bien Phu, only seven miles from the Laotian border, had been strategically important because it sat astride trade routes between China, Thailand, and Laos. Remote and hard to reach, when the French first arrived in Indochina, it was the last place to come under their control—after months of resistance led by a man called Nguyen Van Giap (no relation). Now Navarre decided to stay in Dien Bien Phu for three quite different reasons. Giap relied on the sale of opium grown in the area to finance the purchase of weapons and medical supplies; if that major source of funds—worth millions of piastres a year—could be cut off, some of the Vietminh would wither on the vine. By interrupting the Vietminh's supply lines, he could put an end to insurgency in Laos. Lastly, Vietminh units might be lured into set-piece battles: a heavily fortified camp containing light tanks and artillery would be the base from which strong fighting patrols would flush out and eliminate Vietminh units and dominate the area. Giap again, as usual putting his finger right on the mark:

> Our problem was to try to foresee how the enemy would act. He could defend Dien Bien Phu and Lai Chau at the same time or re-

group to a single position; reinforce that position and transform it into an entrenched camp; or he might withdraw. If he withdrew, he would lose territory. If he sent reinforcements he would scatter his mobile forces. The landing of troops at Dien Bien Phu laid bare the contradiction between occupation of territory and concentration of force; between occupying the delta or the mountains.

Giap underscored the dilemma by making life more difficult for Navarre:

On 7 December the enemy at Lai Chau had withdrawn part of his forces to Dien Bien Phu; the remainder of it was preparing to withdraw. On the tenth we opened fire on Lai Chau, and at the same time sent troops to cut off the retreat to Dien Bien Phu. On the twelfth, we liberated Lai Chau town. After more than ten days of fighting, pursuit, encirclement, and destruction, our troops liberated the remaining part of the enemy-occupied zone in Lai Chau province. The enemy had to reinforce Dien Bien Phu rapidly.

Not content with this:

In order to create a diversion, on 21 and 22 December, Pathet Lao and Viet units launched two successive attacks near the Laos border, destroying two mobile battalions, part of another, and an artillery battalion. The enemy had to transfer units from his mobile force in the Bac Bo (Red River) delta to reinforce the base at Seno in Laos: Seno became another point where he scattered his forces.

Navarre, having decided to stay in Dien Bien Phu, did not see that he must now change his plan. Instead, he carried on as if the withdrawal of forces for Operation Atlante, the launching of an offensive by fifteen battalions farther south in the Fifth Zone (part of Annam), was unaffected by the new situation. Meanwhile, on 26 January 1954 Giap's troops attacked the western highlands and on 5 February took the town of Kontum, advancing as far as Route Coloniale 19. In response, Navarre transferred some troops from the north, the Bac Bo delta, to the western highlands. He then tried to concentrate his forces in preparation for Operation Atlante but again was diverted by Giap, this time by an offensive in Laos. Next, he was obliged to reinforce Luang Prabang with mobile troops withdrawn from the Viet Bac. Despite Navarre's stated aim of creating a sizable central reserve, his opponent was making him disperse his troops. As Giap puts it:

> By March 1954 we saw two noteworthy characteristics. First, our troops were victorious everywhere. Second, the enemy strategic mobile mass was no longer concentrated in the Bac Bo delta; it was dispersed in many directions, and reduced from forty-four to twenty battalions.
>
> Navarre reckoned that despite his casualties he had been able to cope with and check our autumn-winter offensives and that it was now his turn to take the initiative. He ordered that the strategic offensive on the southern battlefield should continue, that relatively big forces should be concentrated in order to resume the Atlante plan, which had been interrupted. On 12 March he started an attack on Qui Nhon, not for a moment believing that on the following day we would launch a large-scale offensive on the Dien Bien Phu fortified entrenched camp.

Giap had harried Navarre and forced him to take his eye off the ball, had made him break two of the basic rules of warfare: first, he had been unable to maintain his aim—the establishing of the central reserve—and second, his concentration of effort had been lost by the dispersion of troops to the Atlante operation. To make matters worse, a big rift had developed between Navarre and General Cogny, his commander in Hanoi.

Cogny, a hard-bitten, experienced fighter, had not taken to Navarre from the start: in their case, it was the repulsion of opposites. In his modern, air-conditioned headquarters in Saigon, surrounded by aides, Navarre moved the chinagraph "goose eggs" around on the map, while in the north Cogny had to cope with the day-to-day problems and irritations of equipment availability and reliability, communication breakdowns, supply and movement difficulties, aircraft and crew readiness, senior officers' appointments and foibles, and the need to escort and fuss over visiting VIPs. It was a classic example of a rift between the thinker and the doer, a rift that in their case would never heal until the day they died, and which was to result in acrimonious litigation in open court in France years after they both had left Indochina.

Both Cogny and Navarre were fighting for their place in the history books: Navarre for justification of his decisions, Cogny to be exonerated for the dreadful consequences of those decisions. Essentially, Cogny blamed Navarre for ever having gone to Dien Bien Phu in the first place and, after he got there, for using troops in what Cogny considered to be a useless diversion from the main crisis instead of attempting a relief operation. In Cogny's view Navarre refused him the use of perhaps twenty battalions for an offensive that might have alleviated the pressure on Dien Bien Phu, yet was willing to commit twice as many in a pointless attack on a sector whose conquest at that time (or whose continued control by the communists) was in no way vital to the outcome of the war.

That dispute was to be in the future. Now, the stage was being prepared for a mighty contest, in a ten-by-five-mile arena near the Laotian border, with the soldiers of a man who had taken to generalship as if born to it.

In December 1953 Giap was forty-two years old—but a young-looking forty-two, still with the fine features, large eyes, and thick jet-black hair above a high brow that had once caused Ho Chi Minh to laughingly tell his friends in Pac Bo that Giap was "pretty, like a woman." But there was nothing feminine about Giap: he was whiplash strong and had a mind to match. He had calmly weighed the facts and determinedly taken the measures that would result in battle. Now he set out cold-bloodedly to grind his enemies into the ground.

Vo Nguyen Giap with his first wife

Vo Nguyen Giap's second wife and their firstborn

The first Armed Propaganda Brigade, 1944

The young Giap

Giap and Ho Chi Minh, 1950

Ho Chi Minh's first administration, Giap second from left

Giap's troops at Dien Bien Phu, 1954

General Marcelle Bigeard

Giap with young officers, 1954

Giap with staff officers

CHAPTER TEN

THE ARENA OF THE GODS

A year ago none of us could see victory. Now we can see it clearly,
like light at the end of the tunnel.

—GENERAL HENRI NAVARRE, 1953

Dien Bien Phu—The Seat of the Border County Prefecture—was the name given to a cluster of little hamlets, in all a hundred or so bamboo houses on stilts scattered along a valley eleven miles long by five miles wide in the northwest of Vietnam. After the French established themselves in Tonkin, it became the home of a lowly—and lonely—official appointed by the French to collect taxes in the area—hence the title.

Settlements had existed there for centuries—as they invariably had to be, beside running water: a small river, the Nam Rom, threaded its way down the valley. To the unfortunate official isolated days away from civilization in Hanoi, there were few compensations, unless he was the sort of man who liked living in the back of beyond with people of the Tai minority as neighbors. If he was, then there were many compensations: new sights to see, new things to learn, new pleasures to be sampled. Time passed slowly and peacefully in a repetitive cycle of seasons, natural and human. There was no cause to foresee that this bowl of land held by a distant rim of hills—called by the Tais the Arena of the Gods—would be the scene of one of the greatest set-piece battles of all time, a battle in which both sides showed exemplary bravery; that The Seat of the Border County Prefecture would be the place where a general would display extraordinary military skills and powers of leadership.

Many sieges have lasted longer than the fifty-five days of Dien Bien Phu's. The Americans held Bataan for sixty-six days, the Germans held Stalingrad for seventy-six days, the British held Tobruk for two hundred and forty-one days. There were 330,000 German troops encircled at Stalingrad by over 1 million Russians: in comparison, Dien Bien Phu's garrison of about 14,000, besieged by about 50,000 Vietminh, was small beer. It was the way in which the battle developed and was fought, and the consequences of the result, that made it one of the most decisive of all time and propelled the name of Vo Nguyen Giap into the history books.

Giap takes up the narrative:

> Early in December 1953 Navarre worked out a four-step plan for defense. He would:
>
> > Slow down the advance of our troops by using air power to strafe our main communication lines;
> > Kick our troops out of Lai Chau by violent bombardment;

Check our attacks on Dien Bien Phu by causing heavy damage
to us;

After these victories he would expand his zones of occupation.

With regard to Dien Bien Phu, he believed that his artillery and
armored forces could intercept any of our approach routes; that our
artillery, set up on the slopes facing the valley and within firing
range—ten to twelve kilometers—would be easily detected and then
annihilated by guns and aircraft; that the fortifications would wear
out and repel any assault, while a mobile force held in reserve
launched counterattacks.

Navarre asserted that with such powerful forces and strong defense systems, Dien Bien Phu was the strongest fortified entrenched
camp ever seen in Indochina. It was "an impregnable fortress." From
this subjective viewpoint he considered that an attack by us would be
very improbable, that if our troops ventured to launch an offensive he
would have the opportunity to inflict an inevitable defeat on us. He
went so far as arrogantly to challenge us to attack!

The fortress created by the French looked like a giant footprint
pointing due north on the flat valley: at the toe was Doc Lap Hill;
the sides of the sole were Ban Keo and Him Lam hills; the ball of the
foot was the central sector; there was a long instep held by barbed
wire and mine fields—with the river running down the middle of it;
the heel was Hong Cum. The perimeter was about thirty miles long,
and fifty battalions would have been needed to hold it safely, but the
theory was that guns and mortars in the central keep would support
the three positions to the north and the one in the south, while other
guns and mortars there would support the center and the north;
taken together, the whole place would be a barbed, bristling porcu-
pine of a fortress.

When planning it the man appointed in command, Colonel de
Castries, gave the main positions the names of French women—
legend has it, his mistresses, all nine of them. (Bigeard says he thinks
this was unlikely: de Castries was "not that strong.") Doc Lap was
Gabrielle, Ban Keo was Anne-Marie, Him Lam was Beatrice. The
center consisted of a ring of strongholds: Huguette, Francoise, Clau-

dine, Eliane, Dominique. The heel was Isabelle. Some of the strongholds were subdivided several times; for example, Dominique 1 to 5, Eliane 1 to 4. In all, there were forty-nine separate defended sites.

The task of creating them was gigantic. Laid out with interlocking fields of fire that gave support to neighboring units as well as defending its frontages, each battalion needed fifty-five dugouts and seventy-five machine-gun bunkers. Foxholes were not good enough: these positions had to withstand artillery fire. To construct them, 2,550 tons of engineer stores and 500 tons of barbed wire would be needed. A total of 36,000 tons of material would have to be flown in to entrench the planned garrison of ten battalions and two artillery regiments. (It could not be brought in overland: that would have meant running the gauntlet of Vietminh attacks down an appalling series of tracks.) The sums were not difficult to work out: twelve hundred flights by C-47 aircraft out of Hanoi and Haiphong were required to lift that tonnage: with eighty of them on average available each day, it would take five months!

Would Giap wait that long? Navarre thought he would: it was inconceivable that he would be able to assemble anything significant in the way of an attacking force for months; and if French fighting patrols sallying out into the hills cut up his troops as they approached, never. No, of course there was no great risk . . . (With hindsight, Bigeard says it was a mistake "to think the Viets could not get there in strength," but as a young officer—at the time he was thirty-eight—he was proud to be leading his men in such an important place, which he thought would be impregnable.)

When the siege began the engineers were more than thirty thousand tons short. With what was available they had managed to put underground the headquarters command post, the signals center, the hospital, and the water-purification plant. To make up for the lack of cement and iron bars, the garrison cut down most of the trees in the valley—which resulted in the Vietminh in the hills having an uninterrupted view of what went on in the camp.

As to manpower, forty men took eight days to dig a dugout for ten men and a gun; the same number took five days to build a machine-gun pit. Doing nothing else, a whole battalion needed two months to prepare itself, so one of the first decisions that had to be made by de Castries was to allocate priorities: should the men dig or strike out from the base on patrol?

Under pressure from Navarre, the answer was patrol, in order to eliminate any Vietminh groups the patrols encountered. (What Navarre did not realize, because intelligence never discovered it until much later, was that a whole army was on the move.) But de Castries's men would also have to dig! Through the last months of 1953 and the first of 1954, strike-groups—sometimes consisting of half the men in the garrison—trudged out for days or even weeks on end to seek out and destroy the enemy. They had some successes, but not enough to justify the 1,037 men who became casualties, most of them through sickness rather than as a result of combat: about 10 percent of the total French losses during the Dien Bien Phu campaign occurred between 20 November 1953 and 15 February 1954, a dilution of combat effectiveness that was to be sorely felt in the weeks to come when the battle started in earnest.

The soldiers went on patrol, and when they didn't patrol, dug. The result was that neither patroling nor digging was allocated enough manpower: bigger patrols might have intercepted the main bodies of Giap's divisions and hacked them about; more digging would have improved the defenses. The men themselves, however, never ceased working. They dug or walked, but either way got stiff legs, sore backs, leech boils, and calloused hands—and sweated out the water they drank from water bottles filled from the purification plant down by the river, which would be operated by one man throughout the siege. (Anyone drinking the river water was sure to get amoebic dysentery. The men knew it, but when the water carriers began to take heavy casualties, there was an understandable lack of enthusiasm for the job and people had to resort to either river or rain water—and wait for sickness to strike. As if they didn't have enough to contend with.)

At one time there was concern that because the tall grasses swaying in the breeze might impede fields of fire they would have to be cut down, which would add to the work load. It was decided to give grass cutting low priority, but as it turned out it never had to be done: between ten and sixteen thousand men, nearly two hundred vehicles, ten tanks, fourteen aircraft, and five bulldozers progressively flattened most of it down into the earth, and what was left was blown away by high explosives.

Another problem was that the tight perimeters in the center and the south allowed no room for alternative gun positions: where they were first manhandled into position—most of them in the central keep—was where they would have to stay. Looking down through their binoculars, Giap's gunners registered each position accurately and gave it an identifying number. From then on they could quickly find the target by reference to the number and its related bearing and elevation and then, to get precise accuracy, adjust by observation to allow for weather conditions on the day. (Their task had been made easier because soon after the siege began the Vietminh captured a large-scale map that had recently been produced by the French from aerial photographs.) It was all too easy: not only were the French guns registered, so were all the important command posts, given away because out of the fourteen hundred wireless sets in the garrison, three hundred of them needed outside aerials.

Before the battle started Giap's headquarters issued a new field manual. It said that "to ensure victory it was necessary to have a three-to-one superiority of manpower and a five-to-one superiority of firepower." Also that "after the opening of the first breach one must immediately penetrate into the interior of the enemy-fortified system and hold that penetration to the bitter end." Giap wrote it: Giap went on to do it, with some Chinese help.

Generals Wei Guo-qing and Li Cheng-hu were his advisers at Dien Bien Phu. (According to Bigeard their presence and influence—and that of their predecessors in former years—were largely responsible for Giap's attitude to casualties: in Korea the Chinese had resorted to human-wave attacks constantly as the only way to overwhelm massed automatic weapons; they persuaded Giap that for him it too was the only way.) In addition to the generals, there were several hundred specialists scattered throughout the force, particularly among the field and flak gunners, where they contributed an expertise that was missing until the Vietnamese learned by experience, which they were very quick to do. One trick they learned was to start an artillery bombardment when there was enough light left to be able to see their targets and register them but not enough left to enable French aircraft and artillery to strike back.

Here is Giap talking about the start of the campaign:

> When we launched the attack the garrison comprised forty-nine strongpoints in three subsectors. The most important was the central subsector, situated in the middle of Muong Thanh village. Nearly two-thirds of the garrison was concentrated there: eight battalions, three of them mobile. It had many resistance centers supporting each other and surrounding the command post, the artillery and supply bases and the hospital.
>
> Dien Bien Phu had two airfields—the main one at Muong Thanh and a reserve field at Hong Cum: they linked with Hanoi and Haiphong in an airlift that daily supplied between two and three hundred tons of goods, or airdropped from about a hundred to a hundred and fifty tons. Dien Bien Phu's isolated position far away from supply bases and not to be reached by road made its supply and reinforcement entirely dependent on airlift. If this was cut off or blocked, this powerful fortified camp would expose all its weak points. In case of danger, a withdrawal would be difficult, even if the fighting spirit of the troops was good.
>
> We resolved to concentrate the overwhelming majority of our picked units, and with them destroy the enemy's most seasoned forces, there in Dien Bien Phu. On other fronts our armymen would scatter and pin down the enemy's forces and reduce to the maximum his ability to reinforce the camp.

Before the attack started Giap had achieved two things of enormous importance: the concentration of an astonishing number of guns and the further dispersion of Navarre's troops. The latter not only made it impossible for Navarre to concentrate his units, in order to attack or to withstand attack, but also overstretched his air transport resources: the need to supply the small airheads that supported the French mobile columns in Laos and northwest Vietnam meant that there were not enough planes available to take supplies to Dien Bien Phu in the quantities needed. Consequently, when Giap's troops began to arrive in the area, de Castries was unprepared.

During late December 1953 and early January 1954, Giap ordered his 308th Division in Laos to step up the pressure, and his newly formed 325th—the Golden Star Division—in the Mekong delta to do the same: as had always been so, his troops in Cochinchina, operating by remote control, were doing their bit in the war. Obliged to respond, Navarre further diluted his mobile reserve until there was nothing of any significance left.

The covert Vietminh buildup had begun as soon as Dien Bien Phu had been retaken by the French at the end of November; the French had thrown down the gauntlet, but because the jungle concealed troop movements it took some time for them to realize that Giap had picked it up. Major General Le Quang Ba's 316th Division, complete with its supporting 980th battalion of artillery, arrived in the middle of December. The seasoned 308th, the Iron Division, commanded by Major General Vuong Than Vu and manned mostly by volunteers from Hanoi, arrived in December, went on to Luang Prabang and then came back to Dien Bien Phu at the end of January, walking, walking all the way. The 57th Regiment of the 304th Division, commanded by Colonel Hoang Khai Tien, arrived on 24 January. More battalions from the 304th, 315th, and the 316th divisions, and from the independent 148th Regiment, tramped over the hills and took their place in the order of battle. And, of course, there were the guns and engineers of the 351st Heavy Division.

By the time the battle started, Giap had twenty-eight infantry battalions—a total, when the gunners and engineers were added, of 37,500 combatant troops—encircling the muddy Arena of the Gods. Another 10,000 teeth-arm soldiers (i.e., close-combat troops—infantry, artillery, and engineers) were in reserve. The whole lot were victualed and supplied with ammunition by around 50,000 uniformed commissariat troops, and four times as many *dan cong*. In total, around 300,000 people were committed to the logistic line of communication, the main route of which led from the Chinese border at Mu Nam Quam over Provincial Road 13-B to the Red River and thence via Provincial Road 41 to Dien Bien Phu. The total distance, much of it under frequent aerial bombardment, was about eight hundred kilometers, nearly five hundred miles.

Giap gives the background to the buildup:

We made thorough preparations for the attacks:

First, Dien Bien Phu was linked with Highway 41 by a mule track nearly one hundred kilometers long. This track crossed an uninterrupted series of hills and valleys with steep gradients and was cut by nearly a hundred big and small streams. To allow our army, especially the artillery, to attack, the first problem to be solved was immediately to convert the track into a motor road. With great difficulty our troops managed to do this and built a dozen bridges in a relatively short time. Until the end of the campaign, our engineer units kept this road in good repair, despite increasing sabotage by the enemy and torrential rains and floods. [The Vietminh had about eight hundred trucks, six hundred of them Russian two-and-a-half-ton Molotovas supplied by the Chinese, the rest American vehicles captured by the Chinese in Korea.]

Second, our troops succeeded in towing the guns to the vicinity of Dien Bien Phu with trucks and then dragged them into position during seven days and nights. Then five roads were made so that we could pull the guns around the valley with trucks and so give them greater mobility. These roads were within range of the French guns and traversed regions where no tracks had ever been before, but with skillful camouflage we were able to conceal and repair them until the end of the campaign. In sections inaccessible and dangerous to vehicles the guns were hauled into position by men's strength. They were not daunted by enemy aircraft and artillery. There were times when soldiers sacrificed their lives to save guns.

Third, we built very solid artillery positions, casemates capable of bearing the brunt of enemy 105-mm and 155-mm shells, built in places entirely unsuspected by the enemy; carved into the mountains and so skillfully camouflaged that they could hardly be detected by scout planes. We also made sham positions to sidetrack the enemy and disperse his firepower in order to waste his bombs and shells.

Fourth, to guarantee continuity of command, for our command posts we built similar solid entrenched positions in other casemates carved deep into the mountain slopes and capable of bearing the fire of enemy artillery.

Last, our supplies were well prepared. The requirements of the campaign in food, ammunition, and medicines were very great. We organized supply lines hundreds of kilometers long. The enemy destroyed the roads—we mended them. Hundreds of men and women *dan cong*, not flinching from any difficulty or danger, enthusiastically served the front and contributed over three million workdays. Truck convoys ran lightless for nights on end, or sometimes took advantage of foggy weather to run in daytime. Tens of thousands of pack bicycles and wheelbarrows, thousands of craft, convoys of donkeys and horses were employed to transport supplies to the front, using roads and tracks, deep rivers and swift streams.

The French were convinced that whatever artillery Giap managed to bring to Dien Bien Phu would have to fire howitzer-fashion at high angle from reverse slopes over the ridge on to the valley below. In fact, Giap's gunners dug them in on the forward slopes, from which they could shoot directly and therefore more accurately.

At first equipped with American 75-mm howitzers captured from the Chinese nationalists by Mao's soldiers, in 1953 the 351st Heavy Division received forty-eight American 105-mm howitzers, mostly newly captured in the Korean war. In mid December 1953 the 675th Artillery Regiment (with 24×75-mm pack-howitzers and 20×120-mm mortars) arrived to support the 308th Division. During the first week of January, the 45th Artillery Regiment, equipped with nine batteries of 4×105-mm howitzers each, also arrived, to be followed by the 367th Regiment equipped with thirty-six Russian 37-mm light anti-aircraft guns. (A whole battalion of infantry was assigned to the protection of the AA gunners.) Later, the 237th Regiment, with 120-mm heavy mortars, joined the others. Giap ended up in control of 48×75-mm pack-howitzers, 48×105-mm field howitzers, 48×120-mm mortars, 36×37-mm anti-aircraft guns, and 60×75-mm recoilless rifles. Finally, at the climax of the battle, he deployed four fearsome Soviet "Katyusha" multitube rocket launchers, which fired twelve 120-mm rockets in a single salvo. In all, he had more than two hundred pieces of above 57-mm caliber, whereas the French had only sixty at the start and, a week after the battle had begun, an average of less than forty each day. (Some guns put out of action by enemy fire were cannibalized so as to provide spare parts for those that were still able to function, hence the figure of guns-in-action varied from day to day.)

French artillery specialists inside the stronghold later estimated that approximately thirty thousand 105-mm rounds and more than one hundred thousand shells of smaller caliber were fired into the perimeter during the battle—about fifteen hundred tons of ammunition. In addition, in an astounding feat that was a tribute to Giap's powers of organization, the logistic troops and the *dan cong* brought in over 8,000 tons of assorted supplies, 4,500 tons of petrol, and 2,250 tons of foodstuffs—including 1,700 tons of rice, 400 tons of which were eaten by the porters on the way! (The rice was brought from a different source, farther south, along another route.)

Hearing of the buildup and assessing the disparity in numbers, Navarre now thought about withdrawing, but an airlift was quite out of the question from airfields under observed fire, even if there had been enough planes to achieve a clean break—to ensure that there were no remnants left who would be overwhelmed after the main body had gone—which there were not. As to withdrawing by road, he was advised that to save four battalions—the ones in the middle, the least reliable because of their doubtful motivation, the Vietnamese and the North Africans—he would probably have to sacrifice the six in the vanguard and rearguard, the paratroops and legionnaires, the cream of the French army. It was not something he could contemplate, even fleetingly. He was committed—or, rather, de Castries and Langlais and Bigeard and their troops from many countries were committed—to fighting it out.

Christian Marie Ferdinand de la Croix de Castries, holder of eighteen citations for valor, wearer of colored neckerchiefs and carrier of a twitching riding crop; aristocrat, dilettante, world-class horseman, gambler, lover. Pierre Langlais, hard-bitten paratroop veteran of many battles—like Bigeard, this was his third two-year tour in Indochina; he had lost count of the battles and his citations for valor. Bruno Bigeard, young, tough, pipe-smoking leader of tough Frenchmen: at the end of it all, when he had gone on to fight many more battles in Algeria, he was to become the most decorated officer in the French army, with twenty-five awards for valor. And, too, there were the thousands of men from Europe and North Africa. (Less than 40 percent of the garrison were Frenchmen.)

There was just one European woman in it, a bonny twenty-nine-year-old by the name of Genevieve de Galard-Terraube, who was there because the plane in which she had flown to Dien Bien Phu as a flight nurse had been hit and she could not leave. She was to win a Croix de Guerre and be appointed to the Legion of Honor for her bravery under fire and selfless devotion to duty in tending the wounded.

There were eighteen other women inside the fortress: seven Vietnamese and eleven Algerian prostitutes, the complement of the two mobile brothels that had accompanied the legionnaires. They came in on the airlift; they left on foot, to what fate nobody knows, after doing their bit as holders of dying hands and disposers of blood-soaked bandages and amputated limbs in the nightmare hospital. (There were also forty-nine thousand bottles of French wine, another essential ingredient to Gallic warfare. Maybe some of them still exist in a forgotten corner of a Tai village, slowly accumulating value with the crusted dust.)

On the morning of 12 March Major General Rene Cogny, six feet, four inches tall in his socks, walked the course with de Castries. The month before, short, tubby, pugnacious-looking Lieutenant General John W. (Iron Mike) O'Daniel, commander of the American army in the Pacific area, had visited Dien Bien Phu and then gone back to his headquarters to write a report for the chairman of the American Joint Chiefs of Staff. By now, American aid was amounting to 80 percent of the costs of the war. (The United States had given $385 million alone to fund the Navarre plan for the creation of the mobile reserve and the bigger National Army of Vietnamese.) Equipment they provided included 1,400 tanks, 340 aircraft, 350 patrol boats—needed to counter the use of sampans and other river craft by the ubiquitous Vietminh on the hundreds of waterways, natural and irrigation, that riddled the country. Washington's concern for the way things were going was such that President Eisenhower had undertaken to commit U.S. air power to the battle should the Chinese intervene directly to help Giap.

Two weeks after O'Daniel's visit, Mr. Malcolm Macdonald, slightly effete and bohemian but clever British resident commissioner in Southeast Asia, son of a one-time prime minister of Great Britain, had also trudged through the mud, then gone back to Singapore to write a report for Mr. Anthony Eden, foreign secretary, who had been appointed joint chairman—with Mr. Molotov, his Soviet counterpart—of a multinational conference that was going to discuss, among other things, the future of Indochina.

As Cogny's plane began its takeoff run, Vietminh shells exploded on the runway and an aircraft on the apron burst into flames. He never came back.

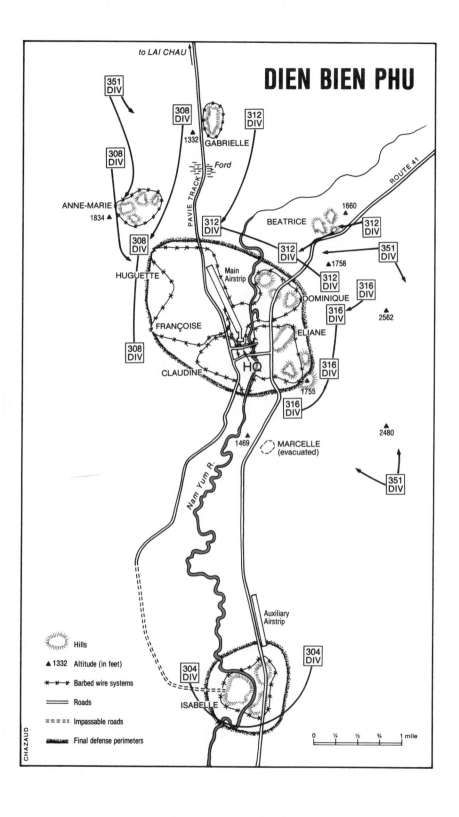

DIEN BIEN PHU

to LAI CHAU

351
DIV

308
DIV

312
DIV

▲1332 GABRIELLE

308
DIV

Ford

ROUTE 41

ANNE-MARIE
1834 ▲

PAVIE TRACK

312
DIV

BEATRICE

1660
▲

312
DIV

308
DIV

312
DIV

351
DIV

HUGUETTE

Main
Airstrip

▲1758

312
DIV

316
DIV

DOMINIQUE

316
DIV

2562
▲

FRANÇOISE

ELIANE

308
DIV

CLAUDINE

HQ

316
DIV

1755
▲

316
DIV

2480
▲

1469
▲

MARCELLE
(evacuated)

Nam Yum R.

351
DIV

Auxiliary
Airstrip

Hills

▲ 1332 Altitude (in feet)

✳—✳—✳ Barbed wire systems

════ Roads

═ ═ ═ ═ Impassable roads

▰▰▰ Final defense perimeters

304
DIV

304
DIV

ISABELLE

0   ¼   ½   ¾   1 mile

CHAZAUD

CHAPTER ELEVEN

THE COUP DE GRÂCE

A battle, no matter how important it may be, whether Issus or Hastings, Philippi or Belle-Alliance, can only represent the high point of a developing situation.

—VO NGUYEN GIAP

An unusual thing about the battle of Dien Bien Phu was that Giap changed the theme of the contest after it had begun. At first it had been his intention to get it over quickly, and orders were issued accordingly. Then, while he was in the wooden house that he used for part of the time as his headquarters, he thought it through and decided that he could not afford to take chances: if he got it wrong and lost, then all the effort of the last seven years would have been wasted; the French army would triumph and it would be years before the Vietminh could build up its strength again. He had second thoughts and changed direction completely, not an easy thing to do: his soldiers might interpret that decision as indecision and lose confidence in him. But it was better to risk that than get it wrong. He explains his reasoning in this way:

In the early stage when we encircled the enemy he was still in small numbers, so we worked against time to profit by his deficiency to do a rapid battle in order to win a rapid victory. An advantage was that our troops were in good fettle and our supply of ammunition and food was assured; however, such tactics could be a great impediment because our troops lacked experience in attacking fortified camps. But within weeks the enemy had reinforced his effectives and had organized a fairly strong defense system; now, a rapid attack would not guarantee complete success. In consequence, we resolutely affirmed the guiding principle: advance cautiously and strike surely.

Accordingly, we no longer conceived the battle as a large-scale siege that took place unremittingly in a short time but as a campaign in which a series of siege battles having the character of positional warfare would be fought for rather a long time. We would achieve absolute superiority, sector by sector, until the whole garrison was crushed.

Overall, the Vietminh had achieved the ratio of superiority in infantry and artillery that was needed for a successful attack. Nevertheless, in order to be sure, Giap needed to concentrate his troops for each battle. He decided to take on the main position from the east in the first instance, since that was where his lines of communication ended, then switch to the west, then take on the center, leaving the most southerly outpost to the last. As he puts it: "Such tactics corresponded to the technical level of our troops but we would raise that by fighting a series of battles that were hard and complex but not very great before proceeding to the destruction of the whole fortress."

Giap put great stress on the health of his soldiers and instructed his commanding officers to ensure that the men ate their fill, had hot food and drink, and slept soundly in the warm, as far as that was possible. Preventative hygiene was also the object of close attention by his medical services, such as they were. Predictably, political work also played a big role by instilling a determination to fight and win in the troops. Many slogans were invented, such as "Zealously to build roads for artillery is zealously to work for victory," or "To maintain the roads in good repair is zealously to work for victory," and "To build fortifications an inch thicker is to create more favorable conditions to defeat the enemy."

As an added lift for their morale, not long before the attack was to be launched, a letter was received from Ho Chi Minh that was duplicated and distributed down to company level, and then passed on by word of mouth to the soldiers:

> You are prepared for the attack. This time your task is very heavy, but very glorious.
>
> You have just attended ideological remolding and military courses and have scored many successes in the ideological, tactical, and technical fields. Many units have won victories on the battlefields. I am certain that you will bring into play the recent victories and are determined to overcome all difficulties and hardships in order to fulfill your glorious task to come.
>
> I am looking forward to receiving reports on your successes and will commend the best units and individuals.
>
> I wish you a great victory.
>
> Kisses.

Giap chose his targets for the first phase of attacks and set in train a battle-winning tactic that would reduce the amount of time his soldiers spent in the open while making their assaults, and therefore their vulnerability to small arms and artillery fire: namely, the digging of trenches from the surrounding hills down to within a few strides of the French positions. Despite strafing and bombing by French planes, the Vietminh dug a system of trenches in total nearly one hundred kilometers long, including many cross-communication trenches that made liaison possible.

The task he set the army in the first phase was to wipe out the three perimeter defense strongholds in the north:

On 13 March at 5:00 P.M. we started to shell Him Lam hill [Beatrice]. The outermost post, it had close relations with Doc Lap Hill [Gabrielle], and Ban Keo [Anne-Marie].

The Him Lam resistance center was the strongest. Defended by a reinforced battalion of legionnaires belonging to the 13th Regiment, considered by the enemy to be one of his most seasoned combat units, it was composed of three strongholds supporting each other and provided with mine fields and belts of barbed wire a hundred or more meters wide. Doc Lap was defended by a reinforced battalion of North Africans and had the task of blocking our attacks from the north. Ban Keo was defended by a battalion of Tai puppet troops. All these three centers were covered by 105-mm and 155-mm guns from Muong Thanh [the central keep] and Hong Cum [Isabelle].

Our infantry and artillery coordinated their action very closely. The first of Him Lam's positions was annihilated after one hour's engagement, the second after two hours. The attack on the third was arduous. The enemy artillery, paralyzed at first, began to riposte more and more vigorously. At 10:30 P.M. we completely annihilated the whole Him Lam resistance center, put three hundred enemy troops out of action, and captured two hundred others.

On 14 March we began the attack on Doc Lap [Gabrielle]. At 5:00 P.M. we began to shell the central command post, the enemy's artillery positions, and the airfield at Muong Thanh. This artillery duel was very murderous. According to the documents taken from the enemy, to cover his positions on Him Lam and Doc Lap hills and destroy our artillery, during three days, from 13–15 March, he fired more than thirty thousand shells. On 14 March his aircraft coming from Hanoi bombed and strafed our positions all night long.

Owing to the heavy rain, which delayed the hauling of our mountain artillery into position, the attack on Doc Lap did not start until 2:00 A.M. on the fifteenth. It ended at 6:30 A.M. with the complete annihilation of this stronghold. At 6:00 A.M. an enemy infantry unit supported by tanks had come from Muong Thanh to attack us, but was forced to withdraw, suffering some casualties from our artillery.

On the seventeenth, at 3:00 P.M., Ban Keo received twenty shells from our artillery. Though threatened by their French officers, the Thai puppet troops there availed themselves of the opportunity when their officers took refuge in their trenches to surrender with their weapons. The enemy tanks that pursued them were halted by our artillery and compelled to fall back.

During these battles the Vietminh broke open the northern part of de Castries's defenses, leaving the central subsector, with its vital command post and principle airfield, exposed on three sides. With the airfield no longer usable, resupply became the most critical problem of all. The longer the campaign lasted, the greater would be the losses suffered in men, weapons, and ammunition, and the greater the need for reinforcements. The great quandary was that the more reinforcements he asked for, and got, the worse de Castries's logistic problems would become.

After the first lunges there was a pause while Giap brought in reinforcements, regrouped, and decided what to do with the large number of wounded who had been captured: he could offer to give them back to de Castries, or he could let them take their chance with his own troops. He decided that it would be better to get rid of them if he could: his own men had enough to cope with, and giving them back would add to de Castries's problems. So, during the battle, a communist officer under a flag of truce approached strongpoint Anne-Marie and handed over a letter addressed to de Castries stating that on the morning of 17 March eighty-six wounded survivors from Gabrielle would be left six hundred meters to the north of Anne-Marie 2, where they could be recovered by stretcher bearers. This offer, as well as similar ones that were to follow until the ferocity and duration of the battle submerged such considerations, put de Castries in a cruel dilemma: if he refused to take back his own wounded, the effect on morale could be catastrophic; on the other hand, his limited medical facilities were already hopelessly over-crowded. He decided that morale was the most important factor, and the men were duly collected.

By now there were nearly 500 seriously wounded men in the hospital, a number that rose steadily until by 4 May there were 1,260. The dead reduced the numbers daily, the dying increased them daily. To make matters worse, the chances of evacuating any-one by air were now nil. (A few had been airlifted out in the early days. On one occasion an evacuation plane was shot out of the sky just after it had taken off.)

In the French hospital conditions had become frightful. It had begun with forty-four beds, but later three surgical teams were parachuted in, with two blood banks, and the number of "beds" was increased. (The men lay on the ground wherever there was any space; there were no beds, as such.) Then the flawless drop out of a clear blue sky of No. 6 Airborne Surgical Team under Lt. (Dr.) Vidal allowed the senior medical officer, Dr. Grauwin, to create a hospital annex on the other bank of the Nam Rum, thus saving the seriously wounded a dangerous trip across the open bridge that spanned the little river (though, as time passed, it became possible to walk over the dead bodies that filled the river and so avoid the bridge com-pletely).

The dark, wet dungeons in which the wounded lay were like a hell conjured up in the worst imaginings of Hieronymus Bosch: lit by hissing paraffin lamps, the surgeons and orderlies, despite their physical exhaustion and limited resources, cut flesh, soaked up spurting blood, sawed bones, stitched wounds, and tried to ease the pain, all the while smelling the ghastly stench of gangrene and lis-tening to the groans and shrieks of the dying. Lying on their stretch-ers outside the operating theater, wounded waited their turn, but often when it came it was too late: from the waiting area and the wards, dead bodies were dragged outside, piled up in heaps, and hurriedly buried at night.

On the reverse slopes of the surrounding hills, similar scenes were being enacted in lean-to bamboo huts, with even fewer drugs and medicines, though Giap's logisticians had made a purchase of peni-cillin from the Chinese in preparation for the battle.

When the Tai soldiers defending the Anne-Marie position broke and ran, or surrendered to the enemy, the commanding officer of the battalion behind them, the 5th Vietnamese Parachute Battalion, ordered his men to shoot the fleeing soldiers; how many did as they were told, and how many died, is not recorded. The partial desertion of the 3rd Battalion Tai, soon to be followed by the total demoralization of the 2nd Battalion Tai and of many of the men of the Tai Light Independent Companies, was a major blow, but was not really surprising: some of the men lived in the area and their wives and families were under communist control; all of them had been bombarded with propaganda as well as shells and were now in real doubt about where their true loyalties lay.

The Vietminh also tried to undermine the determination of the North Africans and of the Germans in the Foreign Legion, addressing them in their own languages over loudspeakers and scattering leaflets by night near the trenches. When dawn came German legionnaires would sometimes pick up tracts in which they were asked why they were fighting for their old enemies. The French too had to fight a psychological battle: when the trenches had crept in until they were only yards away, Giap's men would play over loudspeakers the haunting refrain from the World War II resistance song, "Companions, freedom is listening to us in the night." In response, the French soldiers would sing the "Marseillaise."

As the weeks passed, the Tai deserters were to be joined by more and more Vietnamese—soldiers and Tai auxiliary laborers—and by North Africans, who, though they were professional military men and considered themselves to be every bit as good as the legionnaires, or better, had decided that perhaps this was not their fight, or that maybe they were on the losing side. (At one point in the battle Algerian riflemen took off in panic in front of the waves of approaching Vietminh. Standing up like that, they would have been shot down almost to a man if the vanguard of the 312th Division making the assault had not turned aside to avoid their own artillery fire. Quite often Vietminh infantry advanced so rapidly that they outpaced the forward progression of their own shells. This time, as the Algerians made their escape, the Vietminh soldiers walked into a mine field, where hundreds died.)

Because of the increasing confusion on the battlefield, nobody on de Castries's staff made a count of how many "internal deserters" there were, but later it was estimated that there must have been around three thousand of them: the garrison was being whittled down not only by Giap's guns and bullets but also by forsaken loyalty. The soldiers slowly melted away into the maze of shallow caves and trenches in the cliffs of Dominique, and into holes dug into the banks of the Nam Rum, where in order to live they made nightly forays into no-man's land to steal misdropped parachuted supplies. They even operated a brisk black market—so much so that the men who were still fighting sometimes had to ask them for vital stores, such as radio batteries.

The little airstrip on the north side of Isabelle had been under direct fire from the very beginning, and as the Vietminh closed in on the main position, the one there also became a deathtrap. Brave pilots from the airfields at Hanoi and Haiphong (including some American civilians) gave up trying to land in daylight after the Vietminh AA gunners had their target practice during the first few days, got the hang of it, and then shot them out of the sky. Next, they tried landing at night, a hazardous business that also had to stop when they were picked off on the approach run, on the ground, or as they took off. The only answer was to supply the garrison by parachute, but that was not easy either, for the aircrews or for the people who each night had to collect and distribute more than a hundred tons of assorted supplies before dawn came; frequently, they could not do so, and a backlog built up. Occasionally, pallet loads of ammunition fell into mine fields and blew up. Sometimes, pallets fell right on to the Vietminh lines, giving them a welcome bonus of unheard-of luxuries; the smell of Gauloise cigarettes wafted across the churned-up ground to the noses of the battered and blood-stained French soldiers. And on one occasion Giap's artillery hit a supply depot and among other things set light to reserves of cigarettes and tobacco; clouds of blue smoke drifted out over the hills. What a waste, everyone thought.

Giap's orders to dig approach trenches and tunnels were carried out with amazing energy and determination by soldiers and by laborers impressed from the local population. One man would start and slowly dig down, disappear from view, pass the earth to the rear—where it was put into sandbags—work away and reappear. Then relays of men would go in, like mechanical moles burrowing ever closer to the French so that in the end they were within grenade-throwing and submachine gun range. Perhaps, though, the most astonishing example of their digging ability was that when they took Dominique they did not establish positions on top of the hill, they dug right through it from behind; outwardly, it looked as it always had, pock-marked and rugged: inside it was an ant's nest of weapon pits.

Because of the terrain, the Vietminh had advantages the French did not have. Being mostly on the higher ground, and therefore unobserved, at 11:00 A.M. each day as many as possible of the soldiers in front-line positions were changed over; those relieved went back for a hot meal, whereas the French soldiers seldom if ever got a hot meal. Also, being on the low ground, the French suffered more from the rain when it came; it flooded and stayed in their emplacements, whereas it drained down the hills away from their enemies'.

The French, of course, did not take all this lying down. While de Castries was glued to his radio, in almost hourly conversation with Cogny—giving him reports, asking for more airlifted supplies, telling him the worst while hoping for the best—Langlais and Bigeard planned and directed counterattacks, their men surging out of their slits to try to break the spirit of their adversaries and show that they were not done yet. But the Vietminh fought back resolutely and the French took many casualties. Many Frenchmen had hopes that the United States would intervene to lift the siege, either by sending troops or by bombing the Vietminh. To keep up his men's morale during the battles, Bigeard "kept telling them 'We must hold on for one more day; the Americans will come.' "

To make up for the losses, a steady drain on his combatant numbers, de Castries repeatedly asked for reinforcements. In response, a total of 4,277 were parachuted in, 3,596 of them para-trained—the rest of them had never stepped out of a plane into thin air before. (More than 2,500 men in the French Expeditionary Corps volunteered to go to the relief of Dien Bien Phu; 2,048 Europeans, 451 North Africans, 95 Vietnamese. Even at this late stage of the conflict many Vietnamese remained loyal to the French; the colonizers had done much good for Vietnam over the years and were being repaid, though esprit de corps, pride, and fear of loss of face also played a big part in the astonishing spirit shown by the Vietnamese.)

Giap also sent for reinforcements from his 25,000-man reserve pool. Seeing the success of his anti-aircraft guns, and knowing that without air re-supply the garrison was doomed, he sent for another flak regiment of 37-mm guns—and 720 tons of ammunition for it. In hundred-man groups the reinforcements, who were summoned by him in March, began to arrive in April, to be paired up individually with two experienced soldiers who were made responsible for showing them the ropes. In consequence, during the fifty-five days of the battle, Giap's force only periodically suffered shortages of manpower.

On 23 March, Navarre, speaking on the radio, referred to Giap for the first time as "General." In a way it was a turning point: until then, Giap had been a guerrilla leader; now he was the commander of a field army, a fact that nobody could deny.

The capture of Gabrielle (Doc Lap) had not been easy. According to French estimates, based on aerial photographs, more than a thousand Vietminh soldiers were killed and between two and three thousand of them were wounded; intercepted enemy radio traffic showed that after that engagement Giap needed urgent reinforcements and more ammunition from the rear depots at Tuan Giao. Nevertheless, the Bo-Doi (infantry) of the 88th and 102nd regiments of the 308th Division had good reason to be pleased, for they had fulfilled their pledge made when the divisional commander handed them their new red banner inscribed with the motto QUYET CHIEN, QUYET THANG ("To fight and to win"); they had vowed that they would defeat the enemy at Dien Bien Phu, and they had met that pledge. Gunner Pham Van Tuy, who had dragged a hand-built 75-mm wheeled bazooka to within a hundred and fifty yards of Gabrielle's command bunker scored three direct hits and silenced its guns; he later received a first-class and a third-class combat star for his bravery. At 7:00 A.M. on 15 March a twenty-five-year-old sergeant by the name of Tran Ndoc Doan planted the banner on top of the bunker.

Colonel Pham Duc Doi, in 1990 curator of the Army Museum in Hanoi, once the Citadel, remembers those days:

I was born in Hanoi in 1929 and grew up here. In 1942, at the age of thirteen, I went to a French-speaking school near the West lake. Then in 1946 at the age of seventeen I volunteered to become a guerrilla. I was given a rifle and bayonet that was older than I was!

In 1949 I went to learn to be an officer. I graduated after two years. In those days there was no rank; that didn't come until 1958. People called each other comrade. People knew who were officers either because they had close contact or because they had been told. In 1953 I went to train to be a company commander.

I was twice wounded during the French war. Once I had a blanket and a mosquito net around my chest and a bullet went through them and I was lightly wounded. Another time a piece of artillery shell, a small piece of shrapnel, lodged under my left ear.

I saw General Giap several times during the war, particularly in 1954 before the big campaign. He made many visits to encourage the soldiers, at every level from section to division. From 1950 to 1954 every group in the army tried to see Giap. It was very important for him to see them and for them to see him.

By 1954 several divisions had been formed. There was no significance in the numbering of divisions; they were random numbers intended to confuse the enemy.

In 1954 I was on the General Staff in the headquarters for the battle of Dien Bien Phu. I was a military instructor in politics—at that time there was joint military and political command down to platoon level: that also ended in 1958. My job in the headquarters was to get information about every French position and put it on a map, so that Giap could decide how to fight the battle.

At the beginning, his first thought was to fight quickly and get victory quickly. We closed in. But then we were ordered to withdraw the infantry and artillery back to their first positions because he had changed the tactics: we were to fight slowly, phase by phase, not in waves like the Chinese. Giap said that we should use the soldiers' brains and not their bodies.

While we surrounded the French we lived in the jungle. We slept on the ground, with the leaf of the banana tree, placed on a piece of plastic, as our bed; or maybe on a mat of bamboo sticks. Only a few people had mosquito nets; they were very rare, so everyone got malaria. We only had a little quinine; one tablet in a glass of water was passed around.

I had malaria for three years during the French war; sometimes it was twice a month, but then I would be clear for a time. The fever usually lasted at least seven days—the longest time was a month— but when it lasted only three or four days I worked as usual. Most of the time we took no notice of it. When I had malaria I could not eat anything, but after it had gone I would eat everything easily: rice, sometimes a piece of salt, sometimes meat—beef or monkey. When I eventually came back to Hanoi the malaria had gone on the wind and I was very happy.

There were elephants, even tigers, in the area around Dien Bien Phu, and often we had wild pig to eat.

The local people provided us with necessary things. We often slept in the daylight and worked at night.

The officers in regiments had torches, but at battalion and company level we had lamps: oil lamps, paraffin lamps. At the time of Dien Bien Phu we had no map of the area, but we captured a French soldier and got a map from him. After that we had many printed and delivered to units in preparation for the attack.

We used the classic forms of intelligence gathering, applying many systems: we got information from the ordinary people, we sent reconnaissance troops from our side to get information, we listened to the enemy's radio, we observed closely. [Both sides were using American radios, and so could listen to each other, though because of the shortage of radios most of the Vietminh units used telephone cables strung out between command bunkers.]

I worked in the front of the headquarters, and General Giap was sometimes at the back. He worked in three different locations during the battle.

Giap had the big picture about what was happening in Dien Bien Phu:

> Our forces were absolutely superior to those of the enemy. Our infantry was three times, or over three times, stronger than the enemy's, our mortars and light artillery were many times more powerful. Our anti-aircraft and anti-artillery defense was so well organized that the effects of enemy aircraft and artillery were greatly restricted. Furthermore, our artillery was very accurate; operating in good coordination with our infantry, it caused great damage to the enemy, destroying many of his artillery positions, threatening his airfield, and hitting many stationary planes, while our anti-aircraft batteries shot down many others.
>
> After the first attacks the enemy was awe-stricken by the power of our heavy guns. A few days later the enemy artillery commander committed suicide. [Shamed by his inability to keep his word that Giap's guns would be silenced within hours, the one-armed veteran Colonel Charles Piroth killed himself by pulling the pin from a grenade with his teeth and holding it to his chest.]

On 14 and 16 March General Navarre reinforced the garrison with two battalions of paratroops from Hanoi, enabling de Castries to strengthen the defense of the main airfield and replace his Vietnamese troops with Europeans and Africans.

It was at this time, when Giap was preparing for the second and most difficult phase of the whole battle, that he had problems with the morale of his troops, who by then had been living for months in foxholes and communication trenches. "A negative attitude appeared among the officers and men: a fear of casualties, of fatigue, of hardships; a great underestimation of the enemy. [That is to say, they had become too confident.] At all levels the Party worked to eradicate these attitudes and heighten a sense of responsibility. We had to win the battle."

Giap's aim in this most vital phase of the battle was to occupy the fortified heights defending the eastern side of the central subsector. When that had been achieved he would neutralize and then occupy the airfield. Then gradually he would squeeze the perimeter, and therefore the amount of air space in which the air-drop resupply planes could work.

At 5:00 P.M. on 30 March the second phase began. After one and a half hours the Vietminh had put out of action part of a battalion of paratroopers and occupied a stronghold in the north (Dominique). After two more hours they had mauled the battalion defending another height (Eliane).

> The battle fought on the night of 30 March was the most arduous. We occupied two-thirds of the position. In the small hours of the next morning, the enemy, strengthened and supported by artillery and tanks, re-occupied it. [Bigeard led a very successful counterattack on Eliane 1 with eighty paratroopers, about half of whom died. Later, after he had become a prisoner, Giap told him, after giving him the first cup of real coffee he had had in months, that he was amazed by the nerve and bravery of the attack.]
>
> On the night of 31 March we launched a second attack, which dragged on until the next morning. We re-occupied two-thirds of the position, but after many counterattacks, the enemy retook part of the lost ground. On the night of 1 April we launched a third attack, which degenerated into an arduous tug-of-war. On 4 April we still disputed every inch of the ground with the enemy, who were taking advantage of underground trenches to parry our blows: in the end each side controlled half the height. While this stronghold had not yet fallen, the enemy, reinforced by paratroopers, launched, on 9 April, a strong counterattack in an attempt to re-occupy another position: the battle raged for four days and nights, with that hill also divided into two parts, each under the occupation of an opponent. [The whole of the 312th and the 316th divisions were engaged, with two regiments of the 308th, on the attack on the east of the main position. To lead the attack Giap had chosen Lieutenant Colonel Vu Yen's 102nd Infantry Regiment of the 308th Division, known as the Capital Regiment, a battle honor earned for its defense of Hanoi in December 1946. There were only nine survivors out of the two Vietminh companies that bore the brunt of another French counterattack near Eliane, in which 151 French soldiers died.]

Giap's attacking force kept up the pressure day after day:

We drew our positions nearer and nearer to the enemy—from ten to fifteen meters in some places. We turned the eastern hills into strong defensive positions. Our guns of all calibers constantly kept the enemy under their fire and the battle raged day and night.

Taking advantage of our trenches advancing nearer and nearer to the enemy, we applied piecemeal occupation tactics. From the west, east, and north, our lines of attack advanced toward the airfield, met there and then cut it across. The central airfield was occupied!

We tightened the encirclement and the struggle became even fiercer. The enemy launched powerful counterattacks, supported by motorized vehicles and aircraft; the fiercest took place on 24 April with the aim of driving us out of the airfield. The result was that the enemy were partially annihilated while our positions were firmly maintained and the airfield remained under our control.

The sector occupied by the enemy narrowed down to a square of two kilometers a side. Now the central sector was within range of our guns of all sizes. Our anti-aircraft artillery also moved in and the narrow airspace left to the enemy was no more safe. At that time, to kill more of them, to occupy another inch of ground, was of great significance.

We vied with one another in sniping at the enemy: riflemen, machine gunners, mortar men, and artillerymen did their best, causing greater and greater losses. His morale was sinking, he constantly lived in fear and tension and did not dare move about for fear of being shot as soon as he came out of his fortifications. Our shock units penetrated deep into his lines, destroyed his stores and decimated his force.

Giap's tactic of constricting the airspace now posed tremendous problems for the pilots, and more and more of the supplies dropped fell into enemy territory. The Vietminh not only received a bonus of food and clothing and medicines but also of ammunition, some of which fitted their guns and was fired by them at the defenders. But it was not only the French who were having logistic difficulties:

As the campaign dragged on supply became our biggest problem. As in previous campaigns there were times when our troops had to live on rice gruel and times when we had to consider giving up our plans. In Dien Bien Phu we were hundreds of kilometers from our rear depots, and the supply line was very dangerous because of enemy air attack and unfavorable climatic conditions. Another worry of ours was that the rainy season was coming. This might cause great damage, the roads might be destroyed, the fortifications might become wet, the health of our troops and *dan cong* might be affected.

By 5 April the Vietminh had sustained about ten thousand casualties.

Lt. Col. Bach Dan Hoi, an infantry officer who had become a guerrilla in his late teens, walking from his home northwest of Hanoi to join the Vietminh in the Viet Bac, says:

I was born in November 1924 and was nearly thirty years old at the time of Dien Bien Phu, where I commanded a company.

At the very beginning we got an order that we had to fight fast and win very fast. We were told to annihilate the enemy on Hill A1, but after we had made the necessary dispositions the order was completely changed; now we should fight very firmly and win. This was at the time of Tet. The men got rice cake from the local people and wine and cold meat and vegetables, but it was not a feast. There was no time for that.

At one point I was sent to the head of our artillery battalion in order to explain to him where we would attack. He was a German, who called himself Ho, the family name of President Ho Chi Minh. He had been a legionnaire but had surrendered and joined us, and was now in charge of a battalion. After the war he returned to Germany but is now dead.

Our fighting trench was not far from the enemy's barbed wire, only four or five meters. At the beginning of the attack our heavy artillery opened fire. While this was happening, I organized my soldiers to bring the explosives with which we were going to destroy the French. After the enemy had been destroyed by our artillery, we got out of our trenches and made the assault. From the first minute of the assault until the end was nearly one hour. We captured many prisoners and took the position. Most of them were French parachutists.

After that attack I was assigned to another, to split the main airfield. It was one of many attacks we made in the next days and weeks. We had to fight face to face with the enemy until the end of de Castries. There were many French casualties, but we also lost a lot of men.

Bach Dan Hoi, personally deeply involved, was one who would never forget Dien Bien Phu, but there were also other people, not directly involved, who would carry with them, for the rest of their lives, indirect links with the place; like the infant daughter of Captain Desiré of Les Paras, born in Paris at the height of the battle, who was named Anne-Marie after the place that he had valiantly tried to defend.

With no sign of improvement in the situation, and every indication that they were about to suffer an appalling defeat, the government in Paris was becoming truly alarmed. The start of the Geneva conference was drawing near. Somehow they had to find a solution to the ghastly predicament that was claiming the headlines all over the world: would the garrison of Dien Bien Phu be annihilated or would it, by some last-minute miracle, fend off the attacking hordes?

Clearly the time had long gone when the French could do it alone. They had no money, no equipment, not enough men—but worst of all there was no will to continue the fight, in France or among the French in Vietnam. The Americans too were increasingly twitchy: at all costs, Giap had to be stopped, or communism would sweep through Asia like a plague.

Contingency plans were made, and given code names, as contingency plans always are. "Damocles" was the name for a plan to withdraw French troops to an enclave beachhead around the Red River delta until American forces became available to pull them out of the mire; over the horizon the U.S. cavalry sharpened its sabres. "Vulture" was a putative operation to bomb Giap's troops at Dien Bien Phu using planes from two U.S. aircraft carriers in the South China Sea, reinforced by U.S. air force planes from Clark Field in the Philippines: 60 B-29 heavy bombers, each carrying nine tons of bombs, or 98 Superfortresses, each carrying fourteen tons of bombs, would raid the Vietminh positions, escorted by up to 450 fighters. Here was a fleeting glimpse in the brain, a preview almost, of what was to happen for real ten years later. There was even a plan to drop two or three atomic bombs around the valley to snuff out Giap and his threat; it too was a foretaste of another plan that would be discussed in the 1960s—and, like it, shelved, because it was thought that world opinion would castigate the United States if nuclear weapons were to be used.

Meanwhile on 1 May, in the morning, the Vietminh waved red flags above their trenches and played martial music over their loudspeakers to celebrate Labor Day.

In the beleaguered fortress, the garrison had given up all hope of being relieved. The majority fought on with great courage, but on the riverbanks and in the hills the internal deserters skulked out of sight, waiting for they knew not what but convinced that they had a better chance where they were than standing beside their comrades in the trenches. In that they were mistaken.

The third and final phase began on 1 May. Vietminh troops attacked in the center and took positions at the foot of the western and eastern hills. They also began to put pressure on the isolated detachments at Hong Cum (Isabelle).

On the night of the third they attacked Huguette. By now in some places they were within three hundred meters of the central command post. On 6 May they again attacked the area of the command post. Their engineers had dug an underground tunnel leading to the center of the hill and in it laid a ton of explosives. When it was detonated they fiercely attacked the defending paratroopers and legionnaires, causing many casualties. That night they stormed and occupied a secondary position near the river. Now, de Castries's troops were bottled up in a sector only seven hundred by a thousand meters in size, truly in desperate straits.

Giap continues:

> On the seventh we detected some unusual signs. Except for a few planes that dropped some food all the planes carrying munitions returned to Hanoi without dropping their loads. Here and there explosions were heard, indicating that the enemy was destroying his weapons. We saw a number of soldiers throw their arms and ammunition into the river. We deemed that they were in turmoil.
>
> At 2:00 P.M. one of our units attacked a position near the bridge. They offered weak resistance, and profiting from this victory we annihilated positions on the left bank of the river. White flags then appeared in some places.
>
> At 3:00 P.M. our troops received the order to launch a general attack without waiting for night, as we had planned. Though the enemy still had about ten thousand men left, he was completely demoralized.
>
> At 5:30 P.M. we occupied the command post. All the enemy troops came out and surrendered. They were taken prisoner and kindly treated. Our flag bearing the slogan DETERMINED TO FIGHT, AND TO WIN was raised.
>
> We attacked the southern subsector the same night. There the enemy, two thousand strong, tried to withdraw in the direction of upper Laos. Pursued by our troops, by midnight all of them had been taken prisoner.
>
> After fifty-five days and nights of unremitting struggle we were completely victorious.

A five-man assault team, led by Captain Ta Quang Luat, captured de Castries's command bunker. Lieutenant Chu Ba The, the platoon leader, raised the red flag. In a day or two Major General Vuong Than Vu, commanding the 308th Division, which had taken Huguette, claimed it as his own command post.

Giap's soldiers captured one general (for de Castries had been promoted to the rank of brigadier general during the battle), sixteen colonels and lieutenant colonels, and 1,749 officers and NCOs, as well as enlisted men—in all about ten thousand soldiers.

The Vietminh fired more than one hundred thousand rounds of artillery ammunition of 75-mm caliber or greater. The French fired ninety-three thousand. For six months there had never been a moment's silence in the valley; for the rest of time, it would bear a heavy weight of iron and the pungent smell of explosive chemicals that had originated in Russia and China and America and Europe.

In all, 82,926 parachutes had been dropped on the valley; when the guns at last stopped firing, they covered it like a great white shroud.

In France when the news came the whole nation went into mourning. All theaters and cinemas were shut. The Berlioz Requiem and other solemn music was played all day on the radio.

The same day, in Geneva, they started to discuss the future of Indochina. Giap's timing, fortuitous though it was in some respects, could not have been better.

CHAPTER TWELVE

REQUIEM

Navarre could not visualize the immense possibilities of the People's Army—the remarkable progress of the people and our army. He could see only the strong points of Dien Bien Phu and not its vulnerable points. Also, he made a very serious mistake: thinking that we would not dare to attack, on 12 March he pursued his scheme of launching a strategic offensive on the southern battlefield, an untimely operation that caused him further loss of initiative. But his greatest mistake was to underestimate the situation.

—VO NGUYEN GIAP

In all, 16,544 troops fighting for the French were in Dien Bien Phu at some time or other during the siege. (This figure includes the 165 men of the 1st Colonial Parachute Battalion who dropped out of the sky on 5 and 6 May, just in time to be captured, some of them landing right on top of Vietminh positions.) On 4 May 1,260 men were in the hospital. On the morning of the fifth, 8,158 fit men had answered the roll call. On the morning of the seventh there were 1,293 known dead. An estimated 3,000 "internal deserters" were hiding beside the river or on the hill slopes. Therefore, nearly another 3,000 men were unaccounted for. They were dead, wounded, or missing; or, perhaps, there were more water rats than people thought.

Because things had gone beyond control in the last days, no accurate records of casualties had been kept, but as a general figure it would not be far out to say that when the last shot was fired at Isabelle, in all there were about 5,400 battle casualties, of whom about 2,000 had been killed in action. They came from many places: later, Giap was to say that men from twenty-four different nations had been fighting in the valley.

Rigidly applying his nationalist and sociallist principles, Giap decreed that the wounded would be treated in the order Vietnamese, North Africans, French NCOs, French officers. But he allowed the badly wounded men of all these categories to stay in the camp in the care of some of the French medics; they, and the nurse Genevieve, were later evacuated by French aircraft to Hanoi.

As the Vietminh started to move away from the valley, Giap interspersed the remaining prisoners among his own men to deter the French from bombing and strafing his columns. (It did not. Bigeard and fourteen other officers started the withdrawal to the prisoner-of-war camps in a lorry that never stopped during daylight, so that all bodily functions had to be performed in the vehicle, but after a few days the vehicle was strafed and they continued on foot, carrying heavy loads on their backs.)

Hardly any of the 10,000-plus prisoners ever came back: they died from wounds or malnutrition as they staggered along the road, or later in the prisoner-of-war cages that were hurriedly erected for them hundreds of kilometers away to the northeast near the Chinese border. (Bigeard says they did not die as the result of brutality, a charge subsequently brought against the Vietminh: they died because they were physically worn out by the battle and the lack of food they had endured during it, and because on the way to the camps they were obliged to walk long distances with hardly any nourishment; they lived on two bowls of thin rice gruel a day, which they had somehow to cook themselves, both during the march and subsequently in the camps. Bigeard himself remained as tough as ever: after escaping he was recaptured and beaten black and blue by the guards, but because the Viets respected spirit in a man he became the leader of the prisoners of war, keeping fit by jogging even though on such poor rations.)

In keeping with the Geneva Accords, a first batch of 885 people taken at Dien Bien Phu were allowed to return to Hanoi some five months after the battle ended, including de Castries and his senior officers. They went on foot, mostly, but for part of the journey in trucks. In all, about 2,100 of those prisoners eventually made it back to freedom. (The prostitutes had joined in the trek to the camps. One married a soldier and years later appeared in Hanoi with a family. What happened to the others is not recorded. Maybe some of them lived, but probably most of them died of exhaustion on the jungle trails.)

Deducting 2,000 dead from the 16,500 odd who fought in the Arena of the Gods leaves 14,500. Take away the 3,000 odd who eventually came back leaves 11,500 dead, that being the total French loss figure for the battle (a figure, incidentally, that has never been presented in this way before).

Between the time when the war began in 1946 and the time when it ended—in late July 1954, ten weeks after Lieutenant Chu Ba The planted the gold-starred scarlet flag on top of de Castries's bunker—a total of 36,979 soldiers fighting for the French had become prisoners of war of the Vietminh. Of that total only 10,754 (28.5 percent) were freed after the war ended. (Sixty-one of those died within three months, 49 of whom had been taken at Dien Bien Phu.)

Becoming internal deserters did not save the skins of the North Africans and Vietnamese: they were made prisoners along with those who had stuck to their guns, and in the next few weeks most of them died of exhaustion, dysentery, malnutrition, and malaria, just as the others did. Had they gone on fighting it is just possible that three thousand or more extra rifles might, just might, have slowed down Giap's attacks until the rains came and turned the roads into rivers, cut off his supplies and starved his besieging force into melting away into the hills to find sustenance. More of the deserters might have lived. The course of history might have changed.

Dien Bien Phu absorbed only 5 percent of the French soldiers in Indochina, but eight of the battalions committed were elite units, whose loss was a military disaster. In comparison, the battle tied down about 50 percent of Giap's regular soldiers and used up most of the supplies he had received from China in the preceeding months. But to the French that was small compensation for the tremendous loss of prestige and the psychological defeat they suffered.

In France, people had to find excuses and scapegoats for this new and terrible hurt to their pride that followed all too soon after the ignominy of having to be liberated from German rule by the Allies in the World War II. The politicians got the blame, of course, and the generals, but much of the venom was directed at the German component of the Foreign Legion. It was the Germans who were responsible, people said: they had turned their coats out of resentment against their old enemies the French and let the Vietminh win by not fighting as hard as they should have done; the Wehrmacht was the real culprit. It was an unfair accusation, for, after all, every man had been fighting for his life. In fact only a quarter of the legionnaires at Dien Bien Phu were German, and only a few of them were seasoned soldiers. Unlike those who had joined the legion immediately after the war, their average age was only twenty-three, so most were not old enough to have fought in World War II.

The 6,500 men of the Foreign Legion comprised 24 percent of the garrison. Twelve hundred of them were killed at Dien Bien Phu—a very high proportion of the dead—but when those who died as prisoners of war in the following weeks are added the total figure works out at about 3,730, or 57 percent of them. Rightly, they regard Dien Bien Phu as one of their greatest, hard-fought battle honors; like the Paras and some of the North African and Vietnamese troops, they fought with outstanding bravery against an equally brave but more committed and fanatical enemy.

The French lost 48 aircraft shot down, another 167 damaged by flak above the valley, and another 14 destroyed on the ground. They flew 20,800 missions in support of the ground troops; this is a lot, considering the resources available to them but miniscule in comparison to the airpower that was to be used in the next Vietnam war.

Giap's casualties were around 7,900 men killed, the biggest number being about 2,000 in the assault on Gabrielle by the 308th Division, with another 1,200 dying in the assault on Eliane and 1,000 in the last cheering, surging waves on 7 May. There were a lot of hot rifle barrels around that afternoon. In addition, maybe 12,000 were wounded, but no records exist as to how many of them succumbed. (Induction of soldiers into the Vietminh was not the highly organized affair it is in Western armies. Names, addresses, next-of-kin were variables. Paper was scarce. Long-range signal communications hardly existed, and those that did would have been used for messages of higher priority than the notification of casualties. Virtually everything had to be manpacked, so things like boxes containing personal records were left behind if it came to a choice between them and ammunition or food. More often than not, families never heard of a death officially but had to assume it after months or years of not seeing or hearing from their relatives.) It had been a costly business, but in military terms well worth it.

At the end of it all, when the last gun fired the last round, the French casualties in the Indochina War amounted to 92,797 killed in action and 176,369 wounded—a total of 269,166. A further 48,673 soldiers had been medevac'd back to France during the eight years of conflict.

Bruno Bigeard (the name Bruno was adopted by him because he had been lucky with it when he was first given it as a nom de guerre during a military exercise), who was to become a four-star general, and later, in 1975, secretary of state to the minister of defense in M. Giscard d'Estaing's administration, says that French politicians did not know where they wanted to go in Vietnam, and did not know how to get there. But that was only part of the story.

The war did not end on 7 May 1954. Throughout Vietnam, Giap's troops and guerrillas were harrying the French, and he was determined to keep up the pressure. (It is worth noting that even if he had wanted to stop the fighting he did not have the command and control means to pass a coordinated immediate cease-fire order to all his many formations and units in the delta and the mountains. As was to happen in the 1960s and '70s, Giap pulled long chains to make his puppets jump far away on the other side of the horizon.)

And keep up the pressure they did. Later in the summer, farther south in the central highlands, near a town called An Khe, Vietminh soldiers trapped the thousand men of the "Korean" Battalion of Groupement Mobile 100, which had fought hard and well in Korea beside the U.S. 2nd Division. As it tried to fight its way out along Route Coloniale 19 it was ambushed time and again, until the last survivors were massacred in the Chu Dreh Pass. At the end there were only fifty-four of them still standing.

Though the world gasped at the result of the battle of Dien Bien Phu and could clearly see that the end of French rule in Indochina was a foregone conclusion, it took a little time for this to dawn on most of the French troops there. Cogny, for his part, began to concentrate his units in the Operation Damocles mode, forming a tighter perimeter around Hanoi and Haiphong and abandoning the infantry-costly de Lattre Line. Like the Maginot Line, it would become a military dinosaur: great chunks of damp concrete and rusty lumps of iron slowly crumbling away in clinging wet foliage.

In Saigon, Navarre tried hard to keep up appearances, but he would never be the same man again. Of course, nearly everyone blamed him, but the blame lay squarely with Vo Nguyen Giap. On the best information available to him, Navarre had concluded that if he was to prevent Laos from coming under communist control, he must place a large force in the Dien Bien Phu valley, across the umbilical cord, and strangle the flow of propaganda and weapons and, above all, Giap's soldiers, that was making the Pathet Lao such a threat. Since all his advisers said that there was no way in which the Vietminh could get any significant number of guns to the valley, let alone the great tonnages of ammunition needed to keep them firing, there could be no possibility that the elite troops he sent to the garrison would be greatly at risk. On the contrary, they would become a scourge in the area while he brought the Vietminh to battle farther south, inflicted heavy losses on them, and then, without having to worry about his back, finally turned north to crush Giap's best formations. Navarre was later to write: "I only learned gradually through my intelligence service. When I occupied Dien Bien Phu I expected to have to deal with two divisions, then I was told two and a half, then three. . . . It was not until 20 December that I heard that I would actually be dealing with four. By then it was much too late to evacuate the valley. And if I had we would have lost the war. . . ." The French lost the war anyway, so either way he could not win. Even with hindsight he seems not to have understood that from the early days of Giap's buildup he had had no choice but to fight on: the stranglehold was already locked on.

Even so, everything adds up to a perfectly reasonable decision made on the facts presented. What he had not allowed for was the fervor and determination of the Vietnamese and the physical effort they put into the task. Nor the leadership they got. Ho Chi Minh had given the project the benefit of his considerable analytical brainpower and his blessing (and then his distant support); the Party and the Military Committee had deliberated upon the concept and issued their edicts; soldiers recruited from all over Vietnam and the minority people in the North had done more than any reasonable person could ask of them, but the man who caused the catastrophe, inexorably, deliberately, calmly but with dynamic energy, was Giap; pacing about night after night figuring out how best to pull the noose tighter, going without sleep but not, it seems, needing it. As he watched de Castries and the other prisoners shamble past him out of the wreckage of their unassailable fortress he knew that this was, unarguably, the beginning of the end for French colonial power in Indochina.

The day after Dien Bien Phu fell, on 8 May in Geneva, the conference convened to find a political solution to the eight-year war—to find compromises that were acceptable to both sides and which would bring as little loss of face as possible. It consisted of delegations from the Soviet Union, the United Kingdom, France, Ho Chi Minh's regime, the United States of America, the People's Republic of China, and the administration that the French had set up in Saigon. (Bao Dai had been the titular emperor since 1925. When the Japanese surrendered in 1945 he abdicated; then in 1949 was asked by the French to come back and be reinstated. As a figurehead, with a few Vietnamese in official positions but with the French really continuing to run the show, he was to remain in Saigon until 1955. It was his supposed government that represented the South at Geneva.)

The French had no cards to play and nothing up their sleeves: mentally they were shattered, morally they were exhausted, financially they were bankrupt, and at heart they were terribly bitter. There was no doubt that power in the North was now, by courtesy of Giap's troops, in Ho Chi Minh's hands. In 1949 France had declared Saigon the capital of Vietnam and done away with Annam and Cochinchina as separate administrative entities. Now they had lost the North, but nobody knew quite where it ended. They temporarily retained power in the South but obviously would have to leave, since they had neither the will nor the resources to enable them to stay.

In Geneva, there was much discussion about where the partition line should be drawn. Wanting as much territory as possible, d'Argenleau's Cochinchina creation asked for it to be drawn at the 18th Parallel. For the same reason the North wanted it at the 16th. In the end Molotov, exasperated, ruled that it would be on the 17th. On such things do people's lives and history depend.

At the end of it all, after a formal vote on the military aspects but only a show of hands on the political, the Geneva Accords called for:

Partition at the 17th Parallel;
A five-mile demilitarized zone either side;
The withdrawal of French forces from Vietnam;
Free movement of refugees between north and south for three hundred days;
Free elections in the north and the south in 1956;
An independent Laos and Cambodia.

Because Giap's victory had put them in the driving seat, many people thought the communists had been more reasonable than might have been expected: they could have insisted on reparations, on no elections, on no partitioning, on total withdrawal out of Indochina, but, as ever, they were not in a hurry. According to President Eisenhower's memoirs, nearly everyone thought that the elections would end in victory for the North and the reunification of the country. No doubt the Hanoi Politburo did too. It was better to take things a step at a time, to consolidate their situation in the North before they took on the problems of the South.

Keeping its options open, the United States declined to sign the Accords—but a year later announced that any violation of them would be "a serious threat to world peace." A few months after that, on 8 September 1955, the South East Asia Treaty Organization was formed. Through it America guaranteed the security of South Vietnam, Laos, and Cambodia.

With another anticolonial war festering in Algeria, the French were obliged to rely even more than before on American aid. Responding to American pressure, on 1 January 1955 they revoked Indochina's status within the French Union. Seeing the way things were going, that the French were about to pull out and leave them at the mercy of the north, the administration in the south decided not to wait for the national elections but to beat the gun and hold a referendum in which the people would indicate whether they wanted to be members of one nation. Not surprisingly, with a strong Roman Catholic element in the government influencing events and with most of the population feeling that if they opted for union they would become communist and poorer—the north had always had fewer blessings in the way of climate and natural resources than the South and was sure to suck nourishment from its more affluent cousins—in October 1955 the majority of South Vietnamese voted that they should remain separate. The result was the creation of a republic, with Ngo Dinh Diem at its head.

Diem was a fanatical Catholic whose impassive sureness of manner and quiet personal charm had made a big hit when he met senior Americans in Washington a year before. So much so that Senator Lyndon B. Johnson, gushing compliments, falling over himself, had said that Diem was "the Churchill of the decade; in the vanguard of those leaders who stand for freedom." It would be some time before they realized that he was a stubborn and bigoted man prone to ill-conceived acts to which he would brook no opposition. For example, soon after he became president he claimed that because his administration had not been represented at the Geneva Conference it was not bound by any of its decisions . . . This assumption of the right to impulsive freedom of action was dangerous and made the United States even more convinced of the need to become involved. While France, in a complete reversal of the previous bias of its policies and hoping to avert further conflict, developed ties with the North, in the South, American advisers started to train an enlarging indigenous force that was to become known as the Army of the Republic of Vietnam—ARVN.

The final declaration at Geneva had made it clear that the 17th Parallel was not to be regarded as a border between two permanently separated Vietnamese states: it was to be no more than a temporary dividing line between the two "military zones," which the elections would abolish. A lot of people just did not believe it, and a great exodus began from the North, especially of Roman Catholics. Again, nobody made a count and the numbers are not accurately known, but by some estimates half a million people moved south, though others put the figure at nearer a million.

Before partition there had been just fewer than a million Roman Catholics in the south. Now, about another half million trekked down the narrow waist of central Vietnam, over the two tortuous passes in sight of the sea, to a new life, fleeing from what they were sure would be a repressive atheist regime. Diem gave them special favors in terms of land and money, and whole areas became Catholic enclaves. He also gave them many of the most prestigious positions in government, and nepotism, always a factor of importance in Vietnam, ensured that their power increased. All this exacerbated tensions with Buddhists, who felt they were grievously put upon. It was but one of the many reasons for discontent that were to create great turbulence in the new nation in the next decade.

About two hundred thousand Vietnamese men who had fought for the French in the north also moved to the south, with as many dependants. In among them were five or six thousand hardcore guerrillas and cadres—Party members who would merge into the population and lie low. Tens of thousands of people moved from south to north, many of them Tonkinese Vietminh who wanted to go home, some of them southerners who had fought for Giap and wanted sanctuary in North Vietnam. They too left several thousand cadres behind to work with the ones sent from the north: there was no doubt in the minds of the dedicated few, including Giap, an ultra hawk in the cabinet, that this was not the end of the story but only the beginning of another phase, that these people were the vanguard of a liberation force that would make its move when the time was right. (Something between ten and a hundred thousand Montagnards also changed sides, nobody knew exactly, or cared much.)

In the South, no attempt was made to initiate the political and social reforms that might have created popular support for Diem. In consequence as time passed the people turned away from him, hoping that they would get a better deal from the opposition; that is, the cadres of communism who were beginning to do their work of rebellion everywhere—in the cities, towns, villages, and hamlets. The reforms that might have appealed to intellectuals were not even considered, and in consequence they became a small but important element of the disaffected thousands. While in the North the leadership—the top five—were to remain in power for a quarter of a century, giving continuity, and therefore stability, of government, in the south the next two decades were to bring, one after the other, people who promised but did not deliver.

Discontent over lack of social and economic progress played into the hands of the insurrection that Ho Chi Minh's cadres started a year after Diem's refusal to hold the Geneva Accords' stipulated elections of July 1956. Though only 2 percent of the population were thought to be cadres, they amounted to more than three hundred and fifty thousand dedicated men and women, many of them in key posts throughout the nation—teachers, members of farmers' associations, even government officials. After 1960 this revolt, directed and supported from Hanoi, slowly grew in power and influence until it became a civil war—in which the United States stumbled about going from one expedient to another in vain attempts to pursue an aim that was so vague that it defied definition.

In Hanoi until the end of the 1950s Vo Nguyen Giap remained busy. He expanded and modernized the army, re-equipping it with second- and third-generation Russian and Chinese weapon systems that to them were obsolete or obsolescent but which for his soldiers were a big improvement on what they had. He created new divisions, new training centers, new doctrines. Not far from the demarcation line, at Vinh, he established a commando training camp in which men were taught how to use mines and explosives, how to carry out assassinations and kidnappings, sabotage and demolitions; and how to become experts on concealment, camouflage, fieldcraft, hand-to-hand fighting, and reconnaissance.

On 7 May 1955 he had inaugurated a Vietnamese Maritime Force. Part of the army to begin with, on 12 October 1959 it became a separate entity, the Coastal Defense Force. Then on 1 May 1959 the Vietnamese People's Air Force came into being. At first only a military air transport squadron, nearly six years later it became an offensive weapon when, on 3 April 1965, Vietnamese fighters shot down some American planes.

Domestically, after more than eight years' absence during his campaigns, Giap had moved with his wife into a house adjacent to what had been the residency of the senior French official in the north—a large yellow building known to the inhabitants of Hanoi as "The Golden Cage." His wife, a professor of history and social science, was the daughter of a man who had been the social commissioner in Cochinchina. (In 1990 she was still working, with the Embassy Social Commission in Hanoi.)

The grounds of the residency had been made into a guarded compound in which the senior members of the government lived in comfortable villas, some of which had once been occupied by French administrators. There, Giap settled down, raising a family of four children, two boys and two girls. Sometimes he played the piano, but not often, for he spent long hours at his work, in government buildings or visiting army units, and he read a lot—books about Chinese, Russian, French, British, and American military affairs but also other works; he says French authors are his favorites, but he also likes Goethe, Shakespeare, and Tolstoy. Above all, he likes to read the works of Vietnamese poets, ancient and modern.

In the last years of the 1950s Giap had a great deal of responsibility. He was minister for defense, commander in chief of the People's Army of Vietnam (PAVN), deputy prime minister, and deputy chairman of the defense council, in all of which posts he played a leading part in the collective decision making. In the years to come the single most important matter was, of course, the involvement of his army with the Vietcong in the war against the United States. Within that context the big themes were military action—guerrilla and conventional—the creation and use of the Ho Chi Minh Trail, the air defense of the north. These are dealt with in the following chapters.

By now he was known to many people as Nue Lua, The Volcano Under the Snow—icy self-control hiding seismic energy. It is a name whose invention is ascribed by some to the French, from the early days when Leclerc met him, but by others to his own men. The former seems more likely.

Not far from his home, just a few hundred yards away, his old school, the Lycée Albert Sarraut, had been renovated, had had its own electricity generator installed, and had become the Soviet embassy.

CHAPTER THIRTEEN

THE COMMUNISTS

The struggle must build, however slowly. The way to win is by small defeats, one after another until the coup de grace.

—VO NGUYEN GIAP

In 1955 the first priority of Ho Chi Minh's government was to turn North Vietnam into a communist state. Believing they had a mandate to do so—even though deep-down the majority of people had not fought for a communist government but to be rid of the colonial occupying power—Ho Chi Minh's regime began, with great intensity and as quickly as possible, to apply Marxist/Leninist principles and systems to government.

Power now resided with the Politburo and the army, and there was nothing anyone could do about it. Those who tried to subvert the regime were imprisoned, those who tried too hard were liquidated. It has ever been thus in a communist state: opposition cannot be tolerated. To the leaders of the state it is self-evident that the good of the majority, as they interpret it, must be paramount; if the minorities cannot see this, then they are badly mistaken, dangerous, and must be eliminated for the good of the majority.

In the urban areas socialism was forced on every part of the economy. With financial and technical aid from the Soviet Union, the Republic of China, and other socialist countries, Ho Chi Minh started a big program of industrialization. This was relatively successful, but then the base line had been so low to begin with that any improvements were bound to be significant. Nevertheless, during the first few years North Vietnam began to match similar Asian states in industrial productivity. In the rural areas it was a different, sadder story.

After central planning in Hanoi during the winter of 1954, in the early summer of 1955 hordes of young cadres, armed with ideological zeal and determined to build a brave new Marxist world, flooded out into the hundreds of villages and set about destroying a social order that had existed for two thousand years. The least-qualified people in practical terms but the most qualified in ideological terms, the poorest—and therefore probably the most ignorant and the ones with the biggest grudges—were put in charge of land reform. It was to prove a disaster.

The edict from Hanoi was that everyone must be classified according to their position in society. A and B were the exploiters, C, D, and E were the exploited:

  • A were the elite: the landlords, the scholars—by definition grasping, cynical, ruthless people.
  • B were rich peasants; that is, they owned their own farms or rented land to tenant farmers. They were almost as bad as class A.
  • C were peasants who farmed or rented land on a small scale.

• D were poor peasants who farmed or rented land on an even smaller scale.

• E were very poor landless peasants—the *Ban Co*, people who for generations had been poor.

In a brutally conducted collectivization of agriculture, tens of thousands of totally innocent people were killed or made homeless and driven out of their villages. Tribunals were set up that had enormous powers to try, jail, or execute people who were regarded as "culprits." Quotas were set: so many culprits had to be found in each village, in each hamlet. Regular returns had to be submitted to provincial and central Party headquarters. There was keen competition, so much so that if the quotas could not be met, then the goalposts were moved: definitions of wrongdoing were changed.

All over the North, watched by their fellow villagers, so-called exploiters were brought before the tribunals. Charges were read out, accusations were made, denials were shouted down. There were more denunciations, more recriminations. Men cried out and women wailed. Summary trials were followed sometimes by summary executions; if not, by imprisonment or the confiscation of property. Old grudges were dredged out of the past, old scores were settled. Greed paid off, because false accusations could result in more land being shared out. There was blood, broken limbs, ashes, mourning. All the worst in human nature came out, most of the best was choked off and smothered. Not surprisingly, the chaos led to food shortages and revolt. In panic lest they should lose control, the cadres tightened the screws even more.

Again, nobody knows how many people died, but estimates vary between thirty thousand and a hundred thousand people. As always happens when the masses opt for revolution, instead of evolution, there was wholesale misery. Even the poor hill people, the ignorant, illiterate, half-naked stone-age people, were hounded down and accused of things they did not even know the meaning of.

When realization of what was happening came, recriminations began in the Party. Counteraccusations followed the accusations. Scapegoats were found and many Party members were jailed. In the Party and throughout the nation, there was confusion and bickering, which lasted for months. Then at the 10th Plenum, held between 27 and 29 October 1956, Giap stood up in front of the faithful and performed the official act of contrition:

> Cadres, in carrying out their antifeudal task, created contradictions in the tasks of land reform and the Revolution, in some areas treating them as if they were separate activities:
> We failed to recognize the need to achieve unity with class C.
> We should have formed an alliance with class B, the rich peasants, instead of treating them as class A landlords.
> We indiscriminately attacked all families owning land. Many honest people were executed.
> We saw enemies everywhere and resorted to widespread violence and the use of terror.
> In some places, in our efforts to implement land reform, we failed to respect religious freedoms and the right to worship.
> We also failed to respect the customs of the Montagnard tribes and attacked too strongly their leaders and their hierarchical system.
> We placed too much emphasis on class origins rather than political attitudes.
> We resorted to disciplinary punishment, to expulsion, to execution. Worse still, torture came to be regarded as a normal part of the Party organization.
> There were grave errors. . . .

Indeed there were. What admissions. What an indictment! In these measured phrases Giap gave but a glimpse of the appalling injustices that had been perpetrated.

It must have taken courage for him to stand before the Party and the cadres and the people and admit to such things, but it was better that he should do it, the soldier, the famous victor of many battles, than that Ho Chi Minh or Pham Van Dong or any of the other politicians should get the blame; it would wash off him, it would have stuck to them. But he could not have been forced to do it, and the fact that he did so is indicative of his own feelings of guilt and compassion about the frightful effects of this misdirected zeal.

The next month open rebellion broke out in Nghe An province, and it took a division of infantry to quell it. All over the North, Roman Catholics, many of them culpable by status and all of them suspect because of their religion, had taken a more-than-average share of discrimination. On 8 November, farther south, during a riot that started in a small town near Vinh, offices and vehicles were burned and weapons were stolen from police stations. En masse, the rioters then marched on Vinh, and for three days there was hard fighting between about ten thousand Catholics and twice as many soldiers of the People's Army—two divisions. Hundreds died, two thousand or so were executed, and when it all ended about four thousand were imprisoned. It was a nasty episode, and it would be a long time before peace returned.

The French had been removed from the scene, but it was inconceivable that Giap and the other members of Ho Chi Minh's government would, in the long term, accept the situation and live with a capitalist Vietnamese half-brother state as their neighbor. Though for the moment preoccupied with establishing communism in the North, there could be no doubt that in due course the South would be subverted, either politically or by armed force, or a combination of both. The question was when and how?

The people who would do it, the people who were working with Giap toward that end in the second half of the 1950s, were much of an age, had all gone through broadly the same process of development, and knew each other well.

The source of all power in the nation was the ten-man Politburo, on which, for a long time, Giap was the only military member. It did the decision making and wrote the resolutions, which were then passed on to the Central Committee, whose Secretariat formalized them and transmitted them to the Party departments for execution—a system that still operates today.

At the head of the government, unchallenged, the respected elder, genuinely admired and even loved by his associates—and almost universally by the people of North Vietnam and by millions in the South too—was the experienced, charming, but wily politician Uncle Ho, as he was known to everyone. Aged twenty-one, working as a steward on a cargo boat, and calling himself Nguyen Ai Quoc (Nguyen the Patriot), he had left Vietnam the same year that Giap was born. In Paris he scraped together a living by coloring and re-touching photographs, but he also studied: the works of the great authors—Tolstoy, Dostoevsky, Zola, Shakespeare, Hugo, Balzac—were borrowed from libraries or bought by him from penny stalls on the Left Bank, but his real concern was communism: books and pamphlets by Marx, Engels, Lenin, and Trotsky joined the reading list. In 1920 he became a founder member of the French Communist Party and, after indoctrination in Moscow, in 1925 was sent to China as an agent of the Commintern, the international organ of the Rus-sian Communist Party. Not much is known, even today, about what happened to Ho Chi Minh in the 1930s.

Ho's prime minister was Pham Van Dong, five years older than Giap. When he was twenty-four he had been incarcerated by the French for seven years in the disgusting underground cellrooms of the prison island of Con Son, about fifty miles off the coast of the Mekong delta. Like Giap, he had come early to insurgency, and like Giap he had the inner steel to endure great hardship. He was a thoroughly political animal, in early times a leading member of the Lao Dong Workers Party, which became the ICP and then the Com-munist Party of Vietnam. The number-three man was, of course, Giap.

Three years older than Giap was Le Duan, another Annamite. He too had been imprisoned by the French—for seven years—and had then spent most of the decade of the 1930s organizing the guerrilla infrastructure in the south before going to China in 1940 to join Ho Chi Minh. In 1959 he was made secretary-general of the Party. He was influential behind the scenes, a "fixer," a man who became one of Ho's principal aides.

Three months younger than Giap was Le Duc Tho, born in Tonkin and another founder member of the ICP. The son of one of the few Vietnamese administrators in the French colonial government, he was a fanatical communist, secretive and austere —and for a large part of his life on unfriendly terms with Giap. Another one-time inhabitant of Con Son, he and Pham Van Dong had studied together while there and had indoctrinated other prisoners in the theories of communism. A poet, he wrote, "Rage grips me against the barbaric imperialists; / So many years their heels have crushed our country; / A thousand, thousand, oppressions. . . ." However, his bitter feelings were also directed against his own countrymen, for when he rose to a position of power he ordered the execution of hundreds of "deviationists" who did not meet his rigorous criteria of loyalty. (With someone like Le Duc Tho sitting at his elbow and waiting for a wrong move, perhaps it is not surprising that Giap unwaveringly trod the Party line of communist thought.)

Another veteran leader, and another ex-jailbird—for ten years in his case—was Truong Chinh, secretary-general of the Party after the 1954 triumph but sacked from that post as a scapegoat for the excesses of the agricultural reform program, though he was allowed to remain in the Politburo. He too was sometimes to have differences of opinion with Giap, partly because for a time he supplanted Giap, and in some ways even Pham Van Dong, as one of the favored deputies to Ho Chi Minh.

These men ruled the country in accordance with two major principles. The first, intended to safeguard the security of the regime, was that ministers were multihatted; that is, were involved, not necessarily as chairmen, in, usually, four different ministries. Thus they could keep a finger on the pulse of several activities and at the same time prevent ministerial cliques from forming and conspiring together secretly. The second was that leadership within ministries— and even theoretically at the top in the Politburo, though people generally deferred to Ho—was collective, a matter of consensus; kudos and blame were equally shared. While it was possible for a decision that was highly objectionable to one member to be taken, no decision could be taken that was totally inimical to him. Because leadership was collective, no one person could become too powerful or the focus of a personality cult, and therefore strong enough to challenge the corporate leadership.

Fragmentation of power in this way created in North Vietnam a monolithic, mutually supportive, antidemocratic bloc of people who remained distant from the proletariat they were supposed to be representing—but in that they were no different from any other communist regime.

The military leadership too was theoretically based on consensus. Though Giap told the author that the people and the collective leadership had won the wars, and not him, it is difficult to believe that he was not in the driving seat of the battle tank for most of the time, for two reasons: the first is his personality—dominant, thrusting, intelligent, clear-headed; the second, his unchallengeable position as the clear military victor of the Indochina War. With personality, experience, and success behind him, who could talk him down?

The men who would conduct the war in the South were the members of the National Defense Council. In the late 1950s it consisted of the chairman, Ton Duc Thang, two vice-chairmen—Pham Van Dong and Vo Nguyen Giap—and as members Tran Quoc Hoan (minister for the interior), Nguyen Van Tran (from the Central Committee of the Party), Nguyen Duy Trin (from the Foreign Office) and Colonel Generals Van Tien Dung (pronounced Zoong), Song Hao (the chief political commissar), and Chu Van Tan, the Nung Montagnard.

Within a close group of people dedicated to a fanatical political ideal, unity was not difficult, though they each had alliances based on personal friendships and other ties. Sometimes these were to create difficulties; as when someone sided with China, someone with Russia; as when someone was in favor of armed action and someone else in favor of giving predominance to political action.

Of the officer corps generally, more than 70 percent came from bourgeois backgrounds—education = greater education = power—but two of the three senior generals who were to play a great part in the Vietnam war were genuinely proletarian: Van Tien Dung and Nguyen Chi Thanh.

Van Tien Dung had been number two to Giap for many years. Contrary to his appearance, which is tough and pugnacious, he has an easygoing and modest personality. He was born in 1917 into a peasant family and was a textile worker before becoming a trade unionist and then joining the ICP. After being arrested, escaping, living as a Buddhist monk, being arrested again, and escaping again, he went to Cao Bang and joined Giap as a cadre. From then on he was promoted very rapidly and by 1953 was commanding the 320th

Division. He then became PAVN chief of staff, in which capacity he served Giap at Dien Bien Phu, being largely responsible for the brilliant logistical staff work that was one of the battle-winning factors.

Nguyen Chi Thanh, yet another Annamite, was born into a poor peasant family in 1914. In 1938 he, like Giap, was a schoolmaster, and like him involved in the revolution; and, like him, he too was arrested by the French—but not until 1943. He was then kept in prison until 1945, when the Japanese released him and other political prisoners, after they had ousted the French wartime colonial government.

Before being captured he had been much involved with psychological warfare directed at the North African troops serving with the French; he was to say of himself that his "battlefield was in people's minds." After the war, liked by Ho Chi Minh, he was given much responsibility, including the creation of the Communist Youth Union. Then, in the late 1950s, he moved back into the military sphere, becoming chief of the General Political Directorate of the PAVN and a member of the Party Central Military Committee. Thanh was, therefore, primarily a politician and not a soldier and, extraordinarily, it was not until he was a four-star general that he actually took command of troops, when he became the PAVN supremo in the South. As his military chief of staff, he was to have Le Trong Tan, a southerner who in 1953 had commanded the 312th Division.

It is perhaps necessary to clarify something while writing about generals. In most Western minds the concept of generalship brings visions of pomp: gold braid, staff cars, pennants, aides. In the People's Army of Vietnam the overlying theme throughout the 1950s was poverty: there might be some expensive equipment around, but everything else was peasant-basic—and still is today, for that matter. And at the start anyway, for ideological reasons, there was no rank, as such, and therefore no distinguishing symbols of rank—no gold braid and none of the other trappings. It was, and still is, an untidy, unsmart, no-frills, strictly functional, but efficient and dedicated army.

From its inception, the Indochina Communist Party had believed that there were two ways to advance a cause: by politics or by the use of force—what they called political or armed *dau tranh*. The strength of this concept is that it changes the nature of conflict: whereas previously in history the defeat of a nation's fighting forces meant defeat of the nation, under *dau tranh* if the army is defeated the struggle continues politically; the nation can never be defeated as long as the will of the people remains strong. In the years to come the United States would find that though they might win battles, they could not win the war.

After the 8th Plenum in 1941, the Party had decreed that armed *dau tranh* would be used to mobilize the people—though even then Ho Chi Minh proclaimed that political action was more important than military action: whatever happened, the fervor of the people must be maintained by proselytizing. In 1945 and 1946 political *dau tranh* was dominant. Obviously the war years were an armed struggle, and then, after the French departed, politics again were most important.

In 1955 the People's Army numbered about two hundred thousand. For the next two years it took a back seat, the government inward-looking and primarily concerned with its fumbling implementation of Marxist theories. Then, during the 12th Plenum in March 1957, Giap announced a new slogan:

"Positively Build a Powerful People's Army and Gradually Advance to Professionalism and Modernization."

Acting on this dictum, which of course he had been instrumental in writing, he started to reorganize the army. Academies were opened, a tank corps was planned (actually inaugurated on 5 October 1959), new logistic support units were created, and conscription was once again authorized, to start in 1960. Ranks and insignia were introduced, and men began to be paid, based on length of service, rank, honors won, size of family—but very little, and with small differentials between lower ranks. (This is still the case today. A corporal gets just over twice as much as a recruit private, but a sergeant only 17 percent more than a corporal. Field officers, on the other hand, get more than three times the pay of a sergeant, a much bigger differential than in most Western armies.)

The 1957 plenum also ordered changes in the structure of the guerrilla rump of about ten thousand people that had remained in the South after partition. In October Giap created a new unit, known by the number 250, consisting of thirty-seven companies, most of them in the central highlands of western South Vietnam. Within a year a whole battalion was operating in Thu Dau Mot and Tay Ninh provinces. Then in mid 1958 he ordered the formation of the Eastern Nam Bo Command, comprising three companies of guerrillas and an elite explosives unit. In those two years he established the basis of insurrection in the South.

During the next three years the Vietcong, as these guerrilla units became known, progressively took over more and more of the rural areas in the northern part of South Vietnam and by April 1960 had created a liberated zone around six of them that they closely controlled. (The name Vietcong was a derogatory term used in the South to describe communist insurgents. They were not, strictly speaking, Vietminh, since that name referred to the military branch of the political organization created by Ho Chi Minh in the Pac Bo in 1943, but they were the successors to the Vietminh, both in ideology and in practice.) But that is not to say that the Vietcong were unopposed. The young communist bloods wanted action quickly but encountered stolid refusal to change. Unable to persuade the village elders, who wanted to maintain traditional ways, or the district administrators, who were paid by Saigon, they resorted to terror, and between 1957 and 1960 assassinated thousands of civilians—mostly village headmen—and around one thousand seven hundred government officals—in addition to torturing many thousands more.

Replacing these people as leaders of the local communities the Vietcong were then able to direct the population as they wished. As they took a grip on more and more territory, the legitimate government was able to control only the capital and the towns and, as had happened in the North during the Indochina War, the countryside came to be off-limits except when sizable military operations were mounted.

In January 1959, during the 15th Plenum, the Central Executive Committee of the Party, of which Giap was a member, had decreed through resolution 15 that *thoi co*, the propitious moment, had again arrived, this time for armed *dau tranh* in the South. In effect they were formally acknowledging the existence of the units already in the South and authorizing a buildup of armed force to achieve *truong nhat*—reunification.

In July, Giap activated Logistical Group 599 to open up the Ho Chi Minh Trail as the umbilical cord between the North and the South. As the years passed, this route, originally a narrow track through mountainous jungle, was to become a major arterial highway.

In 1960 the controlling organ of the Party in the South, the National Liberation Front, was formed: it in turn created the People's Liberation Armed Forces, the PLAF. In the spring of 1960 more cadres arrived in the Mekong delta from Hanoi, and a year later the PLAF fielded its first two full battalions. Soon, other minor groups had merged together to create more major units, which within the year began to mount multibattalion attacks, supported at all times by regional and local guerrilla forces.

As in the Indochina War there were three branches of the army: the main force, *quan doi chu luc*—distinguished generally by the hard pith-type helmets they wore—and the paramilitary, split into regional *(po doi dia phuong)* and local *(van quan du kich)* guerrilla forces.

Step by step Hanoi had created the basis of the organization needed to take on Diem's regime and its American supporters.

CHAPTER FOURTEEN

WASHINGTON'S WAR

*I predict that you will, step by step, be sucked into a bottomless
military and political quagmire.*

—DE GAULLE TO KENNEDY, 1962

The main reason for U.S. commitment to the independence of
South Vietnam was belief in the "domino theory." At a
press conference held on 1 April 1954, President Eisenhower had
likened the political situation in Southeast Asia to a row of dominoes: if the one at the end of a series of standing dominoes were to
fall, it would send the rest toppling down one after the other; if
communism triumphed in South Vietnam, it could spread south and

west to Cambodia, Thailand, Burma, Malaysia, Indonesia, the Philippines—even, perhaps, as far as Australia and New Zealand. It would outflank, the theory went, the U.S. island-defense chain based on Japan, Taiwan, and the Philippines; the whole of the eastern seaboard of the Pacific would be under communist control, including the three sea channels that allowed access to the Indian Ocean and the Middle East. U.S. vital interests would be threatened, and so would world peace.

It was most unfortunate that this idea—reminding people of their childhood games—made such a quick visual impression on the brain and was so easily understood that it came to be accepted by millions without question, for it made no allowance for differences of race and culture, topography, religion, and economics in all those disparate nations and assumed that they had pliant, homogeneous populations with no alternative aspirations or historical prejudices. It was doubly unfortunate that it made such a deep impression on the man who would one day be president, John F. Kennedy. (The theory, had, in fact, first been voiced prior to April 1954 during deliberations by the National Security Committee in Washington and was not Eisenhower's own inspiration.)

Five years later, in 1959, President Eisenhower publicly declared the United States' on-going commitment to the continued independence of South Vietnam. By the end of the year there were 750 American military advisers in the South, which then had an army of 243,000 men.

In November 1960 Kennedy was elected president. In his inaugural address he made his famous statement about the American people shouldering any burden, paying any price, for the defense of freedom. In May 1961, in further stirring rhetoric, he told Congress that they lived in extraordinary times and that they faced an extraordinary challenge. "The battleground for the defense and expansion of freedom today," he said, "is the whole southern half of the globe, the lands of the rising peoples. Their revolution is the greatest in human history. They seek an end to injustice, tyranny, and exploitation. More than an end, they seek a beginning! And theirs is a revolution we would support regardless of the Cold War."

Kennedy's concept of a Southern hemisphere spontaneously revolting against injustice was also easily understood but, like the theory of the falling dominoes, was flawed. For who were the tyrants, the exploiters, the perpetrators of these injustices? The people he inferred were responsible for the revolutions in Asia and Africa and parts of South America could only be the French, the British, and the Dutch, the fading imperialists, who surely did not fit that description; their short-lived empires had been a phase of human development and education in which much more was gained by primitive peoples than was lost by them. And besides, those European nations were America's staunch allies in the Cold War; it was no way to speak of friends and was a glib assessment that, applied to American foreign policy, was to cause confusion and sometimes animosity for years to come. Furthermore, South Vietnam came to be thought of in many Americans' minds as one of the nations they were helping to free from old injustices, when in fact the problem was now quite different.

In his speech Kennedy had continued: "The adversaries of freedom did not create the revolution . . . but they are seeking to ride the crest of the wave. Yet their aggression is more often concealed than open. They have fired no missiles; and their troops are seldom seen. They send arms, agitators, aid, technicians and propaganda to every troubled area. But where fighting is required, it is usually done at night, by assassins striking alone . . . by subversives and saboteurs and insurrectionists."

In 1961 the prime minister of the Soviet Union had announced that it would support wars of national liberation, in effect that they would use surrogate forces to undermine the capitalist West. From then on they worked to exploit the turbulence caused by the wind of change that was blowing through the Southern hemisphere. However, the monolithic structure of Moscow-controlled communism had been shattered when first Yugoslavia and then Albania broke away after World War II, to be followed by China. The Soviet Union no longer called the communist tune all over the world. It was nationalism that was the main driving force in the anti-imperialist disturbances of the 1940s and '50s.

Nevertheless, convinced by his advisers of the threat of creeping communism, President Kennedy sent more military men to Saigon.

By the spring of 1962 there were nearly 4,000 of them, by late 1962 11,300. Then in October 1963 the president authorized the deployment to South Vietnam of the U.S. Air Force's 7th Air Division, part of the 7th Air Force, the commander of which was responsible for all air operations throughout Southeast Asia. He had increased the stakes enormously.

Backed by the United States in this way, the Diem government in Saigon should have done well. It did not because it was undemocratic, badly led, badly organized, and biased toward the small minority of Roman Catholics. When reform was desperately needed, nothing was done, and no attempt was made to fill the vacuum left by the departure of the French administrators. Bachelor Diem himself lived like a solitary monk in the palace in Saigon, while his worldly brother Nhu and his beautiful but brash wife milked the system for all they were worth and rode in cavalcade through the streets of Saigon like royalty. While the Vietcong—referred to generally by the South Vietnamese and the Americans and their allies as the VC— were terrorizing the countryside to eliminate anticommunist opposition, Nhu's Can Loa secret police purged the villages of opponents to his brother's regime; one American estimate is that seventy-five thousand people were killed and more than fifty thousand imprisoned by them. The villagers, sometimes in dread of the Vietcong and nearly always in fear of their government, swayed before the storm. Diem, fearing change instead of grasping it as a means of progress, repeated the mistakes made by the French—repression (in his case of Buddhists and the Cao Dai sect), aloofness, and no alleviation of the endemic poverty in the nation. Retribution was not far away.

Diem's major initiative to counter the spread of Vietcong activity and influence was what was known as the Strategic Hamlets Program, the forced migration of villagers into secure compounds where they, in theory, could not be intimidated. The scheme was modeled on measures that had been successfully used by the British in the Malayan emergency in the late 1940s and early 1950s. There, people had been moved into designated areas where they could live in safety until the terrorists around them had been eliminated: any people found outside those areas were classed as enemy and were fair game for the security forces. Unfortunately, the situation in

Vietnam resisted such a solution. For one thing, in Malaya the insurgents were readily identifiable: they were Chinese, and quite different in appearance from the darker-skinned Malays. For another, the Malays are Moslems and do not venerate the graves of their ancesters as the Vietnamese do: though during the emergency they might not have liked being moved from their homes, they had no deep spiritual objections to it, whereas when they were evicted the Vietnamese felt that they were deserting the spirits of their forebears, being torn away from their roots.

Millions of soldiers would have been needed to ensure the individual isolation of the twenty-five hundred villages in the South from the depredations and recruiting swoops of the, then, forty-five known bands of Vietcong. Since that was not feasible, the solution was to transfer people into a smaller, more manageable number of fortress compounds. ("Hamlets" was a very misleading term. A compound could be forty miles in circumference, sometimes a string of guarded barbed-wired enclosures with tens of thousands of people living in them.)

On 3 February 1962 the Strategic Hamlets Program began, a name changed as time passed to New Life Hamlets and then to the Revolutionary Development Program. In Saigon, in an organization known as the British Advisory Mission, a man by the name of Sir Robert Thompson, a veteran of the Malayan insurgency—he had been chief of police there—and an acknowledged expert in such matters, helped the CIA to implement the carefully thought-out scheme.

The South was divided into so-called "prosperity zones": Yellow, under government control (about 32 percent of the population), Red, under VC control (43 percent), Blue—neither one nor the other. The aim was to establish hamlets—yellow zones—inside the red zones and then take them over. The time frame allowed was eighteen months.

First, a protected area had to be established, and in it the wherewithal for life. Next, communists had to be eliminated. (Question: Who was a communist and who was not?) Then U.S. Special Forces cells in the hamlets helped an elected council to control the inhabitants and defend them with their own militia. But quite often the militia let Vietcong into the hamlet at night and then let them out again in the morning—and, of course, some of the militia themselves were Vietcong. It was a Kafkaesque, nightmare situation, typical of what was happening in almost every sphere of activity throughout the South.

Though millions of dollars were poured into the Hamlets plan and a gigantic effort was made to make it work, it was a loser from the start. People were forced to move into places that were lacking in basic amenities because the money to pay for them had been diverted into the pockets of unscrupulous contracters; though they might not have been communist supporters originally, such treatment did nothing to improve their opinion of Diem's regime. Villagers had to have identity cards but to get them often had to bribe officials. They had to work hard in bad conditions, were bullied by people they did not know, and at the end of it all were still hounded by the secret police or attacked by the Vietcong, who naturally regarded the hamlets as prime targets. In 1962 more than 2,000 were attacked more than once, one of them thirty-six times! In one province 105 out of 117 were attacked. In the Mekong delta alone the Vietcong destroyed more than 500 hamlets.

The only thing in the Strategic Hamlets Program's favor from the government's point of view was that the uprooting of the villagers disrupted the network of spies, couriers, and thieves painstakingly created by the VC over the years. But this was no compensation for the turmoil created. Though people in the towns still lived reasonably well, in the countryside these upheavals created even more poverty and discontent. In response, in order to secure his position, Diem abolished the traditional system of village councils and allowed his ministers to appoint their own nominees in place of them: an orderly system of administration, evolved over generations, was swept away—and into the void went the Vietcong.

By the summer of 1963 the South was in revolutionary chaos because of the many injustices of Diem's regime and his personal intransigence to American proposals for greater democracy. It boiled to the surface, and on 1 November he and his brother were assassinated during a military coup that had been connived at by the United States in the hope that another better leader would be found—though they had nobody specific in mind. (It must be said that it was only Diem's removal from the leadership that had been intended; the CIA and the key American politicians who covertly assisted Diem's opponents did so with no thought that their help would end in Diem's death, which shocked President Kennedy, even though he had known of, and approved of, the action. However, his departure did not improve matters: South Vietnam was to be led during the next twelve years by a quickly changing succession of squabbling and incompetent men, military and civilian: repeated political coups, many inspired by the military, took place as Duong Van Minh, Nguyen Khanh, Nguyen Xuan Oanh, Tran Van Huong, Phan Khac Suu, Phan Huy Quat, Lan Phan Phat, Tran Thien Khien, Nguyen Cao Ky, and Nguyen Van Thieu in turn took over the leadership.

In 1964 Diem's immediate successor decided that the Strategic Hamlets scheme was unworkable. American money had been poured down the drain (in that and inumerable other projects that were to be initiated in the future: after the war it was estimated that 60 percent of all U.S. aid to South Vietnam was embezzled or diverted from its intended use).

On 22 November 1963, only three weeks after Diem died, President Kennedy was himself assassinated.

As far as foreign policy toward Vietnam was concerned, the change brought no backing off by the United States. The vice-president, Lyndon Baines Johnson, stepping into Kennedy's shoes, was just as determined to block the spread of communism, of which, like so many Americans, he had a genuine if irrational fear. Up to now the administration had tended to wait and see what happened in Vietnam and hope that things would improve. With Johnson at the helm, according to his biographer Doris Kearns, "brash and vulgar, brilliant and sensitive, tolerant and idealistic but bigoted and vindictive, all at the same time," things would be different. She says that he regarded the Vietnamese as a sort of oriental reincarnation of the Germans of the two world wars: they had been vanquished by American might, "now here he was preventing World War III." He wanted to lead positively and be shown to be effective; wanted to make an imprint on events; wanted to take on the commie threat on the other side of the ocean. And at the start of it all so did most of the nation.

By the end of 1963 the Vietcong had begun to create military formations and had grouped battalions into regiments and were starting to form them into divisions. In support of them, and acting on Vo Nguyen Giap's orders, in early 1964 units of the People's Army (PAVN) began to infiltrate into the central highlands in the South and to standardize their weapons with the Vietcong. From now on there would be two communist military organizations to contend with in the South: the ubiquitous VC and the units of the PAVN sent there by Giap to assist them, or sometimes to play the leading role.

In the face of this threat President Johnson decided that America would "remain firmly committed to the preservation of an independent South Vietnam." From then on there was to be an inexorable escalation of material, manpower, and monetary support: more and more ships, aircraft, men, and dollars flowed across the Pacific. As they did, the Vietcong went from strength to strength.

Most of the time the VC lived in the villages among the people and shared their poverty. Shared their misery and their joys. Shared their concerns. Were protected by them. Though many American policymakers, civilian and military, genuinely believed that the VC were alien northern intruders disliked by the native villagers, and that therefore the majority of the population wanted them out, the VC were not different—they *were* the people! That wholly erroneous outsiders' assessment of the nature of the Vietcong was supported by successive regimes in the South because it was in their interests to conceal the truth: the United States might be expected to take on a minority of intruders who were disliked by the majority, but it was quite another thing to expect it to confront most of the population. If the United States pulled out, the regime would topple, so it was necessary to perpetuate the misconception.

Another very damaging American misapprehension was that the Vietnamese were in the pockets of the Chinese, which even a brief study of history would have shown was highly improbable. It was at the root of the domino theory, still current even in 1964. Then, Adlai Stevenson, a leading politician, was quoted in the press as saying that by being concerned with Vietnam the United States was "pre-

venting Chinese aggression in Asia." The *New York Times* made the
comment that "close to one hundred and fifteen million people could
fall to the Communists if Cambodia, Thailand and Burma, and possibly even Malaysia, were to fall." And yet it was clearly preposterous
to think that Vietnamese would die in their thousands—at the height
of the war in the South as many as two thousand a month, twenty for
every foreign death—in order to hand their country over to the Chinese.

In March 1964 President Johnson agreed to "graduated, overt military pressure against North Vietnam." In August of that year the
Tonkin affair was the reason why the United States executed a "one-
time" retaliatory bombing strike against the North. That incident, of
no great importance in itself but a major turning point nationally and
internationally, was a classic example of American knee-jerk reaction to events.

On 3 August 1964 an American destroyer, the U.S.S. *Maddox*,
patrolling in international waters in the Gulf of Tonkin, went to
action stations in response to being attacked with torpedoes by
North Vietnamese patrol boats. The following night radio operators
on the ship heard messages that gave the impression that another
attack was about to be launched. (Later, it was admitted that these
were in fact warning orders to the Vietnamese boats to be ready to
defend themselves against American warships in the area.) Air-sup-
port pilots summoned from a nearby carrier and flying over the
scene for forty minutes saw nothing of the enemy through breaks in
thunderclouds, but on the *Maddox*, and its accompanying sister-ship
the *Turner Joy*, erratically operating sonars picked up what seemed
to be the tracks of twenty-two torpedoes. For more than four hours
the ships blasted off into the night, though not one sailor on either
ship heard or saw the enemy. In the end the two captains claimed
that they had sunk two or perhaps three patrol boats. However, the
next morning the captain of the *Maddox*, in a panic of doubt, signaled that there had been "no actual visual sightings" and that the
blips on the screen had been due to "freak weather effects." The
blame, he said, lay with an "overeager" young sonar operator.

Unfortunately, on the morning of 4 August, President Johnson, in the middle of a presidential election campaign and feeling that he had to be seen to be a resolute man, acting on the first information received and unaware of the doubts, told congressmen that the destroyers had definitely been attacked and that this time he was going to order retaliation against the North. At this moment the incident took on a momentum that only the president could stop. He did not stop it, and while the captain of the *Maddox*, under great pressure from every admiral in the chain of command, was trying desperately to find confirmation from somewhere that four hours of firing had been at real targets, Johnson announced to the nation on television that there must be a positive reply. There was. On 5 August 1964 America went to war without declaring it—and never did subsequently. Starting at 11:00 A.M. sixty-four air sorties pounded port and oil-storage facilities at Vinh, just north of the 17th Parallel. The Pentagon estimated that in ten minutes 10 percent of the North's oil supply had been destroyed.

Two days later Johnson secured what was known as the Tonkin Gulf Resolution, which gave congressional approval to "take all necessary measures" to repel attacks against American forces, to "prevent further aggression," and to determine when "peace and security in the area had been attained." Under those vaguely worded terms, he and his successor Richard Nixon were to pursue hostilities until 1970, when the Senate repealed the act (by which time it had been announced that America would be withdrawing from Vietnam).

In 1964 President Johnson hung back from declaring war for several reasons: because it would seem ludicrous in the eyes of the world for the mightiest power on earth to declare war on a small and backward nation like Vietnam; because doing so might bring China into the conflict; because attention and resources might be deflected from his Great Society program. However, the fact that he did not do so meant that the people were not committed to the war: without their commitment it was wrong and dangerous to commit the army, a fact that would loom ever more largely as time passed. In 1964 it might have been possible to declare war; after 1965, when the protests began, it was not. Without such a formal declaration he and his successor would fight the conflict solely on their own authority as commander in chief of the armed forces.

America fought an undeclared war but unlike during the Korean War did so without a mandate from the United Nations Organization. Feeling isolated, and wishing to prove that it was not acting out of self-interest alone, Washington tried, in what was known as the More Flags Initiative, to persuade other governments to participate in the preservation of South Vietnam's independence. Initially, seventy-five hundred military personnel were offered, but the numbers grew.

South Korea was paid nearly $1 billion by the United States between 1965 and 1970 to send their twenty-two battalions, and at the peak of their effort deployed fifty thousand troops. Thailand also sent troops. The Australians, concerned that China would spread its influence southward by supporting Indonesia in its confrontation with Malaysia, sent an infantry battalion in 1966 and two more later, and artillery, engineer, and supply units, plus an air element, raising their total, at peak, to over eight thousand servicemen. New Zealand sent a battery of artillery and two rifle companies, in all over a thousand combat troops. The Philippines sent a civic action group with its own armed security force. Other nations contributed welfare or social workers. In all, thirty-four nations were to send material aid (food, medicine, educational facilities), specialist personnel, or teachers; eventually some six hundred people joined the five hundred or so French teachers and doctors who had stayed behind to help the South Vietnamese after the French withdrew. Several other nations promised to send help but never did.

The major European powers declined to be drawn in to an Asian war.

In January 1965 the 9th Division of the People's Liberation Armed Forces (PLAF, the official name for the Vietcong), consisting of three regiments and stiffened by the presence of the PAVN's 101st Regiment, destroyed two ARVN battalions at Binh Gia. It was the first time that the VC had purposely taken on major formations in the South in head-on confrontation. A month later, on 7 February 1965, in response to a massed Vietcong attack on the U.S. Air Force

(USAF) base at Pleiku, President Johnson authorized a one-off, eye-for-an-eye air strike code-named "Flaming Dart." A few days later Johnson was told that four of Giap's regular PAVN divisions had been identified south of the demarcation line. On 13 February he authorized "a program of measured and limited air action against selected targets in the Democratic Republic of Vietnam." Code-named "Rolling Thunder," it was aimed at stopping the flow of Giap's soldiers into the South.

American airmen advocated massive strikes, but the view of the president's civilian advisers was that such action might be taken by the Chinese or Russians as a threat to themselves and bring about an active retaliatory response by either or both of them, leading to World War III. Also in Johnson's mind was the wish to avoid America's being seen in world opinion as a bully-boy thrashing a small nation. For these reasons initially he gave the go-ahead to Rolling Thunder on the basis of gradually applied pressure that would cause Ho Chi Minh to see the light and cease to try to subvert the South—a forlorn hope indeed.

As to World War III, had either Russia or China wanted an excuse to take on the United States, they could easily have already found or fabricated one. The fact was that the Russians were content to see the Americans bleed distantly while they built up their navy and their armory of strategic missiles: they were in no position militarily to take on the United States. The Chinese were even more keen not to get directly involved while they sorted out their "cultural revolution," which Mao Tse-tung was then about to launch. Mao was, besides, concerned about what he regarded as increasing Russian collaboration with the West and quite prepared to worsen Sino-Soviet relationships on account of what the Chinese regarded as heretical Soviet changes to classic communist doctrine. With hindsight it is clear that events in Vietnam were not uppermost in his mind.

During the early phases of Rolling Thunder, therefore, restrictions were imposed. First, targets would be sanctioned only south of the 19th Parallel (just north of Vinh), and then only by the Joint Chiefs of Staff, senior members of the cabinet, or President Johnson himself. (He himself selected most of the targets, usually once a week on a Thursday during a working lunch in the White House, the clatter of cutlery on crockery and the murmur of voices punctuated now and then by the whir of his battery-powered pepper grinder.) Second, even when agreed in principle the targets could not be struck until further authorization was given by the Chiefs of Staff. It was a ponderous, time-consuming business that obliged the most responsible and busiest brains in the country to spend time on mind-stubbing minutiae instead of being able to concentrate on more important matters.

On 2 March the first air strikes were made. On the eighth, U.S. Marines landed over the beaches near Da Nang. Said at first to be a token force sent to protect the air base there, they turned out to be the beginnings of a horde. Soon, the Pentagon drew up plans for four brigade-sized enclaves manned by eighty-two thousand American troops. In addition to Da Nang, the second largest city in the South, major infantry bases were to be established at Chu Lai, Quang Ngai, Qui Nihon, Bien Hoa, and Vung Tai. The U.S. Navy would develop a giant base on the virgin sands of Cam Ranh Bay. Plans for these great increases in American commitment went on despite the fact that Johnson was warned by his secretary of defense, Robert McNamara, that six hundred thousand American soldiers would be needed in South Vietnam if that nation was to be defended from the North, and that even then there would be only a fifty-fifty chance of success. At this point in time it was a very prescient and accurate assessment.

Responding to the peculiar nature of warfare in Vietnam, the Pentagon also decided to send more of the army's Special Forces, the Green Berets. When they arrived many of these were sent into the jungle to act as a screen along the western frontier with Laos and Cambodia and to give warning of enemy infiltration across the borders. To enable them to do so they were to woo, train, and fight with the Montagnards—most of whom had great antipathy toward the plains people generally and the Vietcong in particular—and the large Cambodian minority who lived in southwest Vietnam. (The Green Berets, like the OSS, had been modeled on unconventional forces created during World War II, notably Merrill's Marauders—which in turn had developed from the British Chindits and Special Air Service.)

On 17 April 1965 ex-general Maxwell D. Taylor, one-time army chief of staff, then chairman of the Joint Chiefs of Staff, then security adviser to President Kennedy, and now America's ambassador in Saigon, cabled the State Department in Washington saying that he "badly needed a clarification of our purposes and objectives" in Vietnam. That he did not get, but by then the president had decided that targets north of the 19th Parallel could be hit, except that a radius of thirty nautical miles around Hanoi and ten miles around Haiphong would be "off limits." Further, there was to be no mining of the harbors in the North.

The creation of no-strike zones was an extraordinary decision, for it let the Vietnamese concentrate their war potential and material inside these safe havens; the no-mining order, of course, left the ports open to the 67 percent or so of the total material aid from fraternal socialist countries that came in through them.

In March 1965 Giap had begun the construction of surface-to-air missile sites in the North. In response to that and the increase in PAVN strength, the American troop ceiling was raised: by September 1965 they had more than one hundred thousand soldiers in South Vietnam. That same month, the Chinese foreign minister announced that China would not intervene directly in Vietnam; with that poised dagger removed from behind his back, President Johnson felt free to pursue his obsession with the conflict, the cost and degree of which he concealed from Congress and the American people. By now war expenditure was obliging him to defer his social programs, and he was gripped by a terrible personal dilemma: ever since he had become president his dream had been to be remembered as the greatest social reformer in American history. He cared deeply about the poor, black people, the illiterate, and wanted desperately to make life better for them; now, most of his time and most of the nation's resources were being spent on trying to solve the intractable problem of a war that, no matter how much money and military effort were thrown at it, could not be brought to a victorious conclusion.

By year end 1965 Giap had infiltrated sixty-four thousand soldiers of the People's Army into the South.

CHAPTER FIFTEEN

HANOI'S WAR

It is impossible for Westerners to understand the force of the people's will to resist, and to continue to resist. The struggle of the people exceeds the imagination. It has astonished us too.

—PHAM VAN DONG

During 1964 more than a million *dan cong* were enlisted into service to work on road building and other construction projects and in hospitals. By the middle of the year the Soviet Union had provided enough equipment for Giap to create another division.

There was never a problem about finding the manpower, and the PAVN had been growing steadily in size.

In April 1965 Giap and Le Duan went to Moscow and negotiated a new arms agreement under the terms of which Russia would increase its military assistance. (Later that year, in December, they said they would send even more.) Ho Chi Minh himself mobilized the young people.

In April Ho had decreed a law enlisting the young for war work, civil and military. During the year nearly 300,000 new soldiers, 70 percent of them between the ages of eighteen and twenty-five, were enlisted into the army, 160,000 of them in May alone. Many ex-Vietminh soldiers were recalled into the army in order to give the backbone of experience to the new recruits. The 308th, 314th, 320th, and 325th divisions were reconstituted, and by the end of the year another 2 million *dan cong* had been enrolled. Young people from Hanoi University were sent to the Soviet Union for further studies so as to increase the scientific potential of the nation. The air force was increased from one regiment to three, from 2 percent of the armed forces to 16 percent. A new transport ministry was created to administer the flow of material to the South, mostly by road but also infiltrated by sea via the waterways of the South.

By now PAVN soldiers had been going to the Soviet Union for training for some time. They went by rail, mostly, a long trek across China and into Russia, where they were taught, among other things, how to fly and maintain jet fighters—and how to shoot them down, in the air and from the ground. On the way they passed Soviet advisers going in the opposite direction.

The flow of weapons and munitions had been in difficulties in August 1964 when, because of their ideological differences, the Chinese had denied the Russians land access to Vietnam. But in March 1965 they opened their railway system again and allowed Soviet supplies to get through. The Russians had anyway been sending them by sea from Vladivostok down the coast to Haiphong: now they increased the rate and so became largely independent of Chinese objections.

Over the years the Russians had been upping the stakes in the Cold War and challenging the United States by proxy: aiding the

Vietnamese in order that American assets were slowly bled into Asia and attention was diverted away from Europe, the key theater of operations; as time passed American troops were taken even from the Central Region of NATO's Allied Command Europe to try to achieve victory in Vietnam. The Chinese too had an interest in keeping the United States occupied with other matters while they modernized and built up their industrial base and developed nuclear weapons. As far as most of the Vietnamese were concerned, it did not really matter which of their socialist brothers paid the bill. Only the cynical realized that Russia was fighting to the last drop of Vietnamese blood.

On 27 December 1965 a Party conference took place in Hanoi during which Ho Chi Minh reviewed the progress of the war and then announced a new strategy based on the following priorities:

- First, the government and the army would ensure that they were able to protect themselves in the North but would also support war activities in the South.
- Second, in the South priority would be given to guerrilla warfare rather than "conventional," big-unit warfare.
- Third, more effort and resources would be put into the political education of the people, North and South, so as to convince them that they would win in the end.

Ho Chi Minh told the faithful: "The number of American soldiers can be increased, increased, and increased again; they can send three hundred thousand, four hundred thousand, five hundred thousand soldiers to the South, but we are going to win, and will win. But the victory cannot be pursued by itself. We the Party and all the people from the North and the South have to fight for independence, for freedom, and for the reunification of the country."

A year later—in late 1966—430,000 Americans had been deployed. Their commanding general reported that his men were killing Vietnamese soldiers as fast as Giap could get them into action, but that was not really the point: clearly, the North was willing and able to maintain that number in combat for as long as it took, whereas the United States could not possibly be committed to a conflict of indeterminate length.

On 17 July 1966 Ho Chi Minh stated yet again that time was of no consequence. The war could last even longer than twenty years, he told another Party conference; Hanoi and Haiphong could be destroyed, but the people would never be afraid of the United States because nothing was more valuable than independence and freedom. "When the day of victory has arrived, we will build a more beautiful and better Vietnam." To spur the people on, Hanoi urged them to compete to see which provinces and towns could send the most troops to the war.

The whole of South Vietnam, torn from within by disaffection and confusion, ripped apart by bombs and bullets, disoriented and faithless, was in a state of physical and mental chaos. Under it all, helping to create this situation, was a carefully constructed insurgency organization built in the South but fed and armed by Hanoi: a steel spider's web of intrigue and antipathy. It planned and carried out its own offensives, but it also worked in coordination with forces infiltrated in from the North in accordance with the plans concocted by Giap and his staff in the underground bunker on Hung Vu'ong Avenue in Hanoi.

The greatest problem the Americans faced in South Vietnam was the existence of this deeply hidden, mostly unsuspected, cleverly organized, and very efficient communist infrastructure that was integrated into the community and infiltrated even the highest echelons of the official government. Most of the GIs and their officers who went to Nam to fight their war saw and heard what they were meant to see and hear—in the cities a bustling normality of life and administration, smiling, helpful people, hundreds of honking vehicles, thousands of weaving bicycles, easily available pretty girls, and lots of booze; in the tatty villages hard-working barefoot peasants, wide-eyed children, cooking pots, dung-fuel smoke, buffaloes, and bamboo huts. But they were seeing the shadow and not the substance.

Reading the little manuals based on lessons from the Indochina War the cadres in the South believed that the takeover of the country would be achieved step by step by

- Propaganda, proselytizing, agitprop;
- Creating rebel administrations wherever they could;
- Conducting small-scale terrorist operations everywhere;
- Expanding operations into urban areas, and thus
- Creating the conditions for a general uprising that would sweep away the government.

The raw material with which they were dealing was about 16 million people. Of that number about 1 million were Chinese, nearly all of whom lived in Cholon and because of their unreliability were largely ignored and excluded from politics. (Saigon is one of the most highly populated places on earth, with 2 million people crammed into a few square miles. Cholon is second only to Singapore in the concentration of Chinese people outside China. Its signs are in two languages.) In the southwest of the Mekong delta were around 350,000 people of Cambodian extraction. Up in the hills were over a million Montagnards.

The Mat Tran Dan-toc Giai-phong Viet-nam, the National Liberation Front, which was secretly formed in December 1960, was supposedly an aggregation of Southern groups opposed to Diem—youth, peasant, and worker's organizations, the disaffected religious elements such as the Cao Dai and Hoa Hao—but power really lay with its communist core, the Dong Nan Cash Mang, the People's Revolutionary Party, run by Nguyen Van Linh. Just over a year later, on 1 January 1962, Hanoi openly announced its formation, and that of its cutting edge, the Liberation Armed Forces. To assist them and provide the necessary liaison with the Politburo, Le Duc Tho would head a Committee of Supervision. In the South, Tram Nam Trung was to be defense secretary, Le Can Chan the chief of staff.

In order to assist in controlling the nation, the South was divided into five interprovincial zones plus the Saigon/Gia-Dich special zone. Progressively, the PRP took over existing antigovernment but non-communist groups and began to infiltrate every aspect of life in the South.

Right at the bottom of the organizational ladder were three-man —or woman, or mixed—cells, which claimed all the energies of a person, physical, intellectual, moral and psychological. Men and women were purposely left in constant doubt about whether they were fulfilling the many demands placed on them and so, insecure and anxious, were spurred on to ever greater efforts. The specially chosen cell leaders, as far as possible hard-line cadres, did not represent cell members to higher authority, as is usually the way, but represented higher authority to cell members. (However, they were paternalistic in their attitudes, even though Big Brother stood in the background ready to wield the big stick.) Cells existed not only in every village but in every factory and office block and social gathering place. Members, often young, seventeen or so, helped each other in times of illness and to maintain morale. As time passed, the cells were all armed with weapons brought down what was known as Infantry Route One, the Ho Chi Minh Trail.

Groups of cells formed People's Liberation Committees, which represented every social, ethnic, religious, and economic group and existed at village, district, provincial, interprovincial, and regional— that is, South Vietnam—level. Within the committees three types of mass organizations existed—popular, special-interest (for example, people who joined together to pursue leisure activities such as playing music, reading poetry, cockfighting, wrestling), and guerrilla: all of them containing dedicated cadres, all of them subject to constant agitprop and psychological warfare directed from above.

Because they had the broadest appeal, the popular organizations were represented at village, district, interprovincial, and regional level. Youth organizations got special attention—it was said that young people learn gradually, so they were coerced, not directed— but in addition there were three other important branches: workers, women, farmers.

Once control of an area was effective, these mass organizations were consolidated under People's Liberation Committees, which included some noncommunists elected by the people but, of course, ultimately under the rigid control of Party cadres. (PLCs had executive committees that did the day-to-day business.) But Party control did not extend only to politics; it spread over all aspects of life. For example, in order to disseminate information, in Vinh Long province they had a press secretary, a photographer, and three writers (one a poet); in order to provide entertainment for the Vietcong in the jungle, they had a stage manager, eleven actors, and seven dancers. They even had two orchestras and six singers! In Binh Dinh province, in order to produce funds for the Party, they practiced animal husbandry and trained fishermen and blacksmiths—and then took a proportion of their work profits or traded their goods. To provide logistical backup in Gia Lai province, the Party had vehicles, mechanics, pack animals, even a noodle factory.

As an example of the success of infiltration and recruiting, by 1963 a village in Kien Phong province with a population of just over 2,000 had Party membership of 543, of whom 56 were cadres or youth cadres; in total more than half the villagers were cell members. Everyone except the ancients and the infants were brought into the web of insurgency. As was happening throughout South Vietnam, people carried messages, helped to make and use bottle grenades and nail boards—sharp spikes embedded on a base and buried in a hidden pit or on pathways likely to be used by the security forces—constructed hidden storage rooms for people and weapons, and dug tunnel mazes. As Giap puts it: "Each village, each commune was a fortress, each street a front line. Our millions of fellow countrymen were all millions of valiant combatants."

The People's Revolutionary Party organized population controls by issuing identity cards and travel permits, created a web of informers and an efficient communications system through which to control them and motivate the people, then enmeshed them all in its social organizations, through which it kept an eye on what was going on. In the classic way of subversion, once someone did anything for the Party—and it was difficult not to, given the social pressures and the patriotism and antigovernment and anti-American feelings that existed—they became outside the law of the nation; once outside the law they could be coerced or blackmailed into doing more.

At the top of the pile was the Trung Vong Cue Mien Nam, COSVN, the Central Office for South Vietnam, then situated near the Cambodian border in the so-called Iron Triangle. The original six members of the COSVN were Le Duan, Le Duc Tho, Pham Hung, Ha Huy Giap, Ung Van Khiem, and Thuong Vu. Major General Nguyen Don was the soldier.

On to the civilian structure was grafted and integrated the military organization that existed all over the country. To begin with the leading figure was Nguyen Van Linh. Then in 1964, when the scope of the war increased Nguyen Chi Thanh arrived and Linh became his deputy. But the military did not give orders, they obeyed them. It was an absolutely fundamental principle that the Party exercised control over the army. A good military decision could be bad Party policy, so where there was a conflict the Party always came first, if necessary bypassing the military chain of command.

Hanoi's Politburo and the Military Affairs Department of the Central Committee (in effect, Giap) issued orders to COSVN; COSVN passed them on to Interprovincial Party Committees; they to provinces and they to districts. Eventually they got down to the town or village chapters, which ran guerrilla activity. At every level commanders could liaise with, and employ, units of Giap's regular army, the PAVN, in their locality, as well as control the southern forces, the PLAF. At every level there were branches responsible for military affairs, proselytizing, security, economics; and a miscellaneous section that dealt with special-to-area matters.

Giap sums up the development of the war in this way:

> Between 1960 and 1965 the war in the South developed from a political struggle into an armed struggle, then from an armed insurrection into a liberation war—and then into a combination of both; from guerilla warfare to pitched battles and then to a combination of them. The PLAF were created from political forces. During the war armed self-defense troops developed into two categories: the regular forces and the regional forces formed the PLAF, the mobile force; the militia and self-defense organizations formed the armed forces of the masses, the static force.
>
> The People's War further developed with the appearance of the mobile regular forces of the Liberation Army. Battles involving large concentrations of troops were fought at Binh Gia, Dong Xoai, Ba Gia,

during which whole units of the enemy regular forces were wiped out. The revolutionary war gained new offensive power.

That, then, was the structure of insurgency and depth of personal commitment that existed by the time the Americans arrived in strength, a structure that continued to spread as the country plunged deeper and deeper into chaos. The sabotage caused by the dissidents led to chaos, but the chaos that existed because of mal-administration by the government greatly assisted the insurgency.

Overlaid on this tangled mess but almost totally isolated from it by barbed wire and mental attitudes was the American war machine, sometimes pursuing its aims as if in a vacuum; trying to assess its nearness to victory by counting bodies and refugees, hamlet inhabitants and bombing tonnages, deaths and dollars spent. The military cost of the first year when the United States was fully committed had been budgeted at $214 million, with an equal amount in economic aid to the South provided social reforms were made. This large amount, well over a million dollars a day, was passed virtually on the nod by Congress. But it was nothing compared to the total expenditure that would accrue in the years to come.

In Hanoi, the way to unification had been planned in 1955. First, they would try, with French help, to achieve it through diplomatic action.

The French, not unnaturally after the traumas of their eight-year war and the galling defeat of their army, were not greatly concerned whether the partitioning of Vietnam was rescinded or not. The domino theory anyway had ensured that the Vietnamese were not to be allowed to find their own way to unification. With the French disinterested and the Americans rigidly antipathetic, diplomacy did not succeed.

The alternative course of action was guerrilla warfare in the South assisted materially and psychologically by the North, the aim being to bring down the Diem government and create the conditions in which the fabled general uprising of communist theory would bring power to the people, and hence Hanoi.

From 1964 this plan went well, the Vietcong striking resident (i.e., not mobile) ARVN battalions and eliminating many of them so that they could then take out the rest one after another. But, contrary to expectations, it was this very success that ensured that the United States committed itself fully to maintaining the South as a so-called democratic state. Once that happened the only thing to do was to respond by committing the People's Army's big battalions to the fight, a decision that was to bring dissension about how that battle should be conducted.

The question was, should the Americans be taken on face to face or should guerrilla tactics be given top priority? Giap favored the latter: such a course would avoid heavy losses while enticing American troops into the difficult and wasteful task of trying to infiltrate insurgent-held areas. Meanwhile he would gain time to train bigger forces and infiltrate them into the South. It seemed good sense, but General Nguyen Chi Thanh, who had moved across the border in October 1964 to take up his appointment as overall commander in the South, insisted that the PLAF, bolstered by regular PAVN units, should continue with major offensives; to pause, he argued, would deprive his troops of momentum.

Giap deferred to him for the 1965–66 dry-season campaign, but when that ended their difference of opinion surfaced again. Clearly, there was bad blood between Thanh and Giap, its foundations lying in Giap's somewhat natural lack of respect for the opinions of someone who had never commanded troops in action, and Thanh's defensive reaction to those feelings.

In February 1966, Thanh came to Hanoi to attend a conference and give a review of activities. After it the Central Committee of the Party came to the following conclusions:

• They should extend PAVN and guerrilla activity in the South.
• They should attack government organization in the South and its transportation system.
• They should make greater efforts to involve civilians in the South in the war.
• Finally (the political part), they should increase liaison between the Party and the army.

Thanh, back in the South, writing under his own name and the pen name Truong Son, without directly mentioning Giap by name, took issue with a mythical person who propounded unclear theories, who criticized without offering solutions, whose "conservative spirit prevented him from discovering new facts, who worked in accordance with the old customs, who mechanically copied his own past experiences." He chided this distant but irritating man for being preoccupied with the various phases of war and missing the point that the present situation was a new one.

Though actually only three years younger than Giap, Thanh gave the impression of being a young blood sneering at an old and worn-out man, which was anything but the case. Thanh was sure his smashing of the ARVN at Binh Gia and subsequently in the 1964/65 campaign had obliged the Americans to rethink their policy of using advisers—their "special war," they had called it: everything short of committing troops—and had made them deploy large numbers of troops to shore up the trembling ARVN.

That was true, but then Giap felt that it was not necessarily a good thing. His fundamental tenet about the conduct of the war was that the Vietnamese would outlast the United States not militarily but morally. During his fourth annual review of the conflict, in September 1967, he said it could last five, ten, fifteen, even twenty years. Therefore, fighting was not the point: the point was to make the United States give up politically in the face of stubborn refusal to budge. It was the political side of his experience coming through and smothering his perhaps more natural tendency as a victorious soldier to take on and beat the enemy in battle.

To further counter Thanh's arguments Giap then wrote an assessment of the situation in which he said that the size of main force units telegraphed their intentions. His top priorities for the PLAF were to inflict casualties, hit bases, and erode the ARVN, in that order, which could best be done by increasing the frequency and striking power of guerrilla attacks rather than by attempting to take on major U.S. and Allied formations with big PLAF and PAVN concentrations, which could result in heavy losses to both. In an article published in October 1966, he wrote that "the use of widespread guerrilla actions would oblige the enemy to disperse and so water down their efforts." Guerrilla attacks had already disrupted American attempts to establish bases, had tied down their troops on security duties, and in the countryside had hampered the pacification program: they should be continued. He was right: General Westmoreland told the author that the VC "posed in some ways a more difficult problem for me than the regular troops from the North because by harrassing U.S. and government installations they could tie down more and more troops on defense."

In Giap's view American reliance on firepower used indiscriminately was self-destructive because it caused heavy civilian casualties and brought criticism both within the United States and abroad, let alone among the people whose hearts and minds they were trying to win. Furthermore, big forces were cumbersome and inflexible. He advocated going for logistic supply bases and airfields, which were weak spots. (In an astute aside he said that the more America became involved in the South the more disoriented its government and the ARVN would become.) His views prevailed: large-scale attacks were restricted to large American bases. Da Nang and Tan Sot Nhut air bases were mortared, and spectacular attacks on other bases caused millions of dollars worth of damage.

Thanh was beginning to understand the value of guerrilla warfare when, only fifty-three years old, on 6 July 1967 he died of heart disease in a Hanoi hospital, having been flown back north for treatment. (For years it was thought in the West that he had died as the result of an American bombing raid in the South, but the author was told the true cause of his death by two Vietnamese generals who had been in Hanoi when he died.)

Thanh's place as political head of the military forces in the South was taken by Pham Hung, with, as his deputy, General Tran Van Tra. They were at the end of the radio link with Hanoi, but the person who by then was directing operations on the ground was Nguyen Thi Dinh, who was born in 1920 in Kien Hoa province—an island in the delta forty miles south of Saigon—and whose father was Phan Chu Trinh, who had led anti-French demonstrations in the years before the Great War.

Nguyen Thi Dinh's pocket biography would read: in 1936 joined the revolution, taking messages between headquarters and acting as a guard during meetings. The same year married another resistance fighter. A son born 1939. Imprisoned 1940 and sent to a detention center near the Cambodian border, "a harmful place, of poisonous water, miserable conditions, torture." Released 1943 and joined the Vietminh. Took part in armed rebellion in Kien Hoa province until 1954 and stayed there after partition. When President Diem cemented the South's dependence on the United States, there followed a "bloody year" when anyone thought to be connected with the revolution was arrested and killed or tortured by Nhu's security forces. Then came participation in the Ben Tre uprising, which was followed by others elsewhere in the delta provinces—called by Diem "The Special War," called by the opposition "The Undeclared War." Leaving home, for year after year went into the jungle, walking day after day, living sometimes on half a pound of rice and a few sips of water a day, sleeping rough in hammocks or under houses. Promoted in 1961 to command the headquarters of the central delta provinces, then in 1965 to deputy commander in chief of the PLAF in the whole of the South—a general. Continued in that capacity until 1975 and the fall of Saigon.

Nothing really exceptional there, in comparison with many other North Vietnamese generals, except that Nguyen Thi Dinh is a woman.

In her early days in the jungle she had led units of the *Toc Dai*, the long-haired female cadres who took their share of the fighting, their faces hidden under big conical hats, their weapons hidden under their skirts or in the pole-slung baskets many of them carried. She is proud to say that six of them in Ben Tre became national heroines. "The 'long-haired army' never failed," she says: "We were always victorious. We were fully equal with the men and the Americans were especially afraid of what they called the 'bees.' They were afraid of our bombs, our mines, our spikes. They were even afraid of our arrows! And, of course, we made brilliant spies."

After the North and South were unified, she was transferred to Hanoi, where she became president of the Women's Union and vice-president in the Council of State—and still was in 1990. (Her husband had been arrested six months before she was and died in Paulo Condore—Con Son—prison in 1942.)

It was, of course, lack of regular eyeball-to-eyeball contact that had allowed the confrontation between Giap and Thanh to continue. Both participants were firing over the hill at each other: Giap could not challenge his subordinate directly, and from a distance Thanh could get away with it.

Though Giap had problems with Thanh, his deputy Van Tien Dung was as loyal as ever, methodically but efficiently carrying out the tasks allotted to him. He was in favor of relying on the spirit of the people rather than on the continuing use of foreign weaponry, but in that he was wrong: without weapons the people would have been powerless. But in supporting the southern front he was a tower of strength. For example, he organized no less than half a million people to work on making roads and repairing them after American bombing raids.

Soon after Thanh's death, Giap wrote that large-scale attacks could tie down large numbers of enemy soldiers and resources in places of his choice, leaving other areas open to guerrilla attack. In essence, he had come around some degrees and was now advocating a combination of the tactics that had been the cause of his dispute with Thanh. American failure to flush the PLAF out of the highlands and the jungles north of Saigon was obliging them to increase troop levels and commit themselves to a long-drawn-out campaign. Giap was now in favor of political defiance combined with military attrition.

Publicly, Giap boasted that the United States would need 10 million troops to beat him, but since they would never be able to deploy such numbers—because of public opinion in America and their commitments elsewhere in the world—he would win in the end. He commented scathingly that "Another fifty thousand American troops is like throwing salt into the sea!" Privately, he expected to have to face about a million enemy troops, but thought that because of the huge administrative tail in the U.S. army the actual numbers of combat troops would not increase much. Even so, while addressing a military conference in Hanoi in January 1967 he admitted that there was a threat of invasion.

Meanwhile, Giap had to build up the People's Army even more, in numbers and in fighting spirit.

As he had done before with the Vietminh, he set about inculcating rigid attitudes toward work and conduct. Every recruit had to learn the rules and abide by them. The six points of discipline were preserve secrets, maintain order, look after your weapons and prevent their capture, return what you borrow, pay for any damage you cause, maintain other people's homes as if they were your own.

In addition, there were eight general instructions, which were essentially the same as those which had been the basis of conduct for the Vietminh a decade before:

- Encourage the people to increase production.
- Never hit anyone.
- Speak politely; do not swear at anyone.
- Be fair and honest.
- Love and propagandize the people. [Their words]
- Pay fairly.
- Do not damage crops.
- Do not take liberties with women.

And there was another rule, for when they were in battle: Do not mistreat prisoners, something that, generally speaking, they tried to abide by.

(In the complaints made about Vietnamese treatment of prisoners, there is great similarity between North Vietnam in the 1950s and '60s and Japan in the 1940s: in both cases the perpetrators did not think they were doing anything wrong—these people had been making war on them, what did they expect? The Japanese despised war prisoners because under their Bushido code of military honor it was shameful to surrender; the North Vietnamese treated their prisoners the same way they treated all criminals, which in their view ethically the bomber aircrews and soldiers were. The unsanitary squalor and appalling rations of the Central Prison in Hanoi were not specially laid on for its wartime detainees: they were the normal state of affairs in a penurious nation.)

The life of restrictions and self-denial imposed on members of the People's Army had its compensations, such as comradeship and joint endeavor. It seems, for instance, that there were very egalitarian relationships between officers and men; outside working hours close friendships could grow between people of different ranks without disapproval or embarrassment; inside working hours juniors nearly always obeyed orders precisely.

In any country officers are the executive class of the armed forces; noncommissioned officers are soldiers to whom minor responsibilities are delegated by the officers. In the PAVN, NCOs were drawn mostly from the peasant class, and therefore were generally ill-educated. Nobody from the ill-famed higher classes designated by Hanoi during the Agricultural Reform Program—the exploiters of the poor—was allowed to contaminate the NCO structure, though, strangely, because better educated, they could become officers.

Officers were between eighteen and twenty-five when they entered their training schools. They had to have fifth-grade education and be in good health, but above all they had to demonstrate loyalty to the Party. At officer school they were examined in politics and marked on their attitudes, organizational ability, military tactics, and effort. They were graded at the end of their training: grade 1 became second lieutenants, grade 2 were known as aspirants (probationers), grade 3 did not quite make it and became sergeant majors—the top levels of the noncommissioned ranks.

During the war Vu Ky Lan was the political commissar of a PAVN unit deployed on the Ben Hat River, part of which marked the demarcation line of the 17th Parallel. Because of the nature of his appointment he was privy to information not normally available to lesser, nonpolitical soldiers. After the war, he wrote an account of an attack in which he was involved during 1967. It illustrates the way of life of members of an artillery unit of the People's Army:

My home was in Vinh Linh. I was trained at the military school at Cho Rang, in Nghe An Province. My unit was part of the IVth Military Inter zone of Front B5, which was commanded by Colonel Dam Quang Trung. Regiment 164 (also called the Ben Hai Regiment) had two battalions, one of 100-mm guns and one of 105-mm guns.

Near the demilitarized zone, fighting did not depend on the local Party Committee. Only the Supreme Command in Hanoi had any say in the matter. In November 1966 they told the Army Political Department and the Area Command of the IVth Military Interzone that it was to open a front on Highway 9, which runs from Dong Ha to Laos. Heavy artillery bombardments would prepare the way for our armymen to entice the Americans to fight in the north of Quang Tri province.

I went to hear about it. Sitting in front of a model of the battlefield, I had the impression of learning a lesson in its tiniest details. Then I returned to my unit, which soon moved into its designated area. The last night of November 1966 was the first of a thousand nights I spent in trenches.

Preparation for the attack went on, shrouded in secrecy to the point of appearing ludicrous. All orders relating to the attack were given by word of mouth. Sometimes messengers were disguised as ploughmen, manure carriers, or woodcutters. Telephone lines were laid out from our headquarters to Vinh Thuy battlefront. Telephone calls were limited, and radio communication was forbidden.

Hundreds of militiamen from the Vinh Son, Vinh Thuy, and Vinh Lam communes dug shelters for our guns on the slopes of hills. They worked in the dark, taking measurements by touching with their hands. At daybreak they camouflaged their work with green leaves and suppressed all traces on the hillside. Before the guns moved into position each local household brought two basketfuls of straw to spread on the road just before the guns passed and so remove all sign of their tracks.

Our two artillery battalions had to confront six U.S. artillery battalions and dozens of warplanes, not to mention all the batteries carried by the warships off the coast. If we were detected, this huge firepower would not fail to rain down upon us and cause terrible damage. To defend us, all our anti-aircraft forces in the area (one battalion of

37-mm guns, one of 12.7-mm machine guns, and one company with five armored vehicles armed with 14.5-mm double-barreled machine guns) were sent to Vinh Thuy to defend our artillery positions.

Sham firing emplacements would play a decisive role in the outcome of the battle. When our guns started firing, hundreds of flares from these false firing nests would go off at the same time. The light of them was brighter than that of guns firing and would draw the attention of the enemy to them and away from our guns. If the enemy reacted, these sham nests would receive most of the enemy's shells.

The day came for us to begin the attack. According to our plan our two battalions would fire twelve hundred shells in half an hour, but in the first ten minutes we fired more than a thousand! Le Ngoc Hien gave orders to stop firing for a while.

The enemy's batteries at Gio Linh retaliated. They could shell along a ten-kilometer line from the sea coast to the foot of the mountain, and from Hien Leong to Ha Co. With a firing range of thirty-five kilometers, their 175-mm guns could hit as far as Son Thuy, in Quang Binh province. They fired in our direction even though they could not see exactly where we were. In military terms the result was very poor, but firing at random day and night they were a permanent threat. Gunfire was to be heard sporadically, now in succession, now in the east, now in the west, especially the thunder from their 175-mm guns.

The battle went on, artillery fire being exchanged day after day. Then on 2 January 1967 the 3rd Division of the U.S. Marines began to garrison the enclaves on the other side of the river, replacing one of the ARVN divisions, which was sent south to do "pacification." Dong Ha, a small port at the junction of Highway 1 and Highway 9, thirteen kilometers north of Quang Tri, suddenly became a big military base, the field HQ of the marines and a logistics base for the Highway 9 front.

On 9 February the demilitarized zone south of the Ben Ha river was defoliated. The wind blew the chemicals to Ho Xa and Vinh Hien, and some people breathed them in, or ate food that had been contaminated. The first symptom was unbearable thirst. Then they were ill for several days.

On 17 May 1967, the enemy mobilized big ground, naval, and air forces and put them under the command of the general commanding the U.S. Marines' 3rd Division. He was to launch Operation Hickory in an attempt to pen up the population and destroy the villages in Gio Linh and Cam Lo districts in preparation for the construction of the McNamara electronic wall. Those were the most trying days in Vinh Linh, with nonstop aerial bombardment. But it was nothing new: after the war I heard that, on average, each inhabitant of Vinh Linh received seven tons of bombs and eighty shells.

Because of the danger people were in the habit of putting some of their children into different trenches as a precaution to preserve family members in case a trench was hit. Always there were casualties. Children. Old people. One of the strangest was Ai Danh, a soldier serving on the southern front who was granted leave to see his family in Vinh Tranh. His mother, standing in a trench, saw him coming and turned round to call his wife and children, but he was killed by a bomb at that very moment. He died where, four years before, he had parted from his family to go to the front.

CHAPTER SIXTEEN

WESTY'S WAR

The politicians in Washington just had no idea about the complexity of the situation in South Vietnam.
—GENERAL WESTMORELAND, TO THE AUTHOR

The American officer who in 1964 had been sent to Vietnam as commanding general was William Childs Westmoreland. Born on 26 March 1914 he was two and a half years younger than Giap. A high graduate of West Point Military Academy—first captain of his class (in company with illustrious cadet predecessors Lee,

Pershing, MacArthur), winner of the Pershing Sword—he had commanded an artillery battalion and served on the staff in North Africa, Italy, and Germany during World War II.

In 1950 Westmoreland was an instructor at the Command and General Staff College at Fort Leavenworth in Kansas, and immediately after that at the Army War College in Carlisle Barracks, Pennsylvania, the joint-service college for more mature officers. Then he attended an advanced course at the Harvard Business School. After training as a parachutist in 1952 and 1953, he commanded an airborne combat team in Korea. Then came staff appointments in the Pentagon as a brigadier general: in the army's Manpower Office and then as secretary of the general staff, "a kind of chief of staff to the army chief of staff," as he puts it. (The army chief of staff at the time was General Maxwell D. Taylor, whom he had first met in Italy and served under in Korea.) Westmoreland was the youngest major general in the army when he was promoted to that rank at the age of forty-two, to command the 101st Airborne Division. His next appointment was as superintendent of West Point.

Further promoted, Westmoreland became commander of the XVIII Airborne Corps, then in June 1964 was appointed deputy commander, and then, after a short time, commanding general of the U.S. Military Assistance Command in Vietnam (MACV). He was tailor-made for the job: had seen combat in four theaters of war, had instructed army doctrine in two of the premier U.S. military colleges, had senior command experience, had made tactical innovations (for example, as commander of the airborne division had pioneered the use of massed helicopters), and knew the Pentagon systems intimately.

Like Giap, Westmoreland had read the works of Sun Tzu, von Clausewitz, and other renowned writers on military subjects. Like Giap he was in charge of huge armed forces: at their peak he was to command more servicemen in South Vietnam than had been in the whole of the United Nations' multinational force in Korea. Tall, ruggedly handsome, self-confident, thrusting, he took over the most technically sophisticated forces that had ever gone to war. To meet their support requirements, in his first three years in command, in among thousands of other decisions, he decreed that seven deep-water ports and eight major airports should be built. (To achieve this there were at one time fifty-one thousand American civilian contractors working in South Vietnam.) When he took over as commanding general, American expenditure on the war was half a billion dollars a year; the appropriation for the fiscal year 1968, when he left Vietnam, was 30 billion dollars.

The ultrasophistication of the American war machine was to prove one of the major obstacles to success in Vietnam: the availability of high-tech equipment made American servicemen and politicians alike too reliant on the supposed superiority of modern weaponry in all circumstances and regardless of the caliber of the opposition: just pour on the hot iron and the enemy will melt away. The decisive, battle-winning human factor was too often obscured behind a smokescreen of napalm and lasers and sensors and defoliants.

Also, the American army tended to be hide bound by their doctrine, which had been developed for European armored warfare. Unfortunately, although Westmoreland "was determined that what had happened to the French in 1954 would never happen to the American army," he regarded the Indochina War as "not being really too meaningful. The French were right out on a limb there. They did not have our resources." The Vietnam war was a new kind of war where the lessons of the past had no application. This situation was counterinsurgency on a big scale, the like of which had never before been encountered by the U.S. army. He went on record as saying that "the communists in Vietnam are waging a classic revolutionary war," when in fact that was not the case: revolutionary war is intended to reach a decisive result without outside help, whereas in South Vietnam the Vietcong alone could not do that; they had to have the assistance of Giap's regular army.

Westmoreland had heard Giap's name before he went to Vietnam, but it "was meaningless to me until I arrived on the battlefield, at which time I was quite aware of him, and cognizant of the success he had had at Dien Bien Phu." Giap's campaigns were not studied at Fort Leavenworth or the War College. No staff studies of them were commissioned in the U.S. Army Headquarters in Saigon, nor were the enemy commanders studied "in any depth; there was only a superficial assessment made of them." But "every responsible officer [in Vietnam] was cognizant of Vietnamese history and the experience of the French."

Perhaps Westmoreland's biggest problem, however, was that from start to finish America had no clearly defined political aims in Vietnam—and therefore no direction for its military strategy. From the time they first sent their advisory group to Saigon things just grew like Topsy. (And right to the end this did not change: when Clark Clifford took over as secretary of defense in 1968, he was to say, "It was startling to me to find out that we had no military plan to win the war.") All the brains in the government and the Pentagon never actually produced a cogent long-term plan or strategy that would achieve victory. Most of these clever people realized that the original parameters were mistaken—America should never have become involved militarily in the first place—but by now the United States was too deeply committed to turn back: at home and overseas it would be seen as weakness and reneging on U.S. promises. So, as events occurred, the politicians and military responded, plugging holes wherever they appeared. Time after time the great cornucopia of American wealth was tipped up: money poured out, and soldiers, and weapons.

Westmoreland's predecessors in the U.S. military advisory group in Saigon had recommended that action be taken to "plug up the porous border" with Laos and Cambodia, suggesting that a cordon sanitaire be established. In 1961 the CIA told a special policy group set up by President Kennedy that in its view the border could not be sealed. Later that year the Southeast Asia Treaty Organization produced SEATO Plan 5/61 for the positioning of international forces along the border. In October the Joint Chiefs of Staff in the Pentagon declared that the plan was not feasible. Instead, a proposal was made by the president's special military representative, General Maxwell D. Taylor, that a force of thirty-three hundred ARVN rangers should operate in the five provinces on the borders. Nothing came of that idea either, but in 1962 the CIA started to coordinate the mobilization of Montagnards into defense militias. During the year these units, trained and advised by Green Berets and commanded by their ARVN counterparts, were strung out along the border.

Thus when General Westmoreland arrived in Saigon the strategy for the battle had already been decided: Special Forces units, with the task, he says, of "gathering intelligence about enemy activity, especially any incursions by battalion or regimental-sized units," would guard the open flank; inside it his soldiers and their allies would carry out hunter/killer operations—intelligence-gathering forays into the jungle to find VC or PAVN units and try to eliminate them. As he puts it: "Had I had at my disposal virtually unlimited manpower I could have stationed troops permanently in every district or province and thus provided an alternative strategy. But such a concept would have required literally millions of men"—which is precisely what Giap had forecast. Seeing the problem, as time passed, Westmoreland built up his forces and as soon as possible switched to more positive, bigger-scale aggressive action: search-and-destroy operations by larger formations heavily supported by artillery and air power (a strategy that had already been tried without success by the French).

Now, in scores of operations, under the screaming whine of jet bombers and the thumping beat of helicopter rotors, relatively small combat groups of American and allied troops patroled the jungles and paddies as bait, hoping the Vietcong would show themselves and succumb to superior firepower; or that as they converged with other groups they would pinch enemy units "between hammer and anvil" and destroy them. In fact, the enemy did not show themselves or just slipped aside. It was like trying to catch a trout between fingers and thumb in fast-running water.

An example of the way in which reliance on technology contributed to the lack of real American success in battle was the use of helicopters. In time nearly five thousand of them, each costing around a quarter of a million dollars, would be brought down by enemy ground fire. For years they would whir through the skies in operational and logistic support of the troops on the ground, their crews pumping lead into the paddy fields and jungles, delivering supplies and evacuating wounded men, but at the end of the day they made only one really big impact on the war: because they could descend like the cavalry of old in the nick of time and lift the infantry out of danger, they became an escape route to be used whenever the going got really tough. The withdrawal of soldiers under fire in this way allowed the U.S. army to claim that it never lost a battle: but then neither did it ever crushingly win one.

Since taking and holding of ground was not the aim and with no front line to show on a map, different measures of success had to be found. The body count was one. In their routine reports American commanders were required to say how many enemy bodies had accrued from their activities. Because promotion, medals, rest and recuperation furloughs (to places like Bangkok, Singapore, Hong Kong, Tokyo, Manila, Honolulu), even better rations came in response to a good body count, the solution was simple: you created a body, whether or not it was an enemy body, or you invented one. If a prisoner was taken he had almost no chance of living: not only was it an irksome chore to get him back to base, but what was the point if what the high command wanted was bodies? Because of this mass of dubious information, it became impossible to say with any accuracy how many of the enemy became casualties over the years. By some guestimates there were 350,000 of them—dead, wounded, deserters—between 1965 and 1967. But however many casualties there actually were, there never seemed to be fewer of the enemy around.

Another equally vague—and equally heartless—measure of success was judging the impact of anti-Vietcong operations by counting the number of refugees generated. As time passed thousands and thousands of people surged like waves back and forth across the land. By 1967 there were an estimated 1.2 million refugees, blasted out of their homes by aerial bombardment, shelling, or the "sanitation" of whole tracts of land— the removal of the population in order that the areas could be declared "no-go" and any people found in them treated as VC or their supporters. Refugees were also generated by the Strategic Hamlets Program. The result was the creation of chaos: by 1968 no less than one-third of the population had been uprooted from their ancestral villages and relocated. (Soon after his arrival in Vietnam Westmoreland himself went to Malaya to see the terrain and compare it with Vietnam's, hoping to be able to inject life into what was by now a moribund relocation scheme.)

After Diem's death the VC had redoubled their efforts to eliminate the last remaining Yellow—government-controlled—areas. In
1962 there had been about nine thousand violent incidents, in 1963
nineteen thousand. But in 1964 the number increased to more than
twenty-five thousand and in 1965 to nearly twenty-seven thousand.
Between 1962 and 1965 there were more than forty-five hundred
assassinations alone. Everywhere, knives and bullets cut down people who failed to give the Vietcong the support they demanded.
Leaderless, fearful, and hopeless, the refugees swarmed from place
to place looking for sanctuary.

Nguyen Van Tich is typical of Vietnamese who joined the People's
Army at a very young age and then fought for many years with it.
Inspired by Ho Chi Minh's rhetoric, brainwashed by his cadres, a
dedicated and determined soldier, Tich went through the ranks
steadily, eventually becoming a lieutenant colonel. The knowledge
gained from his long association with the army resulted in his
becoming one of its official historians after he left the service.

During an interview with the author, he describes the conditions
under which members of the People's Army lived and gives a vivid
account of one particular firefight:

> When I first joined the army I followed the normal training for six
> months; then I had to do the special training for those men going to
> the South. We prepared for a very long journey on foot through a
> mountainous area carrying thirty to forty kilos on our backs. We had
> to be ready to work under any conditions. We had to climb up very
> high hills and help each other; to stand on each other's shoulders. We
> had to work all day and all night all week, nonstop. We had to make
> fieldhouses and we slept in hammocks.
>
> We used plastic string hammocks two meters long made from
> American material that we got from the people. We also had a piece
> of nylon. We lay in the hammock at night and used the nylon as a
> blanket. It was very comfortable. I could carry it all in my pockets.
>
> We learned to survive on dry foods and rice that we cooked before

our departure to whatever tasks we were assigned. We were taught
to cook with a very special cooker, the Hoang Cao cooker—named
after the inventor—which made no smoke so that the enemy could
not see where we were. [The smoke from cooking had no outlet
except through a long tunnel dug behind the heat source. The earth
around the tunnel slowly absorbed the carbon particles of the smoke
so that very little escaped into the atmosphere.] Hoang Cao was
made a Hero of Vietnam.

I was lucky because I was in the same unit for twenty-four years. I
fought with the 325th Division, one of the first to be founded. It was
known as the Golden Star Division and was well-known to the Americans and was a special target for them.

I took part in the first fight with the 1st Air Cavalry Division set up
by McNamara, in Binh Dinh province. My division was in the center
of the province and was one of the chief objectives of the U.S. Air
Cavalry. The Americans deployed three regiments against us. The
general aim of their operation was to crush and kill—to search and
destroy, they called it.

Because we had no vehicles we had to divide into many groups on
foot. The cavalry pinned us down and we did not know how to fight
them. Nobody knew what their tactics were, or the tactics of the
American forces generally. Then those who had already fought
against the Americans came and related their experiences, to teach us
how to do it. We began to learn, but decided together that first of all
we had to have enough determination to fight them—then we would
learn the details.

It was decreed that those who killed at least five Americans would
be nominated as Valiant Heroes Third Class. Those who killed ten
would be awarded Second Class, and those who killed more than ten
would be First Class heroes.

I remember particularly the morning of 28 January 1966. We were
in a place called Cat Market about ten kilometers from the sea. Normally it was after breakfast that we deployed to the front, but on that
day it was still very early when suddenly artillery fire descended on us
from land and from their ships out at sea. Only a few of our soldiers
were in their fighting positions. The shells hit the village nearby.

It was obvious that this would be a big operation by the enemy so
we all ran to the fighting trenches in the village as fast as we could. I

heard later that the Americans called the operation by the name given to an article used for polishing rice. Maybe they thought that we in the Liberation Armed Forces were rice and they were the people who were going to polish us!

Next, the planes attacked. There were so many of them that we could not count them. The Americans also used helicopters. They must have had a prepared plan, because many troops entered every village in the area simultaneously. We had many difficulties in keeping contact with each other because we had no radio between units. After the artillery fire stopped some of us had been wounded. They were carried away and taken care of by the local people.

Then a second wave of helicopters came and landed troops in our area, in between coconut trees in a sandy place. The sand rose up in clouds from all the rotors. In all, between two hundred and fifty and three hundred GIs got out of the helicopters and ran in different directions. About one hundred of them came in my direction.

It was a sunny morning, and I remember noticing that they wore short-sleeved shirts and very narrow trousers and steel helmets and high military boots. They were carrying AR-50 guns and M-79s. I looked very hard at them because I had never seen the enemy before. They all looked very young. There were black men there too, and I had never seen them before either.

We were lying there waiting, hidden away, and made no reaction yet. We were anxious about how they would fight. They walked toward us, talking on their walkie-talkies to the helicopters, which did not fire at us from the sky but made a lot of noise up in the air above us. The soldiers came very close, to within about fifty meters of the village. Then I heard someone shout very loudly and the Americans dropped to the ground. Mortar bombs started to fall on the village. We did not react even after the mortar shells fell.

Then I heard more shouting and the Americans, group by group, rushed toward the village. They ran tree by tree toward where I was. When they got really close we started shooting. It was a very short distance. Some of them fell. Then their friends ran to help them and we shot them too. Often we were able to shoot Americans because they came back for their comrades. I killed about twelve of them that day.

They divided the Rice Polisher operation into phases. The first covered an area of three villages, and they spent a whole day on it. They took control of the position that my group was holding, but we killed many of them. Our aim was not to hold the land but to safeguard our force as much as we could while killing as many Americans as we could. After the fighting we withdrew to a safe place.

The next phase was called White Wings. It started one week later, in the Am Lao valley, some distance away from the action of the first operation. They knew the survivors of the first action had withdrawn to that valley. It too lasted a whole week. They made no contact with my unit but only with the guerrilla force in the area. The next phase lasted only a short time; then most of them withdrew.

The Americans controlled the region after the operation, but the people there were very anti them and so they moved them out. In order to evade them, we had to move away too, as the weeks passed deeper and deeper into the jungle.

By the end of the year we had a very serious shortage of food. Shells were falling all day and all night. The people could not suffer such a situation, and all of them left the area, so we had no help from anyone. We had only manioc and rice to eat, the poor rice that grew as the second harvest from what was left after the first good crop had been cut. It was what we found in the rice paddies.

We suffered from a lot of bad skin diseases because of the wet conditions we lived in all the time. Most of us had infections of the feet caused by insect bites and muddy water and the dead bodies in the soil. It made them go bad, and sometimes the infection got right into the bones of the feet. We all had malaria, 100 percent. There were many leeches, and they were the root cause of many of our infections.

Sometimes we had cigarettes but usually not enough. We got American cigarettes after fighting, when we had fought face to face. And chocolate. Many times before fighting we had no food to eat, but after fighting we got food and Coca-Cola and beer from places where the Americans had been.

Our army was successful because we fought in the jungle. We could fight the Americans at any time we wanted, or withdraw whenever we wanted. That is why we were so successful.

CHAPTER SEVENTEEN

GI JOE'S WAR

I have asked General Westmoreland what more he needs to meet this mounting aggression. He has told me. And we will meet his needs. . . . We will stand in Vietnam.

—LYNDON B. JOHNSON

Between July and September 1965 the elite formations of the American army arrived in Vietnam—the 101st Air Mobile Division, the 1st (The Big Red One) Infantry Division, and the 1st Air Cavalry Division—the latter being an infantry division made highly mobile by the use of massed helicopters. Soon these were followed by the 25th (Lightning Flash) Division. They were to be only the first of many: at peak there were to be ten and two-thirds American divisions in South Vietnam.

The 1st and the 25th divisions formed a ring of defensive positions around Saigon while the South Korean "Tiger" and "White Horse" Brigades were given responsibility for the coastline south of the 17th Parallel. Other American formations and later the ANZACs—the Australians and New Zealanders—were deployed in the Mekong delta. Superimposed throughout the country were ARVN units, primarily given the role of "pacification" of the population: that is, by their presence deterring the Vietcong while encouraging the population to support the Saigon government.

By late 1965 the ARVN were losing a battalion of infantry and a district capital every week. In the huge Michelin rubber plantation, the Vietcong 272nd Regiment of the 9th Division overran the ARVN's 7th Regiment, inflicting hundreds of casualties. Then in February 1966 Giap sent the 32nd Regiment of the PAVN to the South, and in August the 33rd, the two commanded by Major General Chu Huy Man. After a fierce engagement, part of the 33rd was cut off by the 1st Air Cavalry and given a drubbing, but that was just a pinprick in comparison with the losses being sustained generally by American and South Vietnamese forces. Something had to be done.

The Americans had three categories of intelligence-gathering agencies in Vietnam: military, operating with American service units and formations; civil, operating with the CIA and with the South Vietnamese army and police; and strategic, which culled information from air and satellite reconnaissance. Using the data presented by these agencies, U.S. army commanders tried to pinpoint the location of enemy units. When a worthwhile target had been identified, they would then strike at it with shattering firepower; the standard doctrine was to find the enemy, then pull back and hit him hard with explosives instead of finishing him at close quarters.

In bigger and bigger numbers U.S. infantrymen and marines moved out into the jungles and paddy fields to take on Charlie Cong, as the Vietcong were known: from the phonetic-alphabet radio call signs for VC—Victor Charlie. But frustration at the lack of success sometimes turned ordinary young soldiers into trigger-happy storm-troopers. The atrocities perpetrated by the Korean Green Dragon Division at Binh Hoa and the 23rd ("American") U.S. Infantry Division at My Lai—in both of which more than five hundred people were systematically slaughtered—were symptoms of rage caused by bafflement at the complexities of a situation that seemed beyond resolution. At Binh Hoa the Koreans slaughtered men, women, and children in a village that had stubbornly refused to stop assisting the Vietcong; at My Lai an American company of infantry ran amok for no special reason except that they had come to hate all Vietnamese. But generally these were aberrations. For years the Americans and their allies conducted military operations, of which there were hundreds, with rectitude and discipline.

Between January and March 1966 Operation Masker (White Wing) in Binh Dinh province claimed a thousand enemy dead and about seventeen hundred suspects taken prisoner. It was to be followed by Double Eagle, which spread into another province, Quang Ngai. During Operations Thayer and Irving napalm was used extensively. Other major operations followed: Five Arrows, Highway 9, Jeb Stuart, Byrd, Pershing, Saratoga, Yellowstone. Dozens of them, all claiming dozens of enemy killed. The whirlybirds rose up out of the combat bases and flocked out over the jungle to places where the enemy's presence had been reported. Supported by massive artillery and aerial bombardment, American soldiers and their allies, sometimes with ARVN support, laid down withering fire, called in the aircraft, and then, usually in the late afternoon, withdrew.

These thousands and thousands of soldiers, aircraft, and weapons were supported from vast bases that spread and spread around Da Nang, Chu Lai, Long Binh, Bien Hoa. But even the bases were not safe: the countryside right up to the fence surrounding the airfield at Da Nang was under Vietcong control, and only during daylight was it possible to get to and from the harbor by road.

Sometimes the Allies achieved high body counts. Sometimes, as at Ban Bang, Nha Do, Cam Xe, Bong Trang, Pleine, Binh Dinh, they lost a lot of people. The names of those places, and the names of many other operations—for example, Double Eagle, Dragon Fire, Shenandoah, Starlight, Silver Bayonet—became firmly anchored in the minds of the tens of thousands of Americans and their allies who took part in them, a never-to-be-forgotten trigger that would remind them all of sweat, thirst, and cursing fear; and, sometimes, wild exhilaration. And bleeding bodies and broken bones and the cries of dying men. And also grinding despair and homesickness and deep depression.

Later in 1966 major offensives were launched: two of them, operations Abilene and Birmingham in April, were followed in June by El Paso. Then between 14 September and 24 November the biggest operation so far was mounted—Attleboro, in which twenty-two thousand troops used twelve hundred tons of ordnance and captured two thousand tons of rice, nineteen thousand grenades, five hundred mines, and a mine-making factory. More than two thousand of the enemy died, about half of them from the effects of air strikes, and one hundred fifty-five Americans.

At the end of 1966 intelligence sources indicated that there were about 280,000 Vietcong and PAVN, controlled by 8,000 cadres, operating in the South. Another massive response was called for.

The biggest operations conducted during the whole war were the interrelated Cedar Falls and Junction City. Nearly thirty thousand troops went into the Iron Triangle, in which, according to intelligence assessments, was a large enemy order of battle: the 272nd Regiment of the PAVN, two battalions of the 165th Vietcong Main Force Regiment, the Phu Loi Battalion, two independent VC companies, and the headquarters of the Vietcong's IVth Military Regiment. And, possibly, the headquarters of COSVN.

The Iron Triangle, so-called because of the shape of the guarded enclave created by the Vietcong in the fork of two rivers, was an area only twenty miles northwest of Saigon. Much too close for comfort, it was honeycombed with tunnels and its roads and tracks were littered with booby traps.

The aim of the operations was to take out the units and headquarters and force the enemy to stand off from the capital. It would be done by sweeping troops southeast—the hammer—and trapping the enemy against a blocking force on the southern side, the anvil.

Cedar Falls began on 8 January 1967 with the evacuation of about six thousand civilians from villages on the perimeter of the Triangle, some of which had been under Vietcong control for more than two years. Then the village of Ben Suc, on the northwest corner, was assaulted and completely destroyed. It took three days for troops to clear, with acetylene gas and explosives, the tunnels in the village, which were on three levels. (Because tear gas was used to flush the enemy out of the tunnels before American troops entered them, U.S. infantry and engineers, Tunnel Rats, as they were known, had to wear gas masks. They carried hand torches and pistols and wore flak jackets during these dirty and dangerous missions, which had to be repeated in almost every village U.S. troops entered.)

While this was going on, the anvil, consisting of the 25th U.S. Division, supported by an independent U.S. brigade and the 7th Regiment of the 5th ARVN Division, took up its positions. Thirteen fire bases were established, during which the troops killed 835 enemy soldiers and found base camps that had been used by COSVN. Unfortunately, the bird had flown.

The follow-up to Cedar Falls, Operation Junction City, began in mid February when the 173rd Airborne Brigade of Task Force Deane (named after its commander, Brigadier General John R. Deane, Junior) was parachuted into position by sixteen C-130 aircraft. Together with the 3rd Brigade of the 1st U.S. Division, it became the hammer. Between 18 March and 15 April, the two formations moved on down toward the anvil, during which phase nineteen hundred enemy dead were claimed.

In retaliation, the 9th Division of the PLAF attacked the American-held villages of Ap Ban Bang, Soui Tre, and Ap Gu: the division was decimated by fighter-bombers using cluster-bomb units that sprayed anti-personnel bombs and fleshettes over a wide area, by B-52s carpet-bombing from high altitude, and by massed artillery fire.

During Cedar Falls and Junction City, American planes dropped nearly 10 million leaflets and made loudspeaker appeals from helicopters urging the enemy to defect under the "Chieu Hoi" clemency scheme, instituted by the South Vietnamese government in an attempt to water down the strength of the Vietcong. Only a few did.

Around 6,000 Vietnamese civilians were treated by American medics as part of the "Medcap" Assistance to the Civil Aid Program. Three minor airfields were constructed. In total 2,728 VC and PAVN were killed during the combined Cedar Falls and Junction City operations. American units lost 282 dead and more than 1,500 wounded.

In Hanoi, Vo Nguyen Giap claimed that Junction City had been a big victory for the Vietcong and that more than 13,000 allied soldiers had been killed. Perhaps this was sheer propaganda, and he knew it was; perhaps it was his version of the body count, gone mad. (For two reasons it is better to discount any casualty figures whether their own or Allied, emanating from North Vietnamese sources: first, whereas in a democratic society there is an obligation not to dissimulate, in a closed society there is no such constraint; second, the Vietnamese always had great difficulty in assessing casualties.)

Certainly, the operation, and others like it, took away the initiative from the Vietcong to some extent. Certainly, it disrupted COSVN's plans—made them move their headquarters and obliged them to position PAVN units and bases in Cambodia, and to use material brought to border sanctuaries down the Trail rather than resources supplied by the local population nearer the scene of action. (Also it meant that PLAF units based in the villages and jungles could not rely on the immediate support of PAVN Main Force units to the same extent as they had before.) Certainly, the Americans put enormous energy into it, at great material and financial cost. The results, though, in terms of enemy casualties and equipment losses, like so many of these weapon-oriented operations, were negligible, primarily because such a huge percentage of bombs and shells exploded in jungle empty of human beings. Two days after the U.S. troops pulled out of the Iron Triangle, the Vietcong moved back in again.

General Westmoreland himself has great admiration for the fighting qualities of his Vietnamese enemies and for the way Giap inspired them; he says that many of the men who died had tattoos on their bodies saying BORN IN THE NORTH TO DIE IN THE SOUTH, and that they did so willingly. General Bernard Rogers, who took part in Junction City, and who would one day become Supreme Allied

Commander Europe, says of the Vietcong that they were "dedicated, disciplined, persistent, tenacious, and courageous."

That, really, was the root of the problem.

To the baffled American soldiers there seemed to be no solution.
They felt they had one arm tied behind their backs because they
were not allowed to take the fight into the North, but how could the
administration permit that when the reason for their presence in the
South was to prevent its takeover by the North? How could the
government condone the sort of aggression which, they had declared, was the reason for their involvement?

Because no amount of military action made any difference, in
May 1965 there had even been discussions of the possible use of
nuclear weapons, but the idea was rejected because of the feared
reaction from world public opinion: in the Cold War the United
States could not afford to lose points with the Third World.

Despite everything that was done the flow of men and material
never ceased down the Ho Chi Minh Trail. Trying to block it by
bombing was proving to be impossible: hordes of *dan cong* filled the
holes and repaired the bridges or built a bypass. In desperation, the
American secretary of defense, Robert McNamara, proposed the
construction of a sensor-laden line that would go from the coast right
across the country into Laos. Operation Die Marker would have
entailed building one hundred and sixty miles of electrified fencing
and sowing it with the latest electronic gadgets. After work had
begun on it in April 1967, the concept was found to be astonishingly
complicated and fantastically expensive and was shelved.

Robert Strange McNamara had been born on 9 June 1916 in San
Francisco, California. A graduate of the University of California at
Berkeley and of the Harvard Business School, he was a "whiz kid"
who, after quickly attaining the rank of lieutenant colonel during
World War II, by 1960 had become president of the Ford Motor
Corporation. In December of that year he accepted the post of sec-
retary of defense in the incoming Kennedy administration and was
serving in that post when Johnson took over.

Because President Kennedy had such a high regard for

McNamara, early on in America's involvement in South Vietnam the Defense Department assumed primary responsibility for policy-making, rather than the State Department as had been the case in the past. Thus it was that through the war years McNamara came to wield so much influence, managing not only the execution of policy but also much of its creation.

Having for many years played such a key part in the conduct of the war, in May 1967 McNamara wrote to President Johnson saying that "the picture of the world's greatest superpower killing or seriously injuring a thousand noncombatants a week while trying to pound a tiny, backward nation into submission on an issue whose merits are hotly disputed is not a pretty one." Predictably, many people in political and military circles did not accept this statement as being a true summary of the situation but interpreted it as a sign that McNamara was cracking up.

In the summer of 1967 McNamara helped to draft the San Antonio peace formula, which proposed discussions with the North Vietnamese in exchange for an end to bombing. In October Hanoi rejected the idea. In November, having finally decided that the military effort he had orchestrated for seven years was "futile and immoral," he told the president that pacification had if anything gone backward and that the Rolling Thunder bombing campaign had neither significantly affected infiltration nor cracked the morale of Hanoi. His advice was that the United States should freeze its troop levels in South Vietnam, consider terminating the bombing, and make covert moves toward peace talks with Hanoi.

This was too much for Johnson, by now totally obsessed with winning the war, to the detriment of the many domestic and international problems that beset the administration. How could he admit that all the lives lost and the effort made had been a waste of time? McNamara departed. (In February 1991, speaking about the Vietnam war for the first time in twenty-four years, he told an interviewer he was still not sure if he had resigned or had been sacked.)

Of course it was not only a land war. In the Mekong delta "Game Warden" patrols operated in small rivercraft with the aim of flushing out or curtailing the activities of Vietcong who used the Rung Sat waterway approaches to Saigon. At sea, ships of the United States 7th Fleet incessantly patrolled the Gulf of Tonkin. Though they had no enemy fleet to contend with, they gave support to the ground forces by using their guns, where distances allowed, to augment artillery bombardment on land, and with the might of the great carriers augmented the power of the United States Air Force, which operated from bases in the Pacific, in Thailand, and in Vietnam. Attacks by planes flown by navy and marine pilots were integrated into the overall targeting plan. For years, ships and men rotated from California to the coast of Asia to play their part in the air war. But in the early days the biggest effort was concentrated on strategic bombing.

Operation Rolling Thunder had begun on 2 March 1965. At the time the staff of the U.S. Pacific Headquarters in Honolulu believed that massive saturation bombing combined with bombardment by the guns of the 7th Fleet would destroy all the North Vietnamese capability to support the war in the South in twelve days. They got it wrong by about twelve hundred days, and even then the bombers did not stop the supplies getting through.

In July 1966, made aware that Rolling Thunder was having little impact, President Johnson lifted the restrictions he had imposed and widened the scope of the bombing to include oil-storage facilities and ammunition depots anywhere in the North. In the spring of 1967, told that there was still no appreciable diminution in the flow of men and material to the South, he allowed the USAF to take on power plants, airfields, and factories in the Hanoi and Haiphong areas, and to mine the harbors in the North. The operation ended on 31 October 1968, preparatory to the commencement of peace talks.

The statistics are astounding: 350,000 sorties flown, 655,000 tons of bombs dropped north of the 17th Parallel, 918 American planes shot down with the loss of 818 airmen.

In the southern part of North Vietnam, the density of attack was twenty times greater than anywhere else. Two million USAF bombs almost totally obliterated all towns and villages south of Hanoi— including An Xa, Giap's birthplace. Five places with populations of between ten and thirty thousand ceased to exist: Phu Ly, Ninh Binh, Thanh Hoa, Vinh, and Ha Tinh.

On 1 November 1968, in the complex of underground "villages" around what had been known as Vinh Linh near the 17th Parallel, seventy thousand people emerged for their first fear-free day in the sun in three and a half years. Like moles, up to twenty feet down they had created cavelike "homes" in the soil, linked together, sometimes with open tunnels. By day they sowed and reaped crops, helped the army, and repaired the roads, ready to leap for cover whenever planes appeared over the horizon—and brought little children up into the light for a few minutes to give their eyes a much-needed change from the pale glow of oil lamps. By night they crept into the caverns and slept in fetid air. Vinh Linh was more intensively bombed, and for longer, than any other place in Vietnam, yet its population were nearly all civilians. Half a million tons of bombs and shells landed there; a quarter of the amount used in the whole of World War II, half the tonnage dropped during the whole of the Korean War.

Phu Ly, a market town with a population of about ten thousand, thirty-five miles south of Hanoi, was hit on eight successive days between 1 and 9 October 1966 and vanished off the map. In Ninh Binh, a provincial capital and trading center of twenty-five thousand people, and once one of the main centers of Roman Catholicism in Vietnam, only the cathedral spire remained standing after the air attacks. Ha Tinh, a provincial capital on the 18th Parallel, was struck 25,529 times between 1965 and 1968: for twelve hundred days there was an air strike every ninety minutes.

CHAPTER EIGHTEEN

CHARLIE CONG'S WAR

I never thought it would go on like this. I didn't think these people had the capacity to fight this way . . . to take this punishment.

—ROBERT McNAMARA

For American soldiers the war in Vietnam posed problems that were not easy to resolve. The army was fighting the Vietcong in short, sharp guerrilla engagements all over the country, but it was also taking on major regular communist formations—battalions, regiments, even divisions. However, the North did not deploy them along a front line, and therefore this was not war in the way wars had been fought in the past, the sort for which the United States had been structured and trained. And because the North had virtually no offensive air force (what there was, Russian MIG-21s mostly, were for the air defense of northern cities and the protection of the supply routes to the South, to which 60 percent were allocated) and because until quite late on there were no PAVN armored units—and then only a few of them—many of the standard components of the U.S. army were superfluous. It was halfway warfare for which it was not prepared.

U.S. forces deployed their immense firepower against Vietnamese field formations only to find that they had never existed, or that they had vanished into the trees; they pumped thousands of tons of lead into empty fields and forests; they fought battles but never took any ground; they defoliated nearly 4 million acres of jungle in order to destroy the enemy's overhead cover and crops; they tried to assess casualties to prove the enemy could not go on, only to find that the enemy never weakened. The sand never emptied out of the hourglass.

For Giap, things in some ways were easier—he had fought just such a war prior to 1954, using main force and regional and guerrilla units in a canny mixture that confused his enemies—but in some ways things were much more difficult. He was no longer at the head of his formations and in close contact with them. He could control the war indirectly through public broadcasts (there were provincial radio stations that relayed coded messages—even at one time a Liberation Radio, pumping out its credo to the population along with covert instructions), and he had long-range radio communications from his headquarters in Hanoi to the main civil and military headquarters in the South, but because of the very nature of the terrain and the scattered deployment of units there was no comprehensive radio network controling all his subordinate units throughout the South. Hence he could not know from day to day, let alone from hour to hour, what was happening, and for much of the time had to be content with promulgating strategy and guidelines.

This he did through the medium of edicts from the National Defense Council, touching the tiller now and then and in that way keeping overall direction of events, making all the really important decisions but also sometimes positively influencing events: for example, soon after the decision had been taken to intervene in the South, he sent individuals and small groups of soldiers of the PAVN to bolster the Vietcong, whose increased activity resulted in the ARVN having to deploy more soldiers to guard static installations, thus diluting its resources.

Not unnaturally, the leaders in the South felt that they were running the war and fighting the battles their way—deciding local tactics and timings, taking the casualties, feeling the heat from the kitchen—but equally the leaders in the North tended to take the credit because they provided the weapons, many of the cadres, and, as time passed, more and more troops. The truth of it was that both made independent but essential contributions. Neither could have done it alone, but even today there is disagreement between Hanoi and Saigon about who actually won the war, and the subject is the source of some bitterness among veterans. Those who fought the French think they had the hardest part (Giap himself is on record as saying that compared to the French the Americans were "greenhorns in the business of war"), while those who felt the blast waves from American bombs and shells are convinced that they must have been tougher to have survived.

As far as international politics were concerned, until well on into the war the Politburo in the North were content to pretend that events in the South were none of their doing and none of their business. In the early 1960s Ho Chi Minh said, "What they do is up to them. It is their problem. They know better than we do what are the possibilities." By distancing himself he could support the pretense that people in the South were independently pursuing the downfall of the government and the expulsion of the United States, thus excusing censure by the United States and avoiding Chinese accusations of widening the war—and also criticism in the United Nations forum that he was violating the terms of the Geneva Accords by sending troops into the South.

In South Vietnam the means most widely used by the Vietcong for transmitting orders was by courier. Thousands and thousands of seemingly innocent people traveled the country day in and day out passing on orders and information. Using passwords and pseudonyms to keep their identities secret, they were the veins and arteries through which the lifeblood of control went back and forth. As in all other branches of the insurgency organization, their rules were comprehensive.

One was that there must be at least two alternative routes from one place to the next. Others were that during travel the names of localities, rivers, and mountains should not be disclosed; that the locations of turning-off points should be kept secret; that people should not pry and should work on the need-to-know principle; that articles such as cigarette butts and paper should not be dropped along the route. There was a Control of Infiltration Routes Section that issued movement documentation, coordinated the setting up of reception areas and liaison stations, and distributed rations. Permanent liaison stations—a shop or someone's house, maybe—were operated mostly by women, who received letters of introduction from couriers, authenticated their documents, and arranged contacts and escorts. (At one of them during one single day six hundred messages were received or dispatched.) Medical centers were operated by public health cadres and midwives. Everyone was warned to be on the lookout for sabotage, both from the enemy and from within, thus increasing feelings of uncertainty and heightening awareness.

Secrecy was, of course, one of the top priorities, and as always there were rules. Never disclose your unit's designation, its weapons, its policies and plans, its location, or the routes it uses. Never reveal your rank, name, or mission to anyone. Never tell secrets to friends or relations. And: uncover and punish violations. Secrecy was especially needed because both sides fielded a large number of spies. At the peak of the war, the CIA had about a thousand paid agents working in the community to provide information, and thousands not on the payroll who were given handouts in cash or kind for giving casual information. (Many, it turned out, were double agents.) The North had an estimated thirty or forty thousand working in the South Vietnamese government, the ARVN, or even among the Americans themselves, who employed many Vietnamese in lowly positions in their bases.

Toward the end of the war American officers discovered some documents emanating from the explosives unit formed by Giap in 1958 as part of the Eastern Nam Bo Command, which had become known as the Demolition Platoon of the 514th Battalion of the PLAF. They give an astonishing insight into the minds of the people who belonged to it—and, no doubt, to other Vietcong units. There are many conclusions to be drawn about how to create a strong corporate feeling in people, how to execute and monitor good administration, how to instill self-discipline in the individual, how to train methodically.

Regular procedures, carried out unwaveringly and supervised by cadres, not harshly but with benign paternalism, were the basis of the system.

Three-man cells had to check once every hour every morning and evening the presence and cleanliness of weapons, ammunition, and stores. And mutually they had to monitor each other's welfare—the food, the conditions they operated in, their health. Every two days, in the evening, there was a recorded roll call and a check of the inventory of weapons, ammunition, and stores. The commander was required to do the same checks for all his sections and cells every three days, at night.

People were of prime importance. People's thoughts, feelings, and motivation were the fuel used for the fight. *Kiem Thao* sessions lasting ten to fifteen minutes were held every day to discuss the performance of individuals, cells, and units. Outstanding achievements and good points were highlighted as well as criticisms. As in all Eastern communist organizations, self-criticism sessions, called *Phe Binh*, were also held regularly, during which everyone had to admit their faults, discuss them, and promise improvement. Like most units they had a wall newspaper, to which everyone was invited to contribute views and writings, and even poetry.

Kiem Thao sessions dealt with leadership and command matters such as ideological leadership, military leadership, man-management, administration, time scheduling, commendations, and punishments. Commendation could be earned for such things as behaving well toward each other, for being modest and polite with each other and with the people generally, and for maintaining unity. Criticism and punishment could be given for not showing affection and understanding, for being bad-tempered, for being inefficient.

To ensure good health everyone in the unit had to participate in sports and physical training. General training was highly detailed and comprehensive. The care of explosives, protection against accidents, the basic theory of the use of electrical power and wiring, camouflage, bayonet fighting, reconnaissance, night-firing of weapons, grenade throwing, overcoming physical obstacles—all were dealt with. Detailed plans were made prior to an attack, often with the assistance of sand models, of terrain, distances, enemy dispositions, and one's own troops' dispositions.

The demands placed on people were enormous, but were compensated for by feelings of unity and achievement. A pattern of relationships was carefully built up through interlocking channels of command and supervision that went down to the lowest levels. The aim was, as far as possible, to "try to help people to love each other as if they were all members of the same family." (The words are those used in their documents.) The system not only allowed people to enter wholeheartedly into everyday life, but also required total commitment from them.

The members of these units worked amazingly long and arduous hours, rising in the dark at a quarter to five in the morning and retiring at nine at night. When not engaged in operations, roll call was followed by calisthenics, personal hygiene, breakfast (unless something happens, one of the timetables said), getting ready for combat, studying, or self-criticism sessions. Then there was a rest break from 11:30 to 1:15. In the afternoon there was more studying, then weapon training, firing practice, weapon cleaning. Bathing and dinner were from 5:10 until 6:00 P.M. Then there was half an hour of leisure time, then more study or discussions. Before settling down for the night there was another roll call, guards were posted, and then fires were doused.

Being in the delta, most of the time the demolition unit lived in villages, hiding in tunnel complexes whenever danger threatened. But Vietcong units away from the delta lived in the jungle for weeks and months at a time. If mobile, they began marching before sunrise, taking only one break before dusk for a riceball lunch prepared the previous night. (The ration per man was two pounds of rice per day, some vegetables and occasionally fish—sometimes, if the tactical situation allowed, caught by exploding a grenade in a stream.) When actively engaged on operations, they had one day's rest per week at base camps that, as time passed and the organization improved, had hospitals, news-printing facilities, and telephone lines from one camp to the next. At each camp the troops received exhaustive briefings on their next assignments.

When actually on the march or bivouacking, the rules were that everyone had to know the plan, that everyone had to be encouraged—by their commanders at cell, section, and platoon level—that all orders had to be communicated thoroughly, that everyone remained vigilant at all times.

Indicating the amount and extent of the demolition platoon's activity, the records show that during December 1966 alone it made two attacks on ammunition dumps, eleven on the Soc Trang airfield, two on the Tan Son Nhut airfield, one on a local hotel—in which they thought were two hundred American pilots—and, by sampan, on two ships in the Gulf of Tonkin. And even one on an aircraft carrier.

Of course, they took casualties and had to notify next-of-kin, so there was a standard pro forma that had to be signed by the commanding officer:

> It is with pain and sorrow that we inform you and your family of the death of ———. The entire unit is deep in sorrow because we have lost a comrade in arms and because your family has lost a loved one. We all offer our condolences. For the 514th Battalion Command Staff. Signed: Doan Minh Quang

Individual entries in the unit documents clearly show that the system worked, both as regards individual commitment and corporate unity:

Phung's mind was at ease and he could concentrate on fighting.

There were no deteriorating changes. I maintained unity and did not have conflicts with anyone.

I overslept. I was reprimanded. I promise not to repeat my error.

I did not maintain unity. I got angry because a comrade checked my ammunition when I was not there.

I maintained secrecy and took good care of my equipment.

The men in the unit also maintained contact with family and friends by letter and recorded their feelings in notebooks. In both their sentiments are often surprisingly poetic. Here is a letter to "the adopted mothers" of the platoon from Be Dahn:

Dear Mothers,
   Tonight I cannot go to sleep. I keep thinking of one thing and another. I am lost in thought under the moonlit sky of the 12th Lunar month, while all the other men are sleeping peacefully. Your son is clutching a carbine in his hands and is looking toward the enemy post. Once in a while a strong gust of wind chills me to the marrow. I think of the waning winter and the coming spring.
   I recall that before, each time the flowers bloomed indicating that spring was coming, everyone was excited and thrilled. But this spring how can we be happy when the Americans are still sowing so many sorrows and miseries, and when many thousands of tons of bombs are falling on our fatherland, destroying and setting houses on fire, stripping the trees bare of leaves, forcing the people to flee and wander from place to place, and reducing them to a life of privation and hardship? How can we be happy when we think of all this? Wherever we go we see only destruction—heaps of ashes and debris where happy homes used to be. What are we going to do? The only thing we can do is to transform our hatred into action and use all our strength to drive away the enemy.

From a notebook of Nguyen Van "Be Danh":

Autumn passes away, winter comes, and then spring returns.
As always I am enraptured of my mission.
Before me, flowers bloom in brilliant colors in front of someone's
house.
A bamboo branch sways gracefully, reminding me of the native vil-
lage I love.
Our unit stops to rest in an isolated area.
My shoes are still covered with dust gathered during the march.
I hurriedly compose this letter to you.
And send you all my love.

Letter from Phuong Trinh to Sau Kim dated 25 March 1967:

My dearest,

My section has received your letter asking for permission to marry
me. I have read this letter and am now keeping it.

During Tet my mother and three young brothers came to see me.
On the seventeenth day of the lunar month my father went to Saigon.
The car he was riding in overturned and one of his ribs was broken.
My mother had to hurry back to take him to hospital and couldn't stay
long here with me. I don't know if my father has recovered and I am
very worried.

My love, I accept your marriage proposal, but let me tell you something. Both of us understand very well the importance of marriage.
Marriage will make one happy or unhappy for the rest of one's entire
life. Loving you means that I have thought things out and have re-
flected on this matter very seriously. But my dear our situation does
not allow us to be married very soon!! Please understand me. We are
both devoted to serving our Party and the fatherland. I am determined to sacrifice my personal life and emotions, to make my parents
happy, and to continue marching on the Revolutionary path that I am
following.

If we wait, this will enable us to gauge the faithfulness of us both,
to see which of us is really faithful. Are you mad at me? But I have
made up my mind. I have given all my love to you and will go on doing
so, but first I must go on fighting.

Biographical notes written by members of the unit were included in the documents. This one is by a youth called Vo Minh Thanh:

> I attended school from the time I was seven years old until I was twelve, when I quit to help my family. When I was sixteen I went to work as a servant to the owner of an ice-cream shop. When I was eighteen I worked as a laborer, catching pigs and helping people clean pigs' hides at the marketplace. I did this until I joined the Province Military Medical Branch on 23 February 1966. Then I transferred to the demolition unit.

And another, by Ngo Rin:

> My parents were poor farmers. I attended village school until I was thirteen, then quit to help my family. I worked as a servant until I was sixteen; then I joined the hamlet self-defense militia. I distributed leaflets, stood guard five times on the road while my unit destroyed a strategic hamlet, stood guard seven times while meetings were held, went with the district force to take over a post in Thanh Phu village, on 20 July 1963 took up a blocking position while my unit intercepted and attacked an enemy platoon going to conscript people and force them to build a strategic hamlet. After that I volunteered to join this unit and was trained by the Province Engineering Unit.

CHAPTER NINETEEN

THE TRAIL

Whether in attacking, counterattacking, or defensive tactics, the idea of attacking should remain central; to always keep the initiative.

—VO NGUYEN GIAP

Trails over the Truong Son Range have existed for eons, worn through the jungle by animals and men, both of them moving from place to place in search of food. Elephants, which until the war existed in large numbers in the thick forest that straddles the borders of Vietnam, Laos, and Cambodia, trampled through the foliage and, as is their way, having made a track continued to use it. Smaller animals—tigers, antelope, boars, monkeys—took the easy way and followed them.

The human animals who trod the same paths were mostly Montagnards, driven out of the plains by the Viets in the Middle Ages; in the north they were of Mongolian/Thai extraction, in the south they had Australo-Asiatic or Malayo-Polynesian genes. All of them, foraging or making a day's journey to a nearby settlement (people always planned to be back home by nightfall), knew the trails, though they kept to their tribal territories. But in the middle of the twentieth century things changed.

At the beginning of 1959 Vo Nguyen Giap gave the People's Army the task of opening a route across the 17th Parallel that would outflank the security forces of the South. Much of it would go through Laos, known for centuries as the Kingdom of the Elephants, and would tail off in Cambodia, hooking in toward Vietnam at several points along the route.

In the spring, two officers and three men set out from the Khe Ho forest at the foot of the range on a reconnaissance. Their first guide was a man of the Van Kieu tribe who carried a machete and a crossbow that fired poisoned arrows. After a night's bivouac, they continued to walk south, led that day by a taciturn old man, the next by a boy wearing a loincloth, the next by a skinny young man smoking a pipe. Having set up a base near Thua Thien the officers retraced their steps to join up with a column of porters who had been sent to a rendezvous point and were waiting for them. Leading them south, each day they left a small detachment of men to build a base in a remote place. In this way they created a sequence of relay stations consisting of two or three small huts on stilts, similar to the shelters the Montagnards erected from which to keep an eye on their crops while remaining out of the reach of tigers.

Week after week the depleting column moved farther south through the jungle, stumbling up and down rocky slopes, fording fast-moving streams, carrying bundles of rifles, boxes of ammunition and other stores, all wrapped in waterproof cloth. Eventually, they reached the place where the trail met the asphalted Route 9 from Khe Sanh to Savanakhet in lower Laos. They crossed it between two positions held by ARVN guards and soon came to the Thach Han River, which they traveled down in sampans. In August, west of Thua Thien, they handed over this first consignment of arms to the Vietcong.

The next year, to avoid security forces in the South who had become aware of the presence of infiltrators, a new route was found farther to the west. It was this that was to become the main artery of the Ho Chi Minh Trail—called the Truong Son Trail by the Vietnamese, meaning High Mountains.

Like Hannibal crossing the Alps the next group of Giap's trailblazers used elephants to help them widen the track over the Mu Gia Pass on the border with Laos. On the other side, the route dropped into a valley but then went even higher over jagged peaks. Once past them it reached a lower plateau of thick forest inhabited by people of the Van Kieu and Lao Thung tribes, and from there entered the western highlands of Vietnam.

Regiment 559 was the unit specially created by Giap to open and maintain the Trail. It consisted of twenty-four thousand soldiers organized in small groups spread out along the length of the Trail, some of them sampan sailors, some of them carrying loads on their backs, the remainder manning the rest camps.

As time passed, Giap's men built a more permanent supply route, gradually broadening and smoothing it so that pack bicycles could be used. These were heavy machines, some of them Peugeots, relics of the Dien Bien Phu campaign, some of them of more modern Czechoslovak manufacture: all of them adapted to carry big loads—not ridden, but guided by a pole strapped to a handlebar and by a steadying tiller fastened behind the saddle. (The tires were stuffed with rags since they burst if filled with air.) Such bicycles had been used throughout the Indochina War by the Vietminh and could transport, on average, 125 kilograms half as fast again as a man could travel on foot carrying a heavy weight. (The record was 420 kilograms, set in 1964 by a man called Nguyen Dieu, who propelled his bicycle for nearly 50 kilometers with that load.)

Much of the time, though, porterage was by men carrying 40-kilogram loads on their backs. Since the average Vietnamese weighs only around 50 kilograms this meant that day after day over this difficult route men were carrying almost their own body weight. (Another record was set by Nguyen Viet Sinh, who, in four years, carrying between 45 and 50 kilos, contributed 1,089 workdays to carry 55 tons over 41,000 kilometers. It was as if he had walked around the world carrying a load equal to his own weight! For this feat he was made a Hero of the Liberation Armed Forces.) Not surprisingly, about 10 percent of the porters died, most of them from fevers made worse by their exertions and the appalling conditions in which they lived. Malaria and amoebic dysentry were the main scourges.

Human porterage lasted from 1959 to 1964, but then between 1965 and 1972 the route was widened to eight meters and in some places asphalted. In 1965 alone the amount of stores transported in vehicles by Regiment 559 equalled the total amount carried by men during the previous five years.

Tens of thousands of people in various types of units worked on the Trail. There were transport squadrons and platoons of mechanics to repair the vehicles, but there were also engineer units to repair the surface and bulldoze new offshoot roads, infantry units to guard the staging points, anti-aircraft batteries to defend everyone against air attack, and signals units to keep communications open along the whole length of the Trail. In all there were eighty thousand PAVN troops in Laos, commanded by General Vo Ban.

The Trail had become the artery for a complex logistic system that sent lifeline stores to Giap's soldiers of the PAVN and the PLAF (Vietcong) in the South and brought wounded men back for treatment in northern hospitals. In what was one of the greatest feats of military engineering in history, it was developed year after year until eventually there were three north-south laterals and seven major offshoots, plus many minor linking roads—in total nearly twenty thousand kilometers of route, along which was a network of repair workshops, stores depots, hospitals, staging and rest camps. Often these were hidden in caves, sometimes big enough only for a team of radio operators, sometimes big enough to hide a command post or a field hospital. But where installations were in the open, the sites had to be chosen very carefully, avoiding places where sudden floods in the wet season could wash a camp or depot away, avoiding places under trees that would shed their leaves in the dry season and expose what was underneath to the pilots of aircraft.

"Shock Youth Brigades Against U.S. Aggression for National Salvation" worked night and day to keep the system functioning—for example, after one bombing raid 286 breaks in telephone lines were repaired by specialist teams. Up to fifty thousand extra people, mostly young women but helped by males as young as fifteen, repaired the roads. There were hundreds of bridges to be built but sometimes, in order to disguise it, streams became part of the route. Sometimes rivers *were* the route, the stores floating down them in watertight plastic bags or on rafts that were camouflaged to look like islands so as to escape detection by American airmen. For the same reason where bridges were needed they were often built a few feet underwater. The Sekong, a tributary of the Mekong, became a sampan/raft route for a distance of more than one hundred kilometers.

A pass through a gorge at the head of the Trail, called by the Vietnamese "Heaven's Gate," was the starting point for the trek south. In the early days Soviet GAZ trucks, relics of the Dien Bien Phu campaign, would go through it, but these were soon replaced by thousands of others sent from communist countries. The best were Russian ZILs, which had a six-ton carrying capacity, six-wheel drive, and good cross-country performance. All the vehicles, draped with camouflaging tree branches and foliage, were driven in relays, new drivers taking over at the staging points. Normally, drivers did one journey each night, leaving a loaded truck and returning with an empty one, since they had to be back at base before daybreak to hide their vehicles.

By 1972 the Vietnamese were able to run convoys straight through to the different fronts without stopping at night: to Binh Tri Thien, the western highlands, Nam Bo. Where the first man-packed columns of supplies had taken six months to make the journey, by 1975 vehicle convoys could do it in one week.

Supplying petrol was a constant problem because, like the porters who ate a large proportion of the food humped down the route to Dien Bien Phu, the trucks drank vast quantities of gasoline along the way. During the early days most of it was supplied by tankers, but as time passed pipelines were constructed over the high passes, needed especially because gun-tractors and tanks, which used enormous quantities of fuel, were traveling down the route. By 1975 a pipeline snaked the whole way from the North to the southern exits, in total some three thousand miles of piping laid over mountains one thousand meters high and through deep rivers.

The U.S. air force attacked the trail relentlessly by day and by night, depending on visual sightings of vehicles or people by day, or the gleam of headlights or a hand torch by night. Attention was focused on the most difficult parts of the route, for example the ravine on the Xeng Phan pass, and the chokepoint at a place called Tchepone, not far from Khe Sanh. According to Vietnamese records, in one month on a two-kilometer section of the road an estimated twenty-one thousand tons of bombs were dropped; on average seven hundred bombs a day—one every two minutes. Day and night the route was the scene of explosions, burning vehicles, wounded men and women, avalanches and forest fires. Fifteen percent of the bombs dropped failed to explode. Bomb disposal men deactivated them and hundreds of time-bombs, dropped in mixed sticks and designed to go off after their neighbors and catch the road-repair teams in action. One of the bombs was known as the "tentacle mine" because on landing it threw out several eight-meter-long snare lines; a touch on any of them would activate the mine and send hundreds of high-velocity fragments in all directions.

Between 1965 and 1973, during operations Steel Tiger and Tiger Hound, the USAF dropped over 2 million tons of bombs on the Trail in Laos. The cost, so the Vietnamese claimed, was nearly twenty-five hundred U.S. aircraft. (U.S. records showed five hundred planes lost, one-seventh of the total destroyed over South Vietnam. Like most of their estimates of casualties the Vietnamese figures were highly exaggerated.) B-52s could drop more than one hundred 750-pound bombs in thirty seconds, cutting a swathe through the forest a mile long and four hundred yards wide. The "Daisy Cutter," a monster bomb weighing fifteen thousand pounds, could blow a crater three hundred feet in diameter. Despite all this the estimated kill ratio was only one Vietnamese for every three hundred bombs—

which cost around $140,000. U.S. statistics show that in 1968, the year of greatest Trail usage, when an estimated one hundred and fifty thousand Vietnamese traversed the route, one hundred and seventy-one thousand tons of bombs were dropped: more than one ton for every infiltrator. Yet nothing could stop the steady movement of supplies down the Trail. Even attempts to change nature: on many occasions the clouds over Laos were seeded in order to drench the trail and make progress more difficult.

And yet there were successes. When USAF pilots obliterated a route, the Vietnamese were sometimes obliged to open up an alternative under the jungle canopy, thus diverting their resources and slowing down resupply. Furthermore, the Pentagon estimated that to get six hundred trucks to their destination the Vietnamese had to start with a thousand, due to the effects of bombing and the roughness of the trail. With such a high rate of attrition, Giap had constantly to top-up the number of trucks in the fleet with new vehicles—but with Sino-Soviet military and economic aid exceeding 1 billion dollars a year, this was not difficult.

In late 1967 the Jason Group—the committee of professors appointed to inject new thoughts and ideas into plans for the conduct of the war—suggested the development of a highly sophisticated system of electronic sensors and radio networks that would trace activity on the route and then consign strike aircraft to targets. Code-named "Igloo White" it consisted of seismic sensors that, dropped on "invisible" parachutes and disguised as young bamboo plants, buried themselves in the ground, or acoustic sensors that, looking like foliage, hung high in the tree canopy. Activated by the shock of landing, or in the case of the acoustic sensors by radio signal, the pressure wave of any passing footfall or the rumbling noise of road traffic was enough to generate signals that were picked up by aircraft in orbit. Sometimes it was even possible to hear voices. The signals were transmitted to Nakhom Phanom in Thailand, where computers in the Infiltration Surveillance Center evaluated them. The "refined" information was then relayed back to fire control centers. Based on these precision calculations, map coordinates were then transmitted to F-111 aircraft waiting "cab rank" in the sky, or to B-52s and other planes ready to take off from their bases.

Usually within minutes the target would be hit. But sometimes the target had moved on, or sometimes there had never been a real target there: only a lone Vietnamese man or woman who saw the sensor and triggered it off on purpose before disappearing into the jungle. Or sometimes the sensor would transmit the sounds of vehicle movement emanating from a tape recorder held by a grinning soldier before he too made a hurried departure. Occasionally an elephant or another animal was the trigger for deadly retribution—elephants, tigers, wild boars, monkeys, and other animals were progressively decimated by the bombs, and by soldiers on both sides who shot them for sport—or in the case of the North Vietnamese sometimes for food. But the development of Igloo White came too late to make any really significant impact on the war of the Trail, though it was of enormous value during the battle of Khe Sanh.

The great irony of all this vast American effort was that early in 1967 the Pentagon had estimated that Nguyen Chi Thanh and his soldiers of the PAVN and PLAF in the South could fight with sixty tons of resupply a day. Three years later it was confirmed that over a period of a year "sixty-eight thousand tons of material started down the Trail and twenty-one thousand tons got there," almost exactly sixty tons a day. Just ten ZIL trucks had to get through to keep the Vietcong in business!

Strategically, the Battle of the Trail was the only one in the Vietnam war that really mattered. It was also the only one that never ceased.

Notes from a diary by Duong Thi Xuan Quy, a young woman journalist and mother who left Hanoi in 1969 to journey down the Trail and was killed by South Korean troops in Quang Nam province in 1970:

9 May.

Ly, my child, you are seventeen months old today! Is the sun shining on you today? Where are you? Are you still in Hanoi? Here I am in a jungle that is bright and dry and glowing with sunshine as if it too is celebrating your birthday. As soon as I woke up I thought of you. My child is seventeen months old, I told myself. How are you? Do you run a temperature? I expect you have forgotten me. I miss you so much I think I cannot bear it any longer. Last year I would fan you for hours to keep you cool. Does Granny do this for you now?

13 May.

The boils on my back hurt me the whole of last night. I could neither sleep nor think clearly. Impossible to lie on my back and torture to lie on my side. Had to rock the hammock frequently to ease the pain. Felt hot all over. Have lost my appetite for several days now. Never thought it could take so much effort to eat.

Haven't had a bath for weeks but must have one now, down in the stream by which the soldiers are busy cooking. Put up a plastic sheet between two trees downstream and wash behind it. Feel good after the bath. Many people warned me not to go to the stream. Many soldiers there, they said. But soldiers or not I had a good bath, and there was no problem at all.

Ill! Oh, my. What a dreadful thing, to fall ill now. I must not break down.

14 May.

Catch up with a big infantry unit that crossed a pontoon bridge over the Sepon river. The men are weighed down with equipment. There are extra rounds of ammunition to carry now that they are nearing the front. In the dim moonlight youthful faces covered with sweat flit by. Laden with rifles, machine guns, grenades, and back-packs, the soldiers still move double-quick. They have traveled like this for three months and now they are nearing the front.

16 May.

In the morning went out with Sac and Oanh to gather sweet potato leaves. I saw a lonely grave, adorned with a small wreath. Guess it was made by a girl. Who made this wreath for you, unknown soldier?

The two boils on my back have erupted, one all by itself, the other assisted by Huong. Have had them covered with sulfamide powder and a bandage, but they hurt badly every time my pack touches them.

18 May.

My skin is peeling and I'm tired out. My knees and ankles give me great pain. It was six when I crossed Highway 9. I had to run because there was an enemy aircraft near. Caught in a shower on the other side of the road. The heat is even more stifling. We were ordered to stop laughing and giggling. "I do not understand why you laugh all the time," Thang complained: "What's the joke?"

Huu protested mildly. "They only laugh because they are young and it's good for them. Leave them alone!" Thang said the Americans dropped devices that could record the slightest sound. So what? Let them record our laughter. That would be fun.

We had a rest and then started off again. We didn't arrive until eight. The advance party had already cooked a big pot of rice soup. I filled my can and gulped it down. Then we groped about in the dark and put up our tents and hammocks.

What a day! My feet and trousers were covered in dirt, but there was no water to wash with. Wiped my feet and lay down to sleep. Up at six.

29 May.

Met a group of thirteen children coming from Gia Lai. They had traveled for a month and a half. The sight of them with their tiny packs fills me with emotion. The youngest is a boy of eleven, with coarse hair and skinny limbs. The oldest is only fourteen. They are going north to study. They carry their own supplies of rice, which they cook themselves. They remind me of Ly. Oh, my child.

All sorts of people travel down the Truong Son, soldiers, civilians, men, and women, but I have never seen children before.

Giap's troops at Khe Sanh, 1968

General Nguyen Chi Thanh

General Nguyen Thi Dinh

General William C. Westmoreland

The author with General Vo Nguyen Giap

CHAPTER TWENTY

THE TET OFFENSIVE

*In all honesty, we didn't achieve our main objective. As for making
an impact on the United States, it had not been our intention—but
it turned out to be a fortunate result.*

—GENERAL TRAN DO

It was the Ho Chi Minh Trail that enabled Giap to launch the
1968 offensives that led to an end of direct American military
involvement in Vietnam. It was down that artery that the tens of
thousands of soldiers and the tons of supplies came in preparation

for the Tet Offensive and the vicious confrontation at Khe Sanh. As Dien Bien Phu had been psychologically to the French so Khe Sanh was to be to the Americans: the focal point of the war.

According to the statistics made available to General Westmoreland—the numbers of enemy dead, deserters, and weapons captured, the miles of roadway opened up for free movement, the increase in the size and number of Yellow, government-controlled, areas—in 1967 the war had gone badly for the Vietcong. Though American casualties had also been rising—2,500 in 1965, 33,000 in 1966, 80,000 in 1967, now was the time to take the initiative.

In early 1968 Westmoreland moved the 1st Cavalry Division and the 101st Airborne Division, together with other American and ARVN troops, into camps about thirty miles east from Khe Sanh as part of a northerly migration of some of his best soldiers into the 1st Corps Military Region in preparation for Giap's anticipated spring offensive. It was odds-on that another dry season would bring more battles, almost certainly in the hills and jungles south of the demilitarized zone. He would be ready for them with nearly fifty battalions of infantry. In all, he intended to have almost a quarter of a million troops there, including men of the Korean Blue Dragon Brigade.

(In conversation with the author, General Westmoreland said that when he briefed President Johnson in Honolulu in 1965 the president asked him what *he* would do if he were in Giap's shoes. Westmoreland replied that he would invade the two northern provinces—which were far from a deep-sea port and had no good roads or airfields, and were therefore inaccessible to quick reinforcement from farther south—and try to take the old capital city of Hue, because its capture would be a great psychological triumph. Three years later Giap was to attack the provinces and go for Hue, but for different reasons of even greater strategic portent.)

Westmoreland hoped to lure Giap into a situation in which he could use the gigantic firepower of his guns and bombers to destroy his best troops. When that had been done he had a plan to strike west and invade Laos with a three-division left hook, the jumping-off point for which would be Khe Sanh. The aim was to cut the Trail, then face about and go eastward toward the coast to link up with a right-hook amphibious marine landing. The two operations would take the battle into the North and pave the way for Giap's final defeat. All he needed was the presidential tick of approval.

But Giap too had plans: he would take the battle into the South in unprecedented force. To this end in October 1967 the Politburo in Hanoi had agreed in principle to his winter/spring campaign, part of which involved a widespread attack in the South at the time of the Tet festivities that on 30 January 1968 would inaugurate the Year of the Monkey.

Giap's 1967/68 dry-season campaign was to be in three phases. The first, in the late autumn, would be a series of probing attacks in the central highlands, intended to test new command-and-control methods and equipment. The second, at the beginning of 1968, was to be the Tet Offensive, a widespread but loosely coordinated campaign of urban warfare, in which units of the People's Army would act as auxiliaries to the PLAF. The third, code-named "Second Wave," was to consist of urban and rural battles combined with a big psychological warfare campaign that would undermine morale in the South and bring about the general uprising. (General Westmoreland did not get it right when he made his appreciation based on the intelligence information presented to him: he thought the campaign would begin with border battles, gear up to a general offensive, and then culminate with another Dien Bien Phu-type battle at Khe Sanh aimed at giving Hanoi weighty diplomatic leverage at any future peace talks as Dien Bien Phu had done prior to the Geneva Accords.)

Giap sent Major General Le Trong Tan and Colonel Le Ngoc Hien to the South to act as his liaison officers, carrying with them, down the Trail, the general outline of a scheme to assault simultaneously the Allied security forces in every place of any importance in the South. After deliberating with the political and military chiefs of COSVN, they reported back that the plan was supported by them. In January, at the 14th Plenum, the Party gave its formal approval to Giap's plan after hearing his assurances that there were more than four hundred safe houses scattered around the South in which the necessary weapons, food, and medicines—and soldiers—could be hidden ready for the attack. It was a plan of enormous complexity, both operationally and logistically, and it would take time to prepare.

To quote from Hanoi's 1988 official history of the war:

> During the summer of 1967 plans were made for a large-scale attack at the beginning of 1968. The aim was to undermine the government of the South by attacking the towns and cities, which were the weakest links. At the beginning of 1968 the whole country would be preparing for the New Year Festival. On 20 January, in order to draw the attention of the American government and military, the People's Army began an attack on National Route No. 9 in the region of Khe Sanh. In response, General Westmoreland substantially increased the numbers of American soldiers in that area.

In October, looking far ahead, Giap had ordered that the necessary men and material should begin to infiltrate down the Trail and across the border. Day and night—but mostly by night—men and stores moved farther and farther south down roads and rivers and tracks until some of them got as far as they could go—right down into the Mekong delta. If the Politburo did not agree to his plan—an unlikely eventuality—the effort would not have been wasted: the soldiers would be integrated into units already in the South, and the supplies would support future operations.

To start Phase 1—the probing attacks—on the morning of 29 October, the 273rd Regiment of the PLAF, supported by the 165th Regiment of the People's Army, captured the government offices at Loc Ninh. A bitter battle lasted for a week before the Vietcong withdrew, leaving 852 counted dead, though some estimates of their casualties went as high as 2,000. During that time Giap's 88th Regiment of the PAVN had also shown itself in the area, as had the 272nd and the 273rd regiments of the PLAF. The PAVN regiment had a lot of new equipment: flamethrowers, grenade launchers, backpack radios, 120-mm mortars, and 122-mm rocket launchers. (During the Loc Ninh battle the American command announced that the magical—and perhaps mythical—"crossover" point had been reached where Vietcong losses were greater than their recruitment capability. It had been assessed that in the last year they had lost 60,000 men but had been able to recruit only 20,000.) Soon after, the 88th Regiment of the People's Army attacked Long Be and the 271st Regiment of the PLAF ambushed and mauled a battalion from the Big Red One U.S. division.

On 15 November Giap's troops attacked the Special Forces camp at Dak To, which had been massively reinforced after a tipoff by a People's Army deserter. The 4th Infantry Division, the 1st Brigade of the Air Cavalry Division, an Airborne Brigade (the same one, the 173rd, that had taken part in Junction City), plus six ARVN battalions were now there looking out on jungle that had been stripped of greenery by defoliants. In a series of vicious engagements over an area of 190 square miles, American troops fired 170,000 shells while USAF and marine pilots flew 2,100 fighter-bomber missions.

At both Loc Ninh and Dak To, Westmoreland used B-52s to augment the firepower of his big 175-mm guns and other artillery, but despite this, except for those suffered during the Tet Offensive, the United States took more casualties in a series of battles at Dak To than anywhere else during the whole of the Vietnam war, more than were to be directly incurred at Khe Sanh. Twelve hundred Vietcong and PAVN died there, but so did 305 Americans. (Of the dead, 124 were from the 173rd Airborne Brigade.) Nine hundred eighty-five men were wounded.

The attack on Khe Sanh preceded the Tet Offensive by ten days and immediately riveted the attention of the media, and thus the people of the United States—to an extent that was out of all proportion to the importance of the battle. Coverage accounted for 25 percent of all time given to reports on the evening news, sometimes 50 percent. It amounted to 38 percent of *all* reports filed by the Associated Press. Westmoreland says that in response to the attack and Hanoi's hints at the possibility of negotiations, the press, Congress, academics, and even government officials "played the role intended for them as if they had had an advance look at the script." In consequence, Khe Sanh became to Americans a symbol of their determination, and its successful defense an act that could somehow brilliantly atone for all the failures and heartaches that had gone before.

Giap benefited greatly from this overreaction because it not only increased antiwar feelings in the United States but, more immediately, enabled him and the leaders of the insurrection in the South to make their last-minute preparations for the Tet battle untroubled by the attention of the American army and the ARVN, both of which organizations had made plans for a sizeable proportion of their strength to be on leave for the duration of the festival, which had always been a time of truce. (This was despite the fact that there had been some indications from intelligence sources that attacks would be made during Tet. However, these were not considered totally reliable; it would have been bad for morale to cancel the leave; and furthermore, quite rightly, it had been assessed that troops farther south could do nothing directly to influence the outcome of a battle near the border.)

Consequently, when the first attacks were made, many GIs and half the ARVN were on holiday. Thirty-six of the forty-four provincial capitals were attacked, as were five of the nation's cities, sixty-four district capitals, scores of other towns, and more than twenty USAF airfields. General Westmoreland says that the enemy penetrated in some strength into thirteen towns and cities. Heavy fighting continued for several days in Kontum, Ban Me Thuot, Phan Thiet, Can Tho, Ben Tre, and Saigon. The coordination of this nationwide assault by an estimated eighty-four thousand troops, mainly PLAF but interlaced with PAVN regular soldiers, was a credit to the COSVN planners in the South and was not something that could have been done in detail in Hanoi.

As urgent calls went out for the security forces to return to duty, every available U.S. and ARVN soldier was rushed into place to try to repel the invaders. In Saigon by the evening of the first day, five American infantry battalions were fighting the Vietcong house by house, street by street. To prevent the enemy from reinforcing the attackers, nearby guerrilla-occupied towns were flattened by air strikes. (That, and the destruction of other places as the PLAF were forcibly removed, increased the refugee population by 470,000 people in a matter of days.)

Even though Giap had put so much thought and preparation into planning the Tet Offensive, on the day, as is so often the case in war, things went wrong. The official history:

> On 30 January 1968 due to a misunderstanding some of the army in the South started to attack and some of them did not. In the South the official New Year's Day was 30 January, one day earlier than in the North, where they were using the old calendar. Some troops attacked on the thirtieth—for example, units in Quang Nam and Quang Ngai—and some the next day. Those that started a day late faced troops who were already alerted, and had a more difficult time.

But the difficulties were not great enough to obscure the message that was sent to the American people. It was suddenly and painfully obvious that even with more than half a million American troops in South Vietnam, let alone another half million Allied troops plus tens of thousands of South Vietnamese local militia, its cities and towns were not safe from attack.

During the next few days, thanks to the skill, bravery, and determination with which the Army of the Republic fought a rash of bitter contests, the Tet Offensive was largely blunted; it was they who took the lead in most of the counterattacks that eliminated the Vietcong and PAVN assault troops. When the sums were added up, General Westmoreland felt he could claim thirty-seven thousand enemy dead. It turned out to be far too high an estimate, but nevertheless it was indicative of the crippling losses suffered by the Vietcong and its PAVN auxiliaries. Everywhere except at Hue they were surrounded, assaulted, and destroyed or captured. By 11 February, a fortnight after it began, the Tet Offensive was virtually over.

Militarily, both sides claimed they had won, but the heavy casualties inflicted were such that the Vietcong would take years to recover. Therefore, in one way Tet was a decisive victory for the South, even though it cost twenty-five hundred American lives. But politically for the United States it was a disaster, not least because it came so soon after the American public had been told that the war was being won. There were reflections of Navarre's "light at the end of the tunnel" in the pronouncement by the American army chief of staff, General Harold K. Johnson, that "We are definitely winning," and in General Westmoreland's assurance, given to an audience at the National Press Club in Washington on 21 November 1967, that "We have reached an important point when the end begins to come into view. The enemy's hopes are bankrupt"—said to encourage his soldiers and the American people, but greatly overstated.

The first stunning intimation of the ferocity of the Tet attacks to appear on television all over the United States was the fierce little brawl to retake the American Embassy compound in Saigon, but the pictures that kept coming up on the screens for twenty-five days were of the battle to retake the ancient capital of Hue. It was to be ten days before the commanders there felt that they had been reinforced enough to be able to make a start. Eventually, eleven ARVN battalions and three U.S. marine battalions did the job, but it was to take them two weeks of bloody, hand-to-hand, house-to-house fighting before the eight battalions of the Vietcong, about 5,000 men, could be prised out. This was partly because the city was never fully isolated from the surrounding countryside—American and ARVN troops ringed it but were unaware that the Vietcong were still able to infiltrate some supplies and reinforcements into the city through alleyways beside the Perfumed River. Acres of Hue were totally destroyed, the small wooden houses burned to matchwood, the stone and concrete buildings pounded to dust and rubble. The Stars and Stripes did not fly again over the bombed ruins of the citadel until 23 February. The ARVN lost 384 dead and the marines 142. Sealed off from major reinforcement by the 1st US Cavalry Division, the enemy lost an estimated 5,000 dead in the city and another 3,000 in the adjacent fighting.

When Hue was taken by the Vietcong, they released all the prisoners in the city jails, especially those who were held because they had been suspected of helping them, but fanatics also killed thousands of the inhabitants whom they regarded as enemies of the people. When it was all over a document was found which listed "1,892 administrative personnel, 38 policemen, and 790 tyrants" as having been executed: cold words that hid the true description of those unfortunate people: civic leaders, upholders of law and order, perhaps citizens whose neighbors were exacting vengeance for a past wrong by making false accusations. Radio Hanoi referred to them all as "lackeys who owed blood debts" and condoned the executions, but in fact it was the commander of the PLAF troops in the city who stopped the slaughter when he heard what was happening.

For the Vietcong the offensive was a disaster. According to Colonel General Tran van Tra: "The Tet objectives were beyond our strength. They were based on the subjective desires of the people who made the plan. Hence our losses were large, in material and manpower, and we were not able to retain the gains we had already made. Instead, we had to overcome a myriad of difficulties in 1969 and 1970." According to a woman member of the PLAF, Duong Quynh Hoa, "Hanoi was guilty of grievous miscalculation, which squandered the strength of the Southern forces." And yet COSVN had agreed to the plan when it was proposed by Giap. They too must have been guilty of harboring subjective desires that clouded their assessment of the true situation.

There are two reasons why the Tet Offensive did not bring about the decisive national uprising—*khoi nghai*—that had been anticipated. One was that many South Vietnamese were not totally convinced that they should become part of a communist state controlled by Hanoi. But the main reason was that, though hundreds of thousands of people were active members of the National Liberation Front, because security demanded that the details and timings of the offensive must remain secret, the bulk of the population had not been prepared for the uprising. The sudden onslaught took them by surprise as much as it did the government and the security forces, and when the day came those who were so inclined did not know what to do.

Giap has this to say about the spring of 1968:

> For us, you know, there is no such thing as a single strategy. Ours is always a synthesis—simultaneously diplomatic, military, and political. Which is why, quite clearly, the Tet Offensive had multiple objectives.
>
> Pacification was a threat to the progress of the war. Our main emphasis was to draw American units away from populated areas in the lowlands and by doing so make it easier for the Liberation Front

to control the people. We deployed two divisions into the northern provinces of Quang Tri and Thua Thien, which drew in American troops from other areas, making them reduce the pacification program. It also stopped their reinforcement of the Mekong delta, where they and their allies were doing well. [Shades here of the moves and countermoves between Giap and Navarre before the battle of Dien Bien Phu.]

At the battles of Loc Ninh and Dak To in the central highlands in 1967, we were able to test our forces against defended positions. The next step was to move a larger force toward Khe Sanh. Again the U.S. imperialists responded.

The force was going to be used for the third phase of the winter/spring offensive, called "Second Wave." In conjunction with military attacks in the northern provinces, we would make appeals to people in the South, saying that the puppet government was finished and asking them to turn against it and the United States. That did not come to pass, but the Tet Offensive proved that in spite of the bombing of the North and search-and-destroy operations in the South, we were stronger in 1968 than at the time of America's commitment of massive forces to the war. Before, their primary aim had been to find and to kill; now, it was replaced by a new strategy of defense.

And that was our biggest victory: to change the ideas of the United States. The Tet Offensive had been directed primarily at the people of South Vietnam, but as it turned out it affected the people of the United States more. Until Tet they had thought they could win the war, but now they knew that they could not. Johnson was forced to decrease military activity and start to discuss with us around the table how to end the war.

For the people of the United States the first few months of 1968 were some of the worst in their history. In Vietnam most of its soldiers realized for the first time that they would never win the war, while at home many people turned away from it with revulsion. During Tet, after the complete leveling of one town, Ben Tre, a weary American officer had told a reporter, "We had to destroy it in order to save it." For millions of Americans that phrase vividly summed up the futility of the war: nobody was winning, nobody could win.

Colonel Mai The Chinh, a bomb-disposal expert who took part in Giap's pre-Tet attacks and in the battle for Hue gave this account to the author:

> At the end of 1967, as part of the offensive leading up to Tet, we were told to open a path through a mine field. It was at a place called Dak To. We had to use our hands to clear the mines, feeling for them in the dark while lying on the ground, and keeping very quiet because we did not want the enemy to be alerted. There were very tricky jumping-mines; if you touched a tripwire they shot into the air and went off, scattering pieces of steel all around. There were also anti-tank mines. And flares, also set off by tripwires. We had to defuse them all. It was dangerous and very difficult work.
>
> We worked from sunset until eleven at night, but we could not clear them all. Finally, because the attacking force had to get through before daylight, we were told to clear a path using big explosive charges, even if we gave our intentions away. We quickly got bundles of explosives and ran forward, but at that moment the enemy saw us and called down artillery fire. Many of my compatriots were killed, but new men came forward to replace them. Early the next morning, soon after dawn, we finished opening the way.
>
> On 30 January the Tet battle began and our forces attacked many posts along Route 9. The aim was to annihilate the enemy so that we could control the northern provinces. After a few days my unit, the 7th Battalion of the Engineer Corps, was sent to Hue, where we fought for several weeks. For our work there the whole unit was named a Heroic Unit. Our forces made many gains and captured Hue, but eventually the Americans drove us out and we retreated into the western jungle.
>
> There were a hundred of us left, and all the food we had was ten kilos of rice. But we had to use that to make soup to give to the wounded, so the rest of us lived on roots and plants. It was a very serious famine situation. We could not shoot wild animals for food because the noise would have given our position away. In addition, we had to suffer carpet bombing and very heavy rain, day after day. There was no cover for the wounded so we tied sheets of plastic together between some trees so that the doctors and nurses could treat them out of the rain.

Because of the constant rain the land began to flood. The situation was very serious. We had no food but we could not move because of the high water. This lasted for some months.

As well as bombs, all the time the Americans dropped leaflets from the air, calling on us to surrender. The liberation war was a legendary story cooked up by our leaders, they told us; we were going to lose, so we should give up now. They waged psychological war, urging all liberation soldiers to go back to their families. In one leaflet they printed a letter from a soldier to his mother saying that he was starving in the rain in the mountains.

Yes, that is what we were doing.

CHAPTER TWENTY-ONE

KHE SANH

I know there is no way you can talk civilized to these people.
—CORPORAL MIKE BROWN, U.S. MARINE CORPS

Like Dien Bien Phu, Khe Sanh was a border outpost. It even lay in the same position relative to South Vietnam as Dien Bien Phu was to the North: in the top lefthand corner. It was only seven miles from the Laotian border and not many more from the 17th Parallel. And like Dien Bien Phu, in itself it was of no great importance. The military value of Khe Sanh lay in the fact that, like Dien Bien Phu, it straddled an important road, in this case Route 9, which went east to west across the most northerly of what was then South Vietnam's provinces and then continued into Laos, and that it was pivotal to defenders and attackers; a key place to hold from which to develop other initiatives.

Khe Sanh village is in Quang Tri province. To the west the hills and jungles make living difficult, so most of the people in the province dwell around the paddy fields in the east, in the strip of land between the coast and Route 1, the French Legionnaires' "Street Without Joy." The village lies in rugged country, with hills rising steeply around it: low hills, high hills, and higher hills, on which grow tangles of canopied trees, thickly belted with undergrowth and laced with vines. The area is prone to fog and downpours of rain that feed the steams and waterfalls that cascade down the slopes. For a lot of the time it is wet, humid, and stuffy—which is why they grow coffee there. The dripping hills, which were never silent by night or by day, were home to many wild animals and a myriad of birds and insects.

In Khe Sanh lived a community of a few hundred people who worked in the surrounding coffee plantations, most of which were owned by French men and women. Nearby were some Bru Montagnards, who in 1958 had been persuaded to move to the village by ARVN troops in order that they could be protected from, and could not support, the Vietcong. Other Bru lived in settlements scattered around in the jungle; in all, there were about eight thousand of them in the area. There were also two French missionaries, who were trying to convert the Bru to Roman Catholicism, and a few Vietnamese nuns.

Two miles north of the village, on a plateau 1,447 feet above sea level, there was a concrete fort built in de Lattre's time, a sort of distant dilapidated offshoot of his Maginot-type fortifications around Hanoi. Beside it was a small grass airfield. In the early 1960s interlocking metal sheets were laid on the strip by an ARVN engineer battalion so that it could sometimes be used as a base for aerial reconnaissance of the Trail.

Seven miles away to the west, on the other side of the border, a lumpy mountain called Co Roc brooded over the pass into Laos. In the far distance to the north Tiger Peak looked down over part of what was, in 1968, the demilitarized zone, the Dee-Em-Zee. Nearer, smaller hills, three or four miles to the north and west of the combat base and about five thousand meters apart, formed a triangle whose commanding heights, giving good observation for the direction of artillery fire, would pose a big military problem for anyone who thought of defending the base: they had to be held.

American troops had been near the village since July 1962, when Green Berets moved into the old French fort. The Special Forces were part of the border screen, and their job was to work with and befriend the Bru: teach them the arts of war, take them on patrol to gain intelligence about the enemy; and eat rats, get drunk on rice alcohol, grow their hair long, get tattooed with local totems, and sleep with Bru women, so it was said.

In 1966 a battalion of marines swept the area for a couple of weeks looking for trouble but found none. When they packed up and walked out along Route 9 they left a company behind in the camp, which they had named Fort Dix. There was no love lost between them and the unconventional soldiers: the marines thought the Green Berets were an ill-disciplined, unkempt rabble, probably high on drugs. The men of the Special Forces thought the marines were brash, hidebound, and downright uncooperative. If marines were going to come and go here, they would rather be somewhere else. They decided to move out, to a new camp in a village called Lang Vei, about five miles down the road nearer to Laos.

Though no contact had been made with the enemy, General Westmoreland was sure that one day it would. A few weeks before, Giap had placed Quang Tri province under his own jurisdiction, taking military control of it away from COSVN and the PLAF: in the future the People's Army and not the Vietcong would fight the battles there, under the control of the Tri-Thien-Hue Military Region. In Saigon, Westmoreland's staff decided to boost the Special Forces team by three hundred irregulars—that is, with a Civilian Irregular Defense Group of Montagnard militia—and also to put a detachment of a Special Operations Intelligence Group beside them. As time passed the troops in Lang Vie would be rotated on the orders of the army, to whom the Green Berets reported, and the CIA, who, with the ARVN, controlled intelligence operations, often without notifying the marines up in Fort Dix. As for the marines, they were proud of their military self-sufficiency—of their own air arm, their own artillery, their own procedures: of the fact that they could operate anywhere in the world without any help from anyone. Because as marines they were traditionally linked with the navy, and because some marine units were permanently afloat in the South China Sea as a reserve, their generals tended to face toward the navy headquarters in Honolulu rather than toward Westmoreland and his army staff in Saigon, which did not make for peaceful cooperation. Another bone of contention was the control of air support. The marines wanted to use their own procedures, but when it came to integrating the big bombers that was not good enough. Determined to maintain their independence the marines created such bad feeling that it became the one issue that caused Westmoreland to seriously consider resigning. In the end he prevailed, and the marines adopted the established army/USAF methods.

In March 1967 another company of marines arrived in Khe Sanh, bringing with them a naval construction team to build new bunkers and living amenities. Almost immediately things began to hot up. Toward the end of April patrols encountered units of the 18th Regiment of the 325thC Division of the People's Army on hills 861 and 881 (named after their height), two of the three high points north and west of the combat base. Twelve marines were killed. An extra company was airlifted by helicopter on to Hill 861 the next day, and a whole battalion (the 2nd, of the 3rd Regiment) and artillery support into Fort Dix. Their arrival signaled the start of what was to become known as the 1967 Hill Fights, a series of brief, savage engagements in which, according to the marines' official history, the 18th Regiment "resisted with great fury." (So much so that as a mark of respect Charlie Cong became known by the marines there as Mister Charles.) According to one of the marine commanding officers, the enemy were "well-led, well-fed, and well-equipped."

The brawls lasted a hard week before the 18th extricated itself—leaving about seven hundred dead—under cover of an attack by a sister Regiment, the 95thC, on the camp at Lang Vei. Twenty-six defenders there were killed and thirty-six wounded before they too withdrew. Rather than repair it, a few weeks later the Green Berets and the other detachments moved to a new camp built a short distance away.

Because it was the highest point in the area, a signal relay station had been established on top of Hill 950. Standing there it was possible to see Co Roc, Tiger Peak, the Laotian hills, and to get a broad view of the DMZ. And even, on a clear day, a glimpse of the South China Sea. On 6 June 1967 Giap's men attacked the hill, killing three soldiers. The next day eighteen marines died on Hill 881 North. After a series of scraps, by late July the total number of dead had risen to fifty-two Americans and two hundred and four of the enemy. When things quieted down again, the various companies of marines were withdrawn and replaced by the 1st Battalion of the 26th Regiment. On 13 June, in order to be able to keep up the pressure of intensive patrolling, another battalion (the 1st, of the 3rd Regiment) joined it. On the fourteenth, a battery of artillery got through by road. Two months later, on 14th August, Colonel David E. Lownds took over as commander of Khe Sanh combat base.

Settling in, the marines began to improve the defenses. But that was not so easy: nearby trees were full of shrapnel from shells loosed off during the Hill Fights, which broke chainsaw blades as soon as they bit into the wood. In any case the trees rotted within weeks of being cut, or were eaten by termites, so hard wood had to be flown in, adding to the logistic load. The base, only four-hundred-by-two-hundred yards in size, began to build up rapidly as relays of aircraft brought in the backup, a small part of the million tons of supplies that were being shipped and flown into South Vietnam every month.

Also in August General Westmoreland decided to upgrade Khe Sanh camp and make it a potential launching pad for the incursion into Laos. Khe Sanh was accessible by road—just, along Route 9, where parts of it were so narrow that trucks could not turn round—but to get there by that means meant running a probable gauntlet of ambushes through Vietcong-threatened jungle, as had been the case at Dien Bien Phu. Consequently, any force there would have to rely on air supply. The airfield was therefore vital, and in August work began to improve it further so that it could take heavier aircraft. Transport planes ferried in men and building materials, trucks brought stone from a quarry a mile away, the metal mats on the runway were ripped up and new, better ones laid. While it was closed a new system, called LAPES—for Low Altitude Parachute Extraction System—was used for resupply; a parachute deployed out of the back of a low-flying aircraft dragged a pallet of stores out on to the ground.

As work went on apace, in September the 1st Battalion of the 3rd Marines arrived. So did more guns, and 4.2" mortars, and a steadily increasing stockpile of ammunition. There were also ten tracked vehicles mounting six 106-mm recoilless rifles. There were even five Patton tanks. And as part of his plan for the future role of Khe Sanh Westmoreland had put two batteries of 175-mm heavy guns into Camp Carroll, about twenty miles away, from where they could support the marines. (He would have put them in Khe Sanh itself, except that they could not get there because of the terrain.) Things were shaping up well when during the late autumn of 1967 surveillance showed that the volume of traffic down the nearby Trail was increasing greatly.

Electronic sensors rumbled and muttered their notification of truck noise and human footfalls to receptors in orbiting USAF planes and to listening radio operators. As well as the sensors that lay in the earth or up in the tree canopy in Laos, some planes and helicopters flying over the Trail carried chemical sniffers that could detect the odors of sweat and urine exuded by enemy soldiers. Others had sideways-looking aircraft radars (SLAR) that could detect movement. Yet others had infrared sensors that responded to heat emanating from men and cooking fires. All these devices indicated that more than a thousand trucks had moved toward Khe Sanh in October, nearly four thousand in November, and considerable numbers of men on foot. On 13 December the 3rd Battalion of the 26th Regiment of marines was sent at short notice to Khe Sanh, diverted in midflight from another operation by General Robert E. Cushman, Jr., commander of all U.S. marines in Vietnam.

On 27 December General Westmoreland sent the Pentagon detailed proposals for the incursion into Laos, using Khe Sanh as the assembly point.

During December 6,315 North Vietnamese trucks had gone down the Trail.

On the evening of 2 January 1968 six men dressed in what some people said looked like U.S. Marine Corps uniforms were seen outside the perimeter of the combat base, apparently surveying its defenses. (Others remember them being clad in the usual black pajamas of the Vietcong.) Failing to respond to a sentry's challenge, five of them were shot dead; the sixth, wounded, got away. Documents on the dead men showed them to be PAVN soldiers of relatively high rank—a regimental commander, his intelligence officer, and so on. The incident was quickly reported up the chain of command, and in Saigon the commanding general was now faced with an identical quandary to that which had caused Navarre to deliberate so anxiously fourteen years before: whether to stay or go.

For psychological reasons Westmoreland was reluctant to retreat. He had recently given the public back home an optimistic appraisal of how the war was going: how would it look if they—and indeed his own soldiers—now heard that he was pulling troops out of the line? In his view it would be "a retrograde step." And there were other considerations. To quote him: "Khe Sanh could serve as a patrol base for blocking enemy infiltration from Laos along Route 9; a base for operations to harass the enemy in Laos; an airstrip for reconnaissance planes surveying the Trail; a western anchor for defenses south of the DMZ; and an eventual jumping-off point for operations to cut the Trail." Like Navarre, he decided to stay and on 5 January set in train the planning for a torrential storm of precision bombing, to which he gave the name Niagara: if Giap's troops attacked Khe Sanh fleets of B-52s would cascade explosives down on them.

Having decided to stay, Westmoreland put himself in the same predicament as Navarre had done: he needed as many troops as possible to defend the base, but because Khe Sanh could only be resupplied by air the more men he put in there the bigger the logistic problems became. However, he had far more cargo planes than Navarre had had, and each of them carried a far greater tonnage.

Even so, there was cause for concern, especially the notoriously un-predictable visibility on the airfield, so he ordered the marines to commit no more troops to Khe Sanh than could be resupplied by air.

As the days passed the troops massing around the Laotian border were identified. Two divisions of the People's Army, the 304th—veteran of Dien Bien Phu—and the 325thC Golden Star, supported by the 24th, 68thB, and 164th artillery regiments, about ninety-six guns in all, were there, a force of at least twenty thousand men. In addition, the 320th and the 324thB Divisions were coming up behind them as reinforcements. (In late December 1967 and early January 1968 Giap had sent the 304th, the 320th, and the 325thC divisions toward Khe Sanh—about thirty thousand men—with one regiment of the 324thB Division—five thousand men—to support the other three. There were not four whole divisions there. Two regiments of the 325thC crossed the DMZ about fifteen miles northwest of Khe Sanh. Two regiments of the 320th, and the supporting artillery, came from the northeast. The rest came down two new roads carved out from the Trail that ended only a few miles west of Khe Sanh. Many of the soldiers walked the approach route in three- or five-man self-sufficient cells, *doans*. Their supply line from Khe Sanh back to Tchepone on the Trail, where two supply points had been established, was short, but first everything had to be brought hundreds of miles from the PAVN's base supply depots.)

Soon enemy snipers began to harrass the marines in and around the combat base, and shells landed nearby as PAVN gunners began to register their targets. (Until Lownds ordered that they should be doused, their job was made easier because they could zero in on the bright lights that illuminated the base at night. Farther down the valley, in Lang Vei, the Green Berets scathingly referred to it as Coney Island.)

On 15 January B-52s hit twelve places near Khe Sanh where it was thought the enemy were hidden. On the sixteenth a third battalion of the 26th Marines (the 2nd) was sent to Khe Sanh. Lownds directed it to Hill 558, where it would be able to give fire support to Hill 861 and would overlook the valley to the east of the base. It was the first time the whole regiment had been in action together since World War II.

On 20 January there was a vicious little battle on Hill 881 North when skirmishers of the 304th Division tested out the defenses. The marines there were pulled back to Hill 881 South. On the same day an operation began to scatter 250 sensors around Khe Sanh to provide close surveillance. Information from them was relayed to an orbiting plane, and by it to the Infiltration Surveillance Center in Thailand. Having been processed there the data was then radioed back to the artillery fire control center in Khe Sanh so that targets could be engaged—or fighter-ground-attack planes called in. (From then on until the end of the battle the surveillance never ceased: apart from all the other information being processed, thousands of feet of film were sent to Saigon for analyses, part of the 3 million taken by photo-reconnaissance aircraft over South Vietnam each month.)

And on 20 January, First Lieutenant La Than Tonc, commanding officer of the 14th Anti-Aircraft Company, which supported the 95thC Infantry Regiment of the 325thC Division, walked up to the perimeter wire and gave himself up to the marines, fed up that after fourteen years of service another officer in his company had been promoted over him. He said an attack would come that night, and that after dealing with the Americans in Khe Sanh the People's Army would go east, liberate the whole of Quang Tri province, and strike at Hue. He gave details of enemy assembly areas and routes. Colonel Lownds quickly alerted Major General Rathvon Tonkins, commanding the U.S. 3rd Marine Division, and the Special Forces commander at Lang Vei. He also ordered the officer's club and the six "cinemas" that had sprouted up in Khe Sanh to be closed. (There was a choice of six movies every night.)

It looked as if the crunch was coming any minute now.

As predicted, Hill 861 was attacked just after midnight on 20 January. Within the hour it had been partially overrun. By 5:15 A.M. it had been counterattacked and cleared of enemy. Then at 5:30 A.M. rockets streaked out of the jungle and hit the combat base. Fifteen hundred tons of stockpiled ammunition detonated. The blast from the huge explosion flattened nearly all the buildings that had been erected in recent weeks, including the post office and the PX, and tumbled parked helicopters away skids over rotors. Shells, mortar bombs, rockets, and grenades rained down over the whole surface of the base and into foxholes and bunkers; some went off but most of them did not, because safety devices in the projectiles needed the tremendous G forces of acceleration in the barrel of a gun or mortar to unlock the fuses. Piles of stored gasoline went up with a huge crump, and black smoke columned up into the sky. In the dawn light, it looked to marines on the distant hills like the explosion of a small atomic bomb. Clouds of choking tear gas bellied up out of the inferno and quickly blanketed the base. As the marines fumbled their respirators on to their faces, some of them imagined hordes of Vietnamese advancing through the smoke. They did not come, but during the next few hours three hundred enemy shells did, crumping down into pools of flaming petrol. It was hell on earth.

Smoke rolled down into the valleys as Vietnamese, Bru, and Americans, startled out of their sleep, stared up at the sparkling pyrotechnic display in the sky. The marines on the nearby hills were sure they must now be on their own—Lownds and the rest had gone, for sure. But making contact with his subordinates by radio, Lownds reassured them: come what may, they were all going to hold on. Then as dawn came on 21 January the 8th Battalion of the 66th Regiment of the 304th Division attacked and took Khe Sanh village. Eighteen Americans died, forty were wounded. Now Lang Vei was cut off.

Up in the base the shattered troops began to take stock. Ninety percent of the ammunition—some ten thousand rounds in all—had gone off in the big bang. Urgent appeals went out over the air for more to be sent, and soon C-130s were being unloaded on the tarmac, bringing, in all, two hundred thousand pounds of ordnance to top up the reserves. Helicopters dragonfly'd in and out, bringing in medics and reinforcements, taking out the wounded (and even, as the days passed and a routine developed, men on Rest and Recuperation furlough.).

Soon after the battle began, the local civilians, in a panic, had fled toward the combat base, looking for food and shelter and safety— but in fact putting themselves in the line of fire. Around fifteen hundred of them congregated near the gates, huddled in what for a few days quickly became a makeshift, squalid camp. There were refugees from Laos—Ca tribesmen and women who had fled after an earlier fight across the border—there were whole Bru families, there were a few of the French men and women who had lived in Khe Sanh for years, and there were the missionaries and the nuns. Hopeless, they all crowded near the gates of the compound.

Inside, Lownds had quite enough to cope with. And besides, he had no way of knowing if some of the refugees were enemy disguised as friends. There was a horde of them and he could not afford to chance letting any of them in. In order to get rid of them, starting on the twenty-second he allowed 1,432 of them to board empty aircraft that had just delivered supplies and fly out to a quickly constructed temporary camp a few miles away. (As time passed many more refugees shambled away down Route 9.) The planes that disgorged the refugees then took on board men of the 1st Battalion of the 9th Regiment of marines and flew them in to Khe Sanh.

On 25 January Westmoreland decided he could not take the marine corps' attitude any longer and established a forward element of his own headquarters in I Corps area in the northern provinces preparatory to the army taking over control of what was happening at Khe Sanh. On the same day he tasked his staff to start planning Operation Pegasus for the relief of the base.

On 27 January 317 men of the 37th Ranger Battalion of the ARVN arrived in Khe Sanh, sent there as an afterthought because it suddenly struck the army staff in Saigon that they had forgotten to include any South Vietnamese soldiers in what Westmoreland had predicted was going to be "the most important battle of the war." Indicative of the lack of trust felt for the Army of the Republic, they were put outside the perimeter of the base, two hundred yards away to the east.

At this point in time, the head count of Americans under Lownds's command was 5,772 marines, 30 soldiers, 228 sailors, and 2 airmen. Appalled, the sailors and the airmen wondered how it was that they happened to be there: why them? Because that's the way it goes, the marines told them. Tough luck! Best start digging—and grab a rifle. (The sailors were Seabees from the Mobile Construction

Battalion that had upgraded the airfield and stayed on to improve the camp. The airmen relayed information from the sensors up to the orbiting planes.)

Half the garrison were inside the perimeter of the combat base. About a thousand marines had been sent to Rock Quarry—a mile away to the west. About a thousand were on Hill 558. Captain Dabney and India Company of the 3rd/26th were holding Hill 881 South, the most westerly U.S. position in Vietnam—the end of the line. (With artillery fire-control officers and signalers, there were some three hundred men there, and within a few days one hundred more would join them.) Captain Jasper and two hundred men of Company K of the 3rd/26th were holding Hill 861. Farther to the east fewer than fifty men guarded the signalers on Hill 950. And of course there were the Green Berets and the Montagnards in Lang Vei. In all, there were seven different defended positions.

Sure that it was only a matter of time, Lownds and the others prepared for the overwhelming assault. But it did not come. Instead, the next days, and then weeks, turned out to be a long, slogging artillery duel, interspersed with small-scale but intense infantry fighting.

In the combat base there were eighteen 105-mm howitzers and six 155-mm guns, twice as many heavy guns as the French had had at Dien Bien Phu. Every day the enemy fired two, three, five hundred shells into the base and at the surrounding hills. (The peak figure for enemy rounds in one day was 1,307.) Two-thirds of them came from the 152-mm guns of the 68th Regiment, which poked their muzzles out of caves on the face of Co Roc, seventeen miles away. Other guns, and mortars, were hidden in a fold of ground called the Horseshoe, closer in, only two thousand yards away from Hill 861 South. There, the men of India Company could see the mortars fire and warn the combat base that bombs were coming: "Arty, arty, Co Roc," would come the cry over the radio and in the compound a marine would press two wired beer-can lids together to complete a circuit and give warning through an old truck horn nailed to a tree. When it blared anybody caught out in the open had to dive for the nearest shelter—with not more than twenty seconds to make it. They called it the Khe Sanh shuffle.

Some days the guns in the combat base and those at Camp Carroll responded with ten rounds for every one fired by the enemy (up to two thousand a day) but though counter-battery officers tried desperately to locate and silence the enemy artillery they could not. As had happened at Dien Bien Phu, after a gun had fired it was pulled back into its heavily camouflaged shelter; roving planes could not find it, and ground observers were not near enough to see it. And besides, some of the PAVN artillery outranged the guns at Khe Sanh and were too far away to be hit by the heavies at Camp Carroll: even if they were seen they could not be hit.

At the beginning of February, radio signals emanating from a complex of caves on the other side of the border indicated that a major headquarters had been established twenty miles or so northwest of Khe Sanh—probably a force headquarters for the command and control of the assembled soldiers. A few days later rumors began to circulate that Giap had arrived there personally to supervise the final assault. In the hope of killing him, B-52s struck it hard, putting the radios out of action for two days. But Giap was not there. His army did not have helicopters, by which means he might have made a quick visit to the front, and in any case he could not afford to be away from the center point of military control in Hanoi, and from his many other, political, duties. And besides, it was not his place to be at Khe Sanh: he was no longer a field commander; he did not need to be there, and past experience had shown that he had good cause to be able to rely on those he had. (In a way it is a pity he was not there: if he had been there might now be a good account of the battle from the North Vietnamese point of view.)

The marines on the hills took the worst of the fighting. The enemy needed the hills before they could attack the base, and from time to time there were bitter engagements, though never massed assaults. Despite the fire directed at them and the bad visibility, helicopters flew in supplies, including water, day after day, often in underslung nets. Every morning on Hill 881 South, one of Dabney's men blew a bugle, then others raised the Stars and Stripes on a makeshift flagpole. (When press reports appeared that it had been shot to ribbons by shell and mortar splinters, American citizens sent fifty-two replacements through the mail. They were duly delivered.)

All the marines fought with great valor, under appalling conditions, but so did the North Vietnamese: according to Chaplain Ray W. Stubbe, who was with the marines "their fire- and camouflage-discipline was outstanding; and their bravery and tenacity." By the end of the first week of February one-tenth of the garrison had been killed or wounded, mostly by artillery fire, and in some ways Khe Sanh was beginning to resemble Dien Bien Phu. Blood there was at Khe Sanh, as there had been at Dien Bien Phu, and gaunt faces. And rain and mud and collapsing bunkers. And hunger. And the never-ending noise of explosions. There were bandages, bombs, and bullets at Khe Sanh; and cold food, wet feet, excrement, muck, and litter. And there were rats—scuttling all over the place, chewing filth, fighting for it, running over men's faces as they slept in their slits and shelters. And, too, there were approach trenches, creeping in closer every day. But there was also helicopter casualty-evacuation of wounded men: there was no blood-reeking lean-to hospital in Khe Sanh, though medics and pilots took a lot of casualties while getting the wounded away.

As had happened at Dien Bien Phu there were times when the garrison in Khe Sanh had to rely on parachute resupply, but for a different reason: not because of the threat from enemy AA gunners but because of the fog. For days on end it blanketed the runway, preventing planes and even helicopters from landing. It came every year at about this time, caused by warm air rising out of the eight hundred-foot-deep ravine at the end of the runway (in which flowed the river, the chief source of water for the base) meeting cold air coming down out of the mountains.

Because the USAF pilots could not see to land, they sometimes used LAPES. They also used the GPES—Ground Proximity Extraction System—whereby a hook dangling out of the back of a plane caught on arresting gear on the ground and dragged the pallet out of the back. However, these novel ideas could not cope with the demand, and in the end parachute drops kept the garrison going until the weather improved. Even then there were hazards for the pilots and crews: the prevailing winds fixed the line of approach of the planes, and farther down the valley enemy soldiers fired blind into the mist and occasionally made a hit.

Intelligence sources now indicated that some of the 320th Division had hooked eastward and were poised for an attack on Camp Carroll. If that fell the heavy artillery support from its 175-mm guns would cease to exist—and so, perhaps, would Khe Sanh base.

Rain and mist still blanketed the area, shells kept falling. In danger and squalor the marines gritted their teeth and hung on.

Then on 6 February at night the enemy overran Lang Vei, using tanks for the first time against U.S. forces, some of them crewed by women. (After the war it was established that they had been used once before in action, against a friendly Laotian government force a few miles away to the west.) On hearing the news a frisson of alarm shot through the staff in Saigon—here was a new dimension to warfare in Vietnam—but they need not have been unduly worried: the tanks could be easily destroyed by the hand-held antitank weapons already on issue to the marines in Khe Sanh. They were Chinese copies of Russian PT-76s, amphibious reconnaissance vehicles weighing only fourteen tons, lightly armored and in no way comparable to the heavy T-72s that were to be used by the PAVN a few years later. Nevertheless, they had a 76-mm gun and a 7.62-mm machine gun, and they helped to make mincemeat of the defenses at Lang Vei. Out of more than 400 defenders in the compound 316 died: 4 companies of Vietnamese soldiers, 3 reconnaissance platoons, one company of Bru irregulars, the Mobile Strike Force—161 Hre Montagnards—and 10 American Green Berets. Only 14 Americans and 60 Montagnards survived. It was a bloody disaster, made worse because, at night and far from the combat base, on the other side of the village, it was not possible to send a relief force to the rescue.

Up in the combat base and out on the hills they were sure it *had* to be their turn now, but still the attack did not come. The main reason was the B-52s.

There was no comparison between the French air support at Dien Bien Phu and the power of the American air armada: the French had had about two hundred planes, the Americans had more than two thousand—and a fleet of B-52s. Every three hours around the clock, day and night, from high above the bad weather, two cells of three B-52s dropped hundreds of bombs on suspected enemy positions. (Because at the time there was also bad weather over North Vietnam, three-quarters of the B-52s intended for Rolling Thunder operations were diverted to Khe Sanh as well. All were brought on target by a computer inside the base.) Including attacks by fighter-bombers, there was an air strike every five minutes on the North Vietnamese positions. Together, all these planes, every day, tripled the tonnage dropped on the peak day during World War II—with an explosive power equivalent to five Hiroshima bombs. The drops were so accurate that the bombs fell within two hundred yards of marine positions.

The B-52s came from Guam, U Tapao in Thailand, Kadena in Okinawa. The fighter-bombers came from all over—from the 1st Marine Air Wing, the 7th Air Force, the Strategic Air Command; from U.S. Navy Task Force 77, from South Vietnamese Air Force bases, and from American Army Aviation units. Thunderchiefs, Phantoms, Sky Hawks, Intruders, Crusaders, and Skyraiders blasted the jungle around the combat base. The planes spread defoliants too, and for miles around the jungle soon became a wasteland of dying vegetation and shattered trees.

The PAVN troops were not able to mount attacks because their plans were constantly disrupted: because all points of reference on the landscape were obliterated and people could not find their way; because platoons and companies of men moving toward the form-ing-up points for attacks were blown sky-high before they ever got there; because the cover behind the start lines had been removed by defoliants, leaving the men bare and wide open to artillery fire. Anywhere within two miles of the defended positions PAVN soldiers could only cower in their earth scrapes and wait for the holocaust to stop. (Fortunately for those farther back the effect of the attacks was reduced considerably because somewhere in the system for tasking the bombers there were communist spies who passed information to Hanoi about the destinations and timings of raids. When received, the warnings were quickly passed down the line, and wherever pos-sible troops took shelter in the caves that honeycombed the hillsides. It was not until after the war that the existence of these under-ground complexes was discovered, though any of the Bru Montag-nards who lived at Khe Sanh could have told the marines about them. One of them tried to but was turned away because it was thought he was a Vietnamese.)

Around 10 February Giap withdrew five battalions—two from the 29th Regiment of the 325thC Division and three from the 24th Regiment of the 304th Division—to relieve the pressure on the PLAF besieged in Hue.

On the night of 29 February a battalion of the 304th Division assaulted the 37th ARVN Rangers at the eastern edge of the camp. The three attacks made by this force during the night were the fiercest of the siege but, it turned out, were a diversion to cover the imminent withdrawal of all People's Army troops from Khe Sanh.

On that day, the fortieth day of the siege, the last day of February, a Leap Year February—thousands of marines were bemoaning the extra day they would have to spend in Vietnam—some approach trenches had come to within one hundred yards of the defended positions. During the next week they crept closer and closer. But there were not many of them—nothing like the maze of trenches that had been dug at Dien Bien Phu. There, Giap had impressed local labor to help the soldiers by relieving them of some of the physical effort; here, there were only the soldiers: they couldn't fight and dig at the same time. And try to dodge the bombs.

With the marines still waiting tensely for the final assault, on 6 March Giap's troops got up and stumbled away through what was left of the jungle. It was forty-seven days since they had attacked, and now, suddenly, they had gone. To Lownds and his men their departure was inexplicable—as was the fact that the enemy had failed to contaminate the one and only source of water for the combat base, the river at the bottom of the ravine. Had they done so, it is possible that the extra logistic load might have affected the outcome. Nobody thought of it for some time, and when they did they thought the Americans, with their huge airlift capability, would get water in somehow.

India Company, which had defended Hill 881 South, took 167 casualties out of a starting strength of 185, but they had been holding the dirty end of the stick. Generally, casualties were light, though not as light as the published figures indicated. Officially, 205 Americans died at Khe Sanh—30 men a week, a much lighter loss rate than was incurred during the Tet battles or at Hue. However, Chaplain Stubbe said he counted 475 marines zipped into green plastic body bags. Also, the figure of 205 does not take into account those killed in the relief operation, or the Green Berets who died nearby. Or the Bru and Hre who died beside them. Or the men of the ARVN Ranger battalion who were outside the compound. Or the 49 Americans who died in a plane crash. In total there must have been well over 600. And then, too, there were hundreds of Laotians and other refugees, and uncounted numbers of Bru who lived in the jungle, victims of the bombing. Based on army intelligence estimates, General Westmoreland had said that the country around Khe Sanh was "virtually uninhabited," but that was not so. Padre Stubbe estimated that 5,000 Bru must have died during the battle.

The official assessment of enemy dead was 1,602, but only 117 rifles and 39 crew-operated weapons were recovered on the battlefield. However, there must have been hundreds—perhaps thousands—of men blown away by the bombs who left no traces of ever having existed: were just pounded into shreds and mixed in with the mud and shattered foliage. In Saigon the staff said that between ten and fifteen thousand had been killed, but that was probably a high estimate.

On 23 March the president announced that General Westmoreland would be returning to the United States to become army chief of staff.

On 15 April, seventy-seven days after the siege began, Khe Sanh was relieved by a force that got through by road. Westmoreland says he "waited until the weather patterns were favorable before committing the relief force; meanwhile we were attriting Giap's troops all the time." During that operation 130 casualties were incurred: 51 marines, 46 soldiers, and 33 men of the Army of the Republic. They too were all attributable to the battle of Khe Sanh.

According to an eyewitness, Major General John J. Tolson, commander of the 1st Air Cavalry Division, who arrived with the relieving force, Khe Sanh "was a very distressing sight, completely unpoliced, strewn with rubble, duds and damaged equipment, and with troops living a life more similar to rats than human beings." Another observer said, "The trees were gone, everything was gone. The place was pockmarked and ruined and burnt . . . like the surface of the moon." And another summed it up: "It was all rubble, bodies, nothing . . ."

On 17 June the combat base at Khe Sanh was bulldozed flat and its bunkers destroyed so that at some future date the enemy would not be able to take propaganda pictures of it. Every vestige of its existence was removed until there was only a scar of red soil on the plateau to show where it had been.

Some people asked why, if it had been so important, it had been given up. Most were just glad it was all over.

Giap makes these comments about the battle:

> Khe Sanh was not that important to us. Or it was only to the extent that it was to the Americans. It was the focus of attention in the United States because their prestige was at stake, but to us it was part of the greater battle that would begin after Tet. It was only a diversion, but one to be exploited if we could cause many casualties and win a big victory.
>
> As long as they stayed in Khe Sanh to defend their prestige they said it was important; when they abandoned it they said it had never been important.

No, Khe Sanh was not that important to Giap. What was important was that he had a force of about thirty-five thousand soldiers on the south side of the demilitarized zone, poised ready to exploit the aftermath of the Tet Offensive; and, after it failed, able to sustain a controlled siege that pinned down troops and planes needed by the Americans elsewhere. If his soldiers had been able to snuff out the marines, so much the better. When it became apparent that Phase Three—Second Wave—would not be possible, and that the B-52s were preventing a successful assault, Giap cut his losses and ordered some of his troops to relieve the pressure on the PLAF in Hue and the remainder of them to retire back into the sanctuary of the Trail.

Westmoreland has been criticized for making the decision to stand and fight at Khe Sanh. His justifications for doing so are quite clear and logical, but even more important, what would have happened if he had not done so? Possibly Giap's force around Khe Sanh would have swung eastward and reinforced the PLAF in Hue. Perhaps that would then have turned out to be a decisive battle like Dien Bien Phu.

Westmoreland, like many other people, criticizes Giap for accepting so many casualties. He says "Giap was callous. He took thousands of casualties without a thought. Had any American general taken such losses he would not have lasted three weeks." But in both the French and the American wars Giap was obliged to accept casualties to compensate for his lack of equivalent firepower: it was a matter of men balanced against material, but if losses were not balanced by results he called off the action.

Compared to other wars American casualties in Vietnam were very light. (And considerably fewer than the French sustained during the Indochina War.) Thirty-six thousand men died during the Seven Days battles of the American Civil War. The British took sixty thousand casualties on the opening day of the Battle of the Somme in 1916, nearly twenty thousand of them dead men. The very same regiment of U.S. marines that was at Khe Sanh, the 26th, suffered twenty-six thousand casualties in an assault against the Japanese during World War II. But attitudes had changed: rampant jingoism was no longer believable; and in the Great War and World War II television broadcasting did not exist—had it, those wars might not have lasted as long as they did.

Also, American and North Vietnamese attitudes to battle casualties were very different. The U.S. military were pressured to avoid them by politicians at home because pictures of coffins lined up on the runway of a South Vietnamese airfield waiting to be loaded for the return flight generated a near-hysterical reaction in the American viewing audience. On the other hand, Giap and the people of the North accepted deaths as part of the price they had to pay. And there was no television in the North.

In America, as the sight and sound of the Tet battles faded from the screens so did the barrage of media coverage about Khe Sanh. After weeks of anxiety, the public realized with relief that the battle was over: not won, exactly, but not lost.

CHAPTER TWENTY-TWO

DISINTEGRATION

We fought year after year in extremely hard conditions which went beyond all imagination—but we continued to live, to work, and to fight.

—PHAM VAN DONG

I t was in the spring of 1968 that two more people became victims of the Vietnam war, and in a sense of Vo Nguyen Giap. One was William Childs Westmoreland.

General Westmoreland has been criticized for making three major mis-appreciations about how to conduct the war. As he put it,

"With their large air-mobile capacity, with their extensive communications and flexible logistic support systems, above all with their tremendous firepower, it was vastly more desirable that Americans fight in the remote unpopulated areas if the enemy desired to give battle there." But other people did not agree. "The real war is among the people, not the mountains," said General Krulak, commander of all U.S. marines in the Pacific. Giap was of the same opinion. Also, Westmoreland's search-and-destroy strategy—which had failed the French—together with his concern about the infiltration routes, dispersed American forces all over South Vietnam and left them open to attack while ensuring that he was unable to concentrate their power if and when a decisive opportunity to smash the enemy presented itself. Furthermore, his concept of widening the war by taking it into the North, a 1960s version of the 1950s landing at Inchon in Korea, which had outflanked the enemy, was by no means a sure thing. There, UN forces had not had to contend with a force like the Vietcong attacking their troops and bases. Giap said of the idea that "Attacking the North means opening another large battlefield. American forces would become more scattered and would be annihilated more easily." It was never put to the test.

Westmoreland says he would have needed at least three times as many troops as he had at the peak of U.S. deployment to have guaranteed the integrity of the frontier in such a way as to force Giap to fight the battle in the conventional mode, one that Giap had no hope of winning. (That is, about a million and a half men.) Westmoreland did not ask for them because it would have been pointless: he could never have got approval to deploy such numbers, given U.S. worldwide commitments and the feelings of Congress and the people. Consequently, it was only along the DMZ that there was partial linear defense; in the rest of South Vietnam, he was obliged to fight a fluid war.

But Westmoreland did a lot to bring modern technology to the battlefield. He used strategic bombers for the first time in the tactical mode, persuading the air force generals to allow B-52s to be used for the close support of troops. Backed by McNamara, he developed the Huey Cobra and other helicopters into airborne gun platforms that could give lethal support to the infantry. In fact, he brought fire and movement to the battlefield in a way that had never been seen before.

As regards Khe Sanh, no man could have done more to ensure that Giap did not achieve a victory there than Westmoreland. He never doubted that it could be held, but to make sure he kept his finger on the pulse of action twenty hours a day. For two months he slept on an iron cot in the Combat Operations Center in Saigon, on call even during his short rest periods. Day after day he lived and breathed Khe Sanh: making decisions, being briefed, writing reports for the president, watching the development of events, personally targeting the B-52s. And for a lot of the time fighting the Tet battle as well. It was a superhuman effort, especially coming as it did after nearly four years of dealing with the politicians in Washington and Saigon, with the generals in the Pentagon, with recalcitrant U.S. Marine Corps generals in Vietnam, with Admiral Ulysses S. Grant Sharp, his boss in the Pacific Arena, and with air force generals all over the place. He had somehow brought it all together.

Today, he says that Khe Sanh was not as important as the battles of the Tet Offensive, which "the American people should have realized was a major victory," but that given the same circumstances he would fight there again. "Khe Sanh *was* an important battle in the sense that if we had not held it Giap's divisions would have pushed on and mingled with the people in the coastal plain. As it was, they got wrapped around Khe Sanh and we destroyed them with our air power."

Westmoreland was in command of gigantic forces for far longer than other famous American generals, such as Patton; and his was a command made even more difficult because some of the information provided for him by the intelligence agencies was highly suspect and misleading. For example, the statistics of air targets eliminated were sometimes ludicrously off the mark: it was claimed by the USAF that they had destroyed 179 railroad switching yards in North Vietnam. How could there possibly be 179 such installations in a few hundred miles of what was predominantly single-track line?

Vietnam had been Westmoreland's hope for a place in the pantheon of America's great military leaders. It was not to be. Though President Johnson had decided some time before Giap started his

1967/68 campaign that Westmoreland should become the army chief of staff, the timing of the announcement of his appointment, coming as it did in the aftermath of Tet and the battle for Khe Sanh, was interpreted by many people as meaning that he was being "kicked upstairs"—being seen off the premises with as little loss of face as possible. Even though that was not the case, he certainly did not leave Vietnam on a high. Effectively, his long and devoted service ended in failure, though he went on to become America's top soldier. Here was no victor coming home full of pride to a ticker-tape welcome down the concrete canyons of New York but a disheartened man who through the coming years would try to pinpoint the reasons why things had gone wrong. It had been a sad episode, and not only for him. As he says, "The young American soldier had to bear the burden of not having the support of the American people."

Like Navarre, Westmoreland had come up against the implacable. Like Navarre, he had tried desperately to find a way around a military problem that was basically insoluble because of *dau tranh:* he could never win so long as the North Vietnamese people were determined to continue the fight; he could never win because the cost of such a war, in lives, money and conscience, once apparent, proved to be unacceptable to the people of the United States. Like Navarre, Westmoreland took a lot of the blame. Someone had to . . .

Westmoreland's generals were simple, dedicated servicemen who, unlike their main adversary, did not realize just how vital public opinion was; did not understand that they had to show respect toward the people they were fighting for—and with—and thus gain their full support; did not comprehend that politics are the taproot of warfare. But even if they had, they could have done nothing about it; military men in the West do what their politicians tell them to do, whereas Giap was unique in the Vietnam war—and indeed in the twentieth century—in having a foot firmly in both camps. He could make the policy—or at least steer it in the direction he wanted—and then implement it.

As most soldiers in his situation would do, Westmoreland thought he could win if only he were given more resources. But even a 20-percent increase in combat effectiveness, in the number of troops actively seeking out the enemy, might have made a significant difference. Instead, the American way of making war meant that most of the soldiers and marines in Vietnam were guarding or administering each other. Almost 3 million soldiers were to go to "Nam" over the years, but of that number a surprising small proportion were ever at the cutting edge of the war. The official proportion of 45 percent support troops is a misleading statistic because many men in combat units spent their time providing the American life-style for their buddies—running the PXs, the cinemas, the clubs. Every week seven thousand of them left Vietnam to go on R&R. In consequence, at any given time only an estimated 5 percent were actively seeking out the enemy.

Giap recognized that "pacification was a threat to the progress of the war in the South," but winning the hearts and minds of the South Vietnamese never featured as high among U.S. priorities as it should have done. The attitude of most military men was summed up for all time in the immortal words of the American general who was quoted as saying "Grab 'em by the balls and their hearts and minds will follow." To make matters worse, back home the politicians slowly lost the hearts and minds of their own people, led by the other victim of the war, Lyndon Baines Johnson.

After the siege began, President Johnson's personal popularity ratings plummeted; but worse than that, 50 percent of the population now said that they did not approve of the war and only 35 percent did. He was haunted by visions of a second Dien Bien Phu. Whatever happened, Khe Sanh must not fall. Feeling that if he took a greater personal interest in what went on there he might be able to influence events favorably, he had a sand-table model of Khe Sanh and its environs built in the basement War Room of the White House and at all hours of the day and night would prowl around it, sometimes in a bathrobe: frowning at it, asking questions about it, demanding frequent updates on the situation. For weeks he went there night after night, obsessed with what was happening, taking his role as the commander in chief of the armed forces of the United States literally, and like other politicians in other places before him interfering with his generals' plans by making big military decisions that were not properly his to make. On 27 January, in an unprecedented step, he had insisted that each of the Joint Chiefs of Staff should individually assess whether Khe Sanh could hold out, and reassure him on the point—"in blood," as he reportedly put it. On the twenty-ninth he got his paper guarantee, signed by them all, that it could. (How he would have responded if they had said it could not is open to conjecture.)

In February 1968 the impact of those television pictures of Saigon and Hue across the whole of the continental United States brought about the biggest reaction yet to the war—and put Johnson hard up against the rock on the question of whether he could continue to spend lives and money on it. Already, because of the financial pressures generated by the war, he had had to defer the social programs that were so dear to his heart—his dream of a Great American Society. He had achieved a lot: votes for black people, one hundred years after Lincoln signed the Emancipation Act; the Medicare Program for the elderly; the Headstart education program for the disadvantaged—but he felt it was not enough. In order to try somehow to balance the war and the dream, he did not tell the American people what was really happening in Vietnam—the numbers committed, the degree of involvement. He did not even tell Congress what it was costing. But in the end, as such things will, it all came out.

On 14 February the administration had allocated $32 billion for war expenditure in 1969. On the fifteenth the USAF reported the loss of the eight hundredth aircraft over Vietnam. On the twentieth the Senate Foreign Relations Committee began a public inquiry to try to determine whether the Tonkin Gulf incident had been an American excuse to broaden the conflict or a North Vietnamese mistake interpreted as an act of war. (Its findings were inconclusive.) On that very day a report had arrived saying that two reinforcing PAVN divisions were moving toward Khe Sanh; that night the attack on Hill 881 South began. Then on the twenty-second Westmoreland's staff announced the highest weekly total of American combat deaths ever during the war: 543 of them. The next day the secretary of defense told him that more soldiers would be needed in Vietnam. To provide them all would have meant calling out the National Guard, which was not a feasible proposition with so much antiwar feeling in the nation. (Westmoreland had asked for the specific units he would need if approval were given to his plan to widen the conflict by striking into Laos and north of the DMZ, and for about 20,000 more to maintain the status quo if it were not. The Pentagon quoted a figure of 206,000, but Westmoreland says that the Chiefs of Staff had arrived at this number in order to rebuild the strategic reserve. "Nowhere," he told me, "will you find a piece of paper with my name on it asking for 206,000 more troops.") On 26 March the president called a meeting of the *Wise* Men, his trusted elders of the nation. Among others, the group comprised Dean Acheson, George Ball, Henry Cabot Lodge, McGeorge Bundy, and retired generals Omar Bradley, Matthew Ridgway, and Maxwell Taylor. It became apparent that they had all ceased to support the war effort: he was the last believer.

Lyndon Johnson was worn out by it all. In a television address to the nation on 31 March 1968 he announced a halt to the air and naval bombardment of North Vietnam, and at the end of his speech said that he would not seek re-election. Three days later Hanoi agreed to open negotiations, and on 13 May peace talks began in Paris. Richard Milhous Nixon took office as president in January 1969.

On 3 September 1969 Ho Chi Minh died in Hanoi, aged seventy-nine. In his testament he had asked that his body should be cremated and some of the ashes enshrined in Hanoi, Hue, and Saigon, in the three principal cities of Vietnam, so that he could remain forever with all his people. Instead, his body was embalmed and then exhibited to shuffling millions of visitors in a glass coffin inside a huge, pink-marble mausoleum in Hanoi, guarded day and night by picked soldiers. By doing this in a sense the Party kept him alive, the symbol of all its endeavors and achievements, a center of veneration. In his place Le Duan became first among equals in the clique that ruled North Vietnam after his death. Ton Duc Thang became the second president of the Democratic Republic, but it was an empty sinecure for him, as it was to be for his successors. Ho remains the venerated father figure.

After years of idolatory Ho's death brought great grief and loud lamentation, but it was a means by which the Party stiffened the resolve of the nation to continue the fight: it was what he would have wanted, the people were told; the least they could do would be to obey his deathbed wishes.

As America became more and more involved in the war, the number of people who thought their government was in the wrong increased. To many Americans it was intolerable that their great nation should be involved in a war that seemed to be exceptionally cruel. Vietnam was being laid waste by bombing and defoliation. Out there, every day, people were being assassinated, tortured, shelled, napalmed.

On 2 November 1965 a young Quaker by the name of Norman Morrison, following the example of Buddhist monks who had done the same thing in Saigon in protest against Diem's policies, had burned himself to death outside the Pentagon in Washington. A week later a member of the Catholic Workers Movement, Roger Allen La Porte, set fire to himself outside the United Nations building in New York. On 27 November thirty-five thousand protestors had marched silently past the White House. Week after week protest marches straggled through towns and cities bearing antiwar banners and chanting antiwar slogans. In November 1967 another estimated thirty-five thousand antiwar demonstrators besieged the Pentagon. In the months to come as unrest continued in university campuses around the nation, effigies of leading figures were burned, including General Westmoreland's. "We, the People" were having their belated say in American policies.

In June 1969 President Nixon announced that American troops would start to withdraw from Vietnam. A month later he unveiled a new doctrine: in the future the United States would honor its treaty obligations and continue to provide a nuclear shield and military and economic aid but would look to the nation directly threatened to assume primary responsibility for providing the manpower for its defense. It was the first step toward finding a way out of the Vietnam straitjacket.

In November 1969 a quarter of a million people gathered in Washington to protest against the war. In May 1970 regular troops had to be called out to deal with a demonstration by one hundred thousand angry dissenters. At Kent State University campus in Ohio National Guardsmen fired into the crowd and killed four students. And also in May Congress repealed the Tonkin Gulf Resolution that in 1964 had given half-hearted authorization for the pursuance of the war. With the military unable to win it, with increasingly large numbers of people vociferously condemning it, and with Congress backing off, President Nixon had to act. In July 1970 he started to implement a four-part strategy to disengage the United States from Vietnam: America would increase aid for the ARVN; make greater efforts toward pacification; withdraw U.S. forces as "Vietnamization" and pacification began to succeed; and also, by diplomatic initiatives, would try to isolate North Vietnam from Russia and China at the same time as peace talks were conducted with Hanoi.

General Creighton W. Abrams, who had taken over from West-moreland in mid 1968, arranged for the withdrawal of U.S. forces to be done in fourteen stages. In quick response to the president's decision to pull out, the first twenty-five thousand left almost immediately. Another thirty-five thousand went in September and another fifty thousand in December. On 20 April 1970 President Nixon announced that another one hundred and fifty thousand would go, leaving only a quarter of a million by the spring of 1971. In an escalating surge of departure, by 1 May 1972 only sixty-nine thousand would be left. The final batch would depart between 1 September and 30 November 1972.

Immediately following the announcement of U.S. withdrawal the scene in Vietnam changed radically. For Giap and his Politburo colleagues in the North, it was a gift: now they knew for certain that they had only to wait and they would win. In the South, the people and their army faced the future with apprehension, but to the U.S. military it was almost a death blow: there is no better way to undermine morale than to announce that there can be no victory. To soldiers, what then is the point of risking their lives? But in Washington Nixon had no choice but to prolong their departure: American troops could not leave until it was felt that the Army of the Republic had built up enough strength to withstand the threat from the North, and that would take time.

Thus it was that the South lost the fight, rather than that Giap and his troops won it, as they had the Indochina War. Then, Dien Bien Phu had been the final coup de grace, after which the French had had no option but to withdraw. In the South there was no decisive end to the war one way or another, only a progressive loss of faith, by both the people of the United States and the South Vietnamese. As the American army withdrew, what was left of it disintegrated, as did the Army of the Republic by its side, leaving the South wide open to eventual takeover by the North.

During the months that the numbers of American servicemen decreased those remaining became more and more demoralized. New arrivals walked into a dispirited, querelous, mutinous atmosphere and in their turn became disaffected. As the contagion spread discipline became an almost forgotten word, and in many units anarchy took the place of an ordered military structure. The army seethed with discontent: at one time or another 245 different antiwar publications were written, printed, and distributed by GIs.

The decision to withdraw was not the only cause of the unrest. In comparison to their opponents, U.S. servicemen, professional, courageous, and proud of their traditions though so many of them were, were not motivated to the same degree. They may have been trained to be physically tough and technically proficient, but mentally they did not have the same edge, partly because many of them were not convinced that they were fighting for their country in the same direct way as their fathers had in previous wars. But a bigger factor in the blunting of their keenness was that all of them, except some of the Special Forces operating deep in the jungle, lived what was known as "American-style," with everything they needed to achieve that high standard transported to them by sea and air over thousands of miles. The generals and the politicians were proud of this, but in fact it was the root cause of many of their problems.

Bomber crews would leave luxurious air-conditioned bases in Thailand, the Philippines, Vietnam itself, fly sometimes nerve-racking missions and then come back to comfort and normality. Sailors never saw the war at close quarters. Even the soldiers and marines who were the cutting blade of the war lived rough for only fleeting periods of time and after riding back in their helicopters from a firefight could eat steaks, fries, ice cream, and drink cold Coke. Even in the midst of battle iced beer would sometimes appear, heliborne, out of the skies. (Army engineers built 2.5 million cubic feet of refrigerated stores in the big bases.) A colonel was given a Silver Star bravery award for delivering frozen turkeys by helicopter to a Special Forces camp on Thanksgiving Day. In some officers' clubs the air conditioning was so sharp they had to build fireplaces. For some servicemen, there were barbecues on Sunday. For nearly all of them TV all year round, a movie every night if they wanted to see one. How could they concentrate on waging war when their senses were dulled by physical overindulgence and mental make-believe? The stark contrast between real life, with its long-term stresses and occasional bursts of blood and guts, and the artificiality of their existence was too much for many servicemen to reconcile mentally and was a major reason why large numbers of them suffered psychological traumas, both during and after the war.

General Westmoreland says that amenities were provided for his troops in order to sustain morale, to keep them off the streets and prevent their free-spending from adversely affecting the shaky South Vietnamese economy; but the never-ending expenditure on easy living was unreasonably profligate. When American servicemen finally quit Vietnam they left behind them 71 swimming pools, 160 craft shops, 90 service clubs, 159 basketball courts, 30 tennis courts, 55 softball fields, 85 volleyball fields, 2 bowling alleys, 357 libraries. And there were post exchange shops full of jewelry, perfumes, lingerie, booze. As someone put it, it was like a walk down Fifth Avenue.

And, too, there was the night life. The arrival of American troops, well paid, ready to spend, destroyed the morality of most South Vietnamese, who became avid to make money, eager to forget the ethics of their ancestors. In Saigon in 1966 an estimated thirty thousand war-orphaned child prostitutes—and the rest—catered to every variation of the basic need; around the big bases trailer camps full of them could hardly cope with the demand. One in every four American soldiers contracted veneral disease. On top of that the climate hospitalized thousands with malaria and other tropical ailments—not to mention the toll taken by drug abuse. Only 17 percent of those admitted to hospitals were battle casualties. The use of drugs became epidemic. By 1970 marijuana was being smoked by 58 percent of GIs, heroin was being injected by 22 percent, and hallucinogenics were being swallowed by 14 percent. In 1971 fewer than 5,000 soldiers needed hospital treatment for combat wounds, but 20,529 were treated for serious drug abuse.

Soft living was not the only problem. Army officers did only six months with a front-line unit—effectively five months, after deducting time for settling-in and R&R. They would arrive on normal scheduled airline flights from the United States, step off an air-conditioned plane, and quite often be told by a pretty air hostess to "Have a nice war!"—which they might or might not do, depending on the luck of the draw. Starting their tours of duty they were often far less experienced than some of the kid soldiers they commanded—their average age was nineteen, they were scarcely more than boys. After doing their five months—too short a period of time for them to get to know their men adequately—the officers would move on to work on the staff or in ARVN training units.

Soldiers served 365 days in Vietnam; the marines served thirteen months. To the day. Their date of estimated return from overseas—their DEROS—was imprinted on their minds and by some stenciled on their helmets—sometimes even gouged into the sides of their foxholes with a sharp stone. The authorized one-year's service for soldiers was the shortest duty tour of any war in the nation's history. (General Westmoreland had "hoped the one-year tour would extend the nation's staying power by forestalling public pressure to 'bring the boys home.'") They were "trickle-posted" to replace outgoing soldiers, which meant that units never achieved the feeling of corporate unity that is essential to good morale, the feeling of buoyant mutual support and comradeship that comes from working for months and years with the same people.

Another reason for low morale was that the method of conscription was unfair to blacks, hispanics, and poor whites. People with money and influence, especially WASPS—white, Anglo-Saxon Protestants, the core makers of American policy—could avoid the draft in several ways, mostly by invoking on-going further education as an excuse for postponing service. Blacks, who in the 1960s were agitating for civil rights, found the unfairness of the draft a source of further contention, which added to disaffection in the ranks. Martin Luther King declared that "negroes are dying in disproportionate numbers in Vietnam" and urged that black Americans should declare themselves to be conscientious objectors. In fact, they comprised 13 percent of the troop force in Vietnam, less than the proportion of blacks in the nation, but a disproportionate number of them, 28 percent, ended up in combat units.

In an attempt to stop the rot, officers were relieved of their command if their soldiers disobeyed them, so they avoided giving orders that might cause offense, especially if they were likely to result in risk to life. And if they did insist, they were likely to be killed. Either shot—usually in the back during operations against the enemy—or by the explosion of a fragmentation grenade tossed into their bivouac or vehicle. An exploded grenade left no fingerprints. Between 1969 and 1971 there were 730 "fraggings," as a result of which eighty-three officers were killed. Sadly, they were often the best, the ones who were trying to maintain discipline. Their next-of-kin were not told how they had died, of course: they thought they had laid down their lives bravely in combat—which, in a sense they had.

Throughout the war, in an attempt to keep up morale, the U.S. army had resorted to that old bait, used ever since men banded together to fight in an organized way—the award of medals. As Napoleon once said, "A bolt of ribbon can win many wars." Medals on the chest are meant to count for something, to show gallantry or merit, but over-issuing medals in Vietnam debased the whole coinage. During the war the army awarded more than a million and a quarter bravery medals—800,000 of them air medals—in comparison with only 55,258 in Korea. And the numbers increased as the combat effort declined: 416,693 in 1968 when there were 14,592 Americans killed in action, 522,905 in 1970 when only 3,946 were killed.

Another factor that perniciously pervaded the scene in South Vietnam was the Phoenix Program.

In the years up to 1968 several American and South Vietnamese intelligence agencies were active but uncoordinated. In an attempt to correct this and improve the security forces' knowledge of the guerrilla infrastructure, the CIA instigated, and financed, a control system code-named "Phoenix." Somehow the CIA wanted to infiltrate the communist cadres and supporters who riddled the South and get a grip on the windpipe of the Vietcong.

Phoenix began with the issue of identity cards so that people could be traced, one of the main aims originally being that U.S. aid would get to the right people. Information on the cards was progressively entered into computer data banks until eventually some 8 million names were recorded in Saigon. Next, Phoenix offices were established at district and provincial level, each with an American adviser, often seconded from army intelligence. In a way Phoenix mirrored the communists' own cellular and administrative structure —low-level units working upward to a centralized control point.

The idea was that collated information would be used to enlarge access into the Vietcong network, which would in turn provide more information, which would give greater leverage to anti-VC operations, which would then provide more information and so on, eventually resulting in the security forces eating away the insurgency infrastructure from the inside and killing it. That was the theory, and as was usually the case with U.S. initiatives it was logical and worthy. But as Americans who themselves worked for the organization said, Phoenix became "the vehicle by which we [the United States] got into a bad genocide program."

From information gathered from the central computers and from local sources, the Phoenix offices tasked their provincial reconnaissance units on the ground. "Hit teams," South Vietnamese police working with—and run by—U.S. Special Forces, then scoured towns and villages for suspects, arrested them, and took them to one of the eighty Phoenix interrogation centers for questioning. The system was often random in its selection of victims yet once they were arrested was ruthlessly systematic in their execution.

Each sector office was issued different printed forms that were filled in according to whether the suspected communist was thought to be a leader, a cadre, or just a follower. One of the problems, though, was that nobody defined exactly what a communist was, and therefore any contact admitted by a suspect, whether voluntarily offered or coerced, and however remote, was taken as punishable guilt and therefore an excuse for more coercion. Given the circumstances in Vietnam at that time almost everyone was bound to have some contact with the insurgency infrastructure, so almost everyone, pressured enough, was sure to admit it.

If the suspect was classified as only a follower, then the CIA was officially not interested and the suspect, man or woman, was meant to be released. If the suspect was thought to be a leader or cadre, they were supposed to be dealt with judicially. In fact, nobody who was taken for questioning to one of the Phoenix interrogation centers ever came out alive. In sworn testimony before a Senate hearing in 1971, an American who worked on the program said, "I never knew in the course of all those operations a detainee to live through an interrogation. They all died. There was never any reasonable fact that any one of those individuals was in fact cooperating with the Vietcong. But they all died."

The use of torture in Phoenix interrogation centers was routine, and though some people succumbed from prolonged hardship most people died immediately and directly from its effects. Phoenix, instead of being an intelligence-gathering system, became an execution machine. An ex-Phoenix operator thinks that maybe thirty thousand people died. But that is only an estimate of the number who expired directly at the hands of the system's executioners. Thousands died indirectly. For example, a sector office, often on the basis of totally unconfirmed and uncorroborated "evidence," would report that a suspected VC was going to be in a particular village at a specified time; in response, a B-52 strike would eliminate the whole place and everyone in it.

Phoenix was a tragic and appalling episode. Some of the American soldiers who had been told to go out and win the hearts and minds of the Vietnamese people lost their own. Everywhere in South Vietnam it was a bleak picture, and as time went on the acronym for Search And Destroy took on a new meaning; now to many of the soldiers the whole business of American involvement in the war was "SAD."

It was not only the American army that was going through a bad time.

After 1954 the Army of the Republic of South Vietnam declined badly because U.S. aid ceased when the French departed. Moribund and lazy and ignoring the tactical lessons of the Indochina War, the army kept to the main roads and avoided the villages, thus leaving the villagers wide open to Vietcong influence and inviting ambush attacks on themselves. At its peak, the ARVN and the South Vietnamese Air Force and Navy numbered half a million men (together with regional and popular force nonregular troops, there were over a million South Vietnamese in uniform), but like the country as a whole, they were badly organized and badly led. The peasants in the lower ranks were centuries distant from their officers from the urban middle class. Everyone was very poorly paid: an ARVN soldier got one-sixteenth the pay of a GI; an ARVN colonel got seventy dollars a month but an interpreter working for the Americans got three hundred dollars.

The Americans expected great results from their efforts but got poor ones because many of the ARVN soldiers and officers, contemptuous of their government, beset by doubts, open to social pressures, fearful of the future, did not really believe in what they were fighting for. Also, to them, belief in what astrologers told them was perfectly natural whereas to Americans it was incomprehensible and contemptible. Unwilling to engage the enemy if the signs were not propitious, wary of casualties—but suffering them nonetheless—their operations came to be scathingly described by Americans as "Search and Avoid." It was a vicious circle: poor results brought lack of confidence, which brought bad morale, which brought poor results. Another factor was that, as General Westmoreland says, "The territorial nature of those units made them dislike moving away from their families on operations. If, to circumvent that problem, their families were sent into the same area with them, they too hated it."

Discipline was lax because seniors were reluctant to punish in case their juniors had political connections. Senior officers sold off U.S. equipment on the black market, embezzled, exploited prostitution, dealt in drugs. Lower ranks bullied and robbed the population. Considered too unreliable and inefficient for joint operations with American and other Allied troops, they were relegated to "pacification" duties, working in the countryside to keep the Vietcong at bay and encourage the villagers to support the government. But of course in that situation they themselves were wide open to Vietcong propaganda: ARVN soldiers were called on to turn their guns against the U.S. troops or hand them over to the People's Liberation Armed Forces; all units that defected en masse would be rewarded and their commanders given responsible positions in the PLAF. Thousands of them took the bait: in 1966 desertions in the army exceeded one hundred thousand. Some of them were men who had decided to join their brothers in the PLAF—for, as had been happening for decades now, families were torn apart when the communists abducted one son in the night and maybe days later government agents conscripted another.

Bad morale also affected the highest echelons of the South Vietnamese government. One-time President Nguyen Cao Ky, an air force major general who was one of the military men who followed Diem (and after the war was to run a liquor store in California), went on record as saying: "Every time the Press wanted to know about the war they asked the Americans, but never the leaders of South Vietnam. The Communists in the North regarded us as puppets, but then so did the people of the United States."

By 1967 the U.S. command considered the ARVN to be 80 percent ineffective. Indeed, they were so much distrusted that in General Westmoreland's headquarters in Saigon there were hidden nozzles that could spray the "elite" ARVN honor guard with tear gas should they suddenly defect. Only the Americans knew where the gas masks were kept. Asked about his own attitudes to the Army of the Republic, Westmoreland told me, "I like the Vietnamese. I think they are good people, hard-working, energetic, the smartest of all the oriental people. The problem with the ARVN was the leadership; there were just not enough competent officers."

Giap himself saw the ARVN as puppets, forced to serve the regime by conscription or economic necessity, and therefore not motivated soldiers. Nevertheless for most of the time the ARVN were more often at the sharp end of the shooting war than the great majority of foreign troops: by the time the Allies left Vietnam more than one hundred thousand of them had died.

CHAPTER TWENTY-THREE

NIXON'S WAR

As Tacitus said of Rome, "They made a desert, and called it peace."
Can we ordain to ourselves the awful majesty of God: to decide what
cities and villages are to be destroyed, who will live and who will die,
and who will join the refugees of our creation?

—SENATOR ROBERT KENNEDY

The air operation that followed Rolling Thunder was code-
named "Linebacker." It was in two phases. The first, Linebacker I, which began in May 1972, was in reaction to Giap's Easter
Offensive, which is described in the next chapter.

It was President Nixon's decision to increase the bomber force in the Pacific and Thailand that saved the army of the South during that offensive. As soon as the president was told of the scale and intensity of the attack, he ordered the return of air squadrons that had already left Vietnam and turned back navy carriers that were on their way home across the Pacific to the United States. The crucial retaliatory element, the B-52 force, was increased from 83 at the end of March to 171 by mid May.

After the end of the Easter Offensive, with the augmented force on station and with the post-Rolling Thunder peace talks again stalled, Nixon decided, in order to break the spirit of the communist regime once and for all, to take the war to the North in a way that had never been done before. (The peace talks had begun in May 1968 and had continued on and off ever since, the North Vietnamese stalling for time and concessions, the United States trying to find an honorable way out of its commitment in Vietnam.)

On 9 May 1972 the first attacks began with the mining of North Vietnamese ports. From then on, day after day, flights of tactical strike aircraft hit inland targets. But not without retaliation. When Linebacker I began, the North Vietnamese Air Force had 204 Russian MIG-21s, deployed on seven airfields. In the early phases of the operation between 15 and 40 of them at a time would take on the USAF planes, which were also likely to encounter barrages of up to a hundred un-guided surface-to-air missiles (SAMs), in this case the Russian SA-2. By firing them "free," without using the guiding radar beams up which they normally rode, the Vietnamese were able to conceal the location of their SAM sites from the electronic gear in the planes that could pick up the track of a missile and trace it back to its point of origin; which, thus identified, could be attacked by supporting planes. Also, the appearance of missiles on the radar screens of the USAF planes diverted the attention of the aircrews long enough for the MIGs to get into position to attack from the rear. On 11 May 1972 they got through with this tactic, and the first U.S. plane to be lost over Hanoi, an F-105G, was shot down.

During September 1972 the USAF added to its strike potential by deploying 48 F-111s with all-weather night-flying capability to a base in Thailand. Able to carry enough high octane to complete a sortie without refueling, these ultrasophisticated planes, with their new terrain-following radar, could come in low over the mountains that distantly ring Hanoi and drop their bomb loads automatically. Using on-board computers that kept track of the distance traveled, and fixed the position of the plane relative to geo-static satellites in the sky, the pilot could release the bombs at precisely the right moment without ever having to see the target.

The rationale behind aerial bombardment was summed up by ex-General Maxwell D. Taylor, then ambassador in Saigon: "I was convinced we could get at least three advantages in the use of our air power. First, morale in South Vietnam: it would give them the feeling of striking back, which would mean a great deal to them. Secondly, a great deal of war equipment and manpower was being sent in by the North. I had no impression that we could stop that, but at least we could inflict losses—we could slow it down. Finally, I felt the air arm gave us a device by which, if used gradually and decisively, we could convince Hanoi that the price was too great to pay. We visualized a progressive movement of air strikes of increasing intensity toward Hanoi until they were faced with the obliteration of the capital if they didn't come to the negotiating table and seek a solution."

As to morale, it is doubtful if the South Vietnamese man and woman in the street knew much about the bombings, or cared; their concerns were closer to home. As to slowing down the flow of material, yes, Linebacker I seriously disrupted the rail supply network in the North, but the logistic supply system was urgently adapted to the use of road transport, which made up for the loss of rail-carrying potential. As to increasing the intensity of bombing, that did come to pass, and helped to bring the North to the negotiating table.

By the autumn of 1972 Giap's Easter Offensive had diminished in force, primarily because of the carnage created by the B-52 bombing of his infantry. With the government of the North proposing that peace negotiations should be renewed, in October the air war was restricted to targets below the 20th Parallel; that is, selectively against the southward flow of supplies near and over the demarcation line. Expecting a cease-fire, the U.S. command maintained this lower level into December 1972.

On 18 December 1972, with the peace talks stalled yet again and with reports of continued infiltration by PAVN troops into the South, President Nixon ordered the resumption of air attacks north of the 20th Parallel. Linebacker II, with its massive strikes against transportation, power, and storage facilities around Hanoi and Haiphong, was the most intense use of American air power since World War II. Round-the-clock attacks were made, in darkness by F-111 and B-52 all-weather bombers, in daylight by tactical strike aircraft.

Night sorties reduced the ability of North Vietnamese fighter planes to find the bombers and prevented surface-to-air missiles from being directed visually on to them. They were incredibly complex and precisely timed operations.

An integrated swarm of planes assembled high in the sky and then, like a great cloud of eagles surrounded by falcons, flew over the frontier to hit targets selected by photo-reconnaissance and "seen" from above by radar screens in the bombers. F-4 fighters escorted the B-52s, which used their ECM (electronic countermeasure) equipment to deflect and baffle the Vietnamese radar beams searching for them. EB-66 ECM planes orbited around the B-52s to thicken up the electronic barrage while chaff corridors (swathes of foil dropped fluttering through the sky to resemble the "signature" of an aircraft on radar screens, and cause further confusion) were laid by F-4s escorted by other F-4 aircraft: they could produce a chaff corridor five miles wide and a hundred miles long, enough to blanket the entire entry and exit routes of the bombers. Other F-4s flew anti-MIG Combat Air Patrols (MIGCAPs) above and around the bombers, ready to ward off any night fighters that tried to engage them. As further protection F-105G Wild Weasel aircraft carried antiradiation missiles that homed in on enemy radars (though they usually destroyed only the radar vans in the center of the site and left the SAMs undamaged). Tanker aircraft flew above the formation to refuel aircraft en route as required. With everything thus fully integrated, the mass of planes then flew steadily, a locust horde in the sky, into what was known as Route Package Six—a designated area that included Hanoi and Haiphong—picked out their targets and attacked them. It was a masterpiece of coordinated air warfare, the like of which had never been seen before.

But first, F-111s took out SAM sites and airfields in what was known in air force jargon as a Low-Low One-Time pass. Using their terrain-following radars, they flew in undetected at low altitudes (radar beams cannot bend around the earth's curvature, so planes can sneak in below them), slammed and then scooted, still at low level, just minutes before the B-52 bombardiers opened their bomb bays. In effect, they made the Vietnamese air defenses keep their heads down until the heavy stuff arrived.

The F-111s struck throughout the night, bracketed by waves of B-52s with all their associated protection. Often three waves of B-52s, one after the other, would hit railways, power stations, warehouses, SAM and gun sites in a single night. The attendant planes, after being resupplied and changing pilots, then supported the daylight strikes.

Daylight "Tacair" attacks were made by F-4 and A-7 aircraft that carried heavy loads of bombs and rockets designed to take on ground targets with devastating effect. If visibility was poor, the planes were guided in by F-4 Long Range Navigation-equipped (LORAN) Pathfinders. If it was not, F-4s equipped with laser-guided bombs struck high priority targets with pinpoint accuracy; a pilot would point a laser beam at a target, which would reflect an upended cone of light into the sky into which a bomb fitted with guidance systems would be dropped and then, "contained" within the cone, hit the target. (On one day in May 1972 the USAF destroyed five railway bridges in this way using only twenty-four bombs: more than two thousand would have been needed to do it by conventional means.) Support for daytime strikes was similar to that for night attacks except that U.S. Marine Corps pilots flew the anti-MIG shield instead of USAF pilots.

In the eleven days of what became known as the Christmas Bombing of 1972, B-52s flew seven hundred sorties and F-111s a thousand. (A typical B-52 bomb load was 84 × 500-pound bombs carried internally and 24 × 750-pound bombs slung under the wings: twenty-seven tons of explosive ordnance. They flew so high that to ensure accuracy of bombing their on-board computers made allowance for the spin of the earth through the firmament.) On 18 December the flock of bombers comprised 121 B-52s—and over a hundred thereafter on every day of the offensive.

By 29 December 100,000 bombs had been dropped. The USAF estimated that in response Giap's soldiers fired 1,242 SAMs at their planes. American pilots shot down eight MIGs for the loss of twenty-six B-52s (each of them costing nearly eight million dollars)—three of them downed by MIGs, the rest by missiles. The Vietnamese admitted 1,318 deaths in Hanoi, but gave no figures for elsewhere—primarily because they did not know what they were.

On 18 January 1973 a ceasefire came into effect. After that it was words and more words as the details of the peace were ironed out.

It has been said that Linebacker II finally brought about the end of the Vietnam war, but Giap says that this was not so. It hurt the North, yes, but having faith in the ability of the people to withstand the raids, Hanoi was confident that the war could have gone on. The Politburo interpreted the end of the Christmas Bombing as the culmination of a last desperate effort by the United States to end the war. Now, they argued, the Americans would be prepared to make concessions; now was the time to cash in and avoid further bloodshed and damage.

One of the reasons why the people showed such spirit was that the government had made practical arrangements to cope with the air attacks. In December nearly all schoolchildren, nonessential workers, and government offices had been evacuated out of the city. Many air-raid shelters had been constructed during the Rolling Thunder attacks, and also every few feet along most streets in Hanoi and Haiphong there were one-person bolt-holes made of concrete piping sunk into the verges. In Hanoi there were about three for every person in the city. (The principle was one shelter close to home, one close to the place of work, and one along the way, in case people were caught between home and work.) Each shelter had a thick concrete cover that could be pulled over the top. When the sirens sounded, virtually the whole of what remained of the population vanished from sight. Another measure was that it was compulsory for children to wear green camouflage on their way to and from school so that in the event of a raid they could run and hide in the fields.

In addition, throughout North Vietnam no less than 2 million men and women had been formed into what were called "Shock Brigades," which went wherever they were needed to repair the effects of air-raid damage, especially to roads and railways. The slogan for them and for workers in the factories was "Combat and Construct." With so many men away in the army, 70 percent of the brigades were women—and half the self-defense forces in the villages and towns were women too, all trained to fight with anti-aircraft guns, rocket launchers, grenades, and rifles. (Young women plaited their hair in pigtails to keep it away from the bolts and triggers of their rifles.) Production sources were dispersed over sometimes dozens of locations to minimize the effect of the loss by bombing of any one of them. And families too were split up for the same reason.

Everyone shared the danger, everyone lived at a basic subsistence level. The rice ration was less than two pounds per person per day. The cloth ration was five yards per person per year, which was enough for two new shirts and a pair of trousers. All workers, even the members of the Politburo, were paid the equivalent of ten dollars a month.

With such highly integrated modern weapons, the Vietnamese could engage American planes from ground level up to close on one hundred thousand feet, the SA-2's maximum effective height. Missiles were directed to their targets by radar beams; MIGs were vectored on to attacking planes by ground controllers. Often, spies in American headquarters and near their air bases, as had happened during the Khe Sanh battle, warned the high command in Hanoi of the structure of the attacking force and its destination as soon as it was airborne, a priceless asset to the North. But even when that sort of information was not available, by studying radar screens and watching the buildup of the strike force as the planes took station in the sky, the Vietnamese could soon get a good indication of the line of flight, the target, and when the bombs were likely to start falling, enabling them to take preventive action. Their Ground Control Intercept (GCI) tracking radars gave about forty-five minutes' warning, enough time to get the MIGs into the sky and into battle far away from the targets and while the USAF planes were heavy with bombs and fuel and at their least maneuverable.

But not only sophisticated weapons were used. A wall of small-caliber bullets fired, however inaccurately, at low-flying aircraft was surprisingly effective in shooting fast jets down. The slightest puncture of the metal skin of a plane flying near the speed of sound was enough to rip it apart. Giap comments:

> The militia and self-defense forces played a great role during the war. With "plough in one hand and rifle in the other," young and old people, men and women, in the countryside and the towns, actively participated in shooting down enemy planes, forming a low-altitude anti-aircraft fire network that covered the whole country. They closely cooperated with the air defense force and the air force in forming a fire network for different altitudes and directions, one that was mobile and able to fight in different conditions, covering large areas but concentrating on the defense of a number of key objectives. Using infantry weapons, militias and guerillas shot down many modern American jet planes and captured a large number of pilots. They also defused tens of thousands of tons of bombs and mines of the latest types. Shooting at enemy planes flying at low altitude was clearly a new form of warfare in the land-against-air people's war.

Giap offers a scathing general indictment of American tactics in the air war: "There were far too many targets, and so they dispersed their effort. They used planes worth millions to attack a bamboo pontoon bridge!"

But primitive tactics like that were only a small part of the story. The air defense that Giap created was amazingly complex and by 1972 was rated by the world's greatest experts in the field—the Americans themselves—to be comparable only to NATO's highly sophisticated network for the defense of Western Europe, better even than that deployed for the protection of the Ruhr in Germany in 1945.

To Giap pride of place went to the twenty-seven-foot-long Russian SA-2s and their guidance systems, which he received soon after the USAF first began attacking the North. Within weeks he had more than two hundred operational SAM sites. In second place were his Soviet MIG-21s, fast interceptor fighters flown by Vietnamese pilots trained in Russia. (Giap had also obtained his first MIGs in 1965.) Backing them up were around four thousand guns of calibers between 23mm and 100mm, two thousand of them alone deployed to defend Hanoi and Haiphong. Their fire, and the launching of the missiles, was directed by two hundred or so radars which, together with the fighters, were coordinated by three major GCI stations at Bac Mai, Phuc Yen, and Kep. Overall command of the air defenses was exercised from a control center located at Hanoi's Bac Mai air base. Giap had a total of 125,000 men and women operating his air defenses—plus several thousand Russian advisers in key posts in the system.

Though by today's standards the SA-2 is a dinosaur, in its day it was a weapon to be reckoned with. Highly mobile, the launchers could be moved half an hour after firing and be back in action again an hour after that, their missiles at the ready. Such flexibility, making the sites very difficult to find, was a great asset, as was the SA-2's high reach into the sky.

Throughout Linebacker I and II there was a constant move and countermove of tactics as the attackers and the defenders tried to beat each other. One gambit was for the SA-2 operators to launch an unguided missile and then switch on its guidance radar at the last moment, allowing just enough time for the missile to be guided on to its target but not long enough for the anti-SA missiles carried by the planes to lock on to the radar beam and destroy the SA-2s. (On 22 November a SAM found its quarry and brought down a B-52. One of the lessons learned by the Americans from that incident was that the relatively narrow chaff corridors through which the bombers flew did not provide protection if winds blew the chaff out of the planned B-52 routes.) Another ploy was to launch at least two SA-2s in sequence. The first, fired high, would cause the target to take evasive electronic action. While its defensive mechanisms were so engaged, others fired behind it rode the track of the first until they locked on to the target and destroyed it.

But the Vietnamese did not have it all their own way: because of the effectiveness of the USAF anti-radiation missiles and cluster bomb units, SAM acquisition radars could only be used in short bursts if they were to avoid giving away their location and thus becoming a target. Also, the launchers had to be moved frequently, causing disruption and loss of efficiency.

The number of bombs dropped on North Vietnam during Line-backer I and II was: by B-52s 35,544, on 734 targets; by F-111s, 1,424, on 139 targets; by F-4s, 2,271, on 254 targets; by A-7s, 1,702, on 226 targets, making a grand total of 40,941.

More bombs were dropped on Vietnam in the three months of April, May, and June 1972, when Nixon was president, than fell on the country in a whole year during Johnson's bombing campaigns. During Nixon's tenure of office, while American troops were being withdrawn from Vietnam, the people of Vietnam, Cambodia, and Laos were bombed more than during the whole of Johnson's time in the White House.

Between 1964 and 1971, in the whole of what had been French Indochina, 6.2 million tons of bombs were dropped—three hundred pounds' weight of bombs for every man, woman, and child; twenty-two tons of bombs for every square mile. Add the amount dropped during Linebacker I and II, and the total becomes nearly 8 million tons, four times the whole tonnage by all forces everywhere during World War II.

In addition to bombing, in total during the war years the USAF carried out more than nineteen thousand defoliant missions: over much of South Vietnam and parts of Laos and Cambodia, Agent Orange was used to strip hardwoods and mangroves of their leaves, Agent White to kill off underbrush, Agent Blue to shrivel the green shoots in the rice paddies.

American aircraft losses during the entire Vietnam war were: helicopters, 4,869 (12 over the North), fixed wing 3,726 (2,651 due to enemy action, 1,100 over the North). They cost $225.2 billion. More than eight thousand American airmen died.

Here are two contrasting views of the air war, seen from opposite ends of the telescope.

Captain Frank D. Lewis of the USAF, taken prisoner by the North Vietnamese and incarcerated in the "Hanoi Hilton," was to write:

I had been asleep about a couple of hours when I was awakened by the air-raid sirens. I had completely forgotten that the old USAF would be back to bomb these turkeys again tonight. I was elated! The sirens went on for about fifteen minutes and then it was dead quiet. None of the background prison noises that I had heard were present. Then the anti-aircraft artillery began firing and picked up in intensity. I could hear close and distant reports. It was all over the place. And then I heard two of the most beautiful sounds I had ever heard. *Kablammm!* And a few seconds later another *kablamm!* I instinctively knew that two One-elevens had passed close by, low and supersonic. The shutters shook. Dust and plaster fell off the ceiling on to me. A few seconds later there followed *boom, boom, boom, boom boom, boom* . . . I could hear their bombs going off. I couldn't keep quiet and danced around my cell like a fool, yelling and cheering. The sounds of AA fire died off in the distance. Everything was quiet again. I knew what would be coming pretty soon.

About ten minutes later the sirens went off again and the AA started up. The sirens quit but the AA continued intermittently. I could hardly wait. Then a new sound occurred. It was a low-level *whooosh*. It had to have been a SAM. Then there were more *whooshes* and heavy-caliber AA explosions. And then the sound came, off in the distance, faint at first but louder as it approached: overlapping explosions of the B-52 strings were marching across the ground in the distance around what must have been the outskirts of Hanoi. Each separate string lasted a long time. They seemed to be coming nearer. It sounded like Godzilla was crunching around the city. Three of these bomb strings started pretty close and came in my direction. Their overlapping explosions were so intense that the walls of the cell shook; the bars and shutters shook so violently that I thought they would fall out; plaster and debris fell all around me. It was absolutely the most awesome sound show I had ever heard. I recall hoping that the navigators had remembered to set their offsets. The AA reports were intense and the *whooshes* of the SAMs came more frequently. I jumped around and yelled with delight. . . .

Never again in the next three months would I ever feel alone. It was the ultimate deus ex machina. I prayed for the men, the crews, and the aircraft they flew. To me they had become the hand of God that had reached out to bring me an inner peace and strength with which I could endure this cruel land.

Nyguyen Thi Huynh:

I am thirty-one years old, unmarried, and the only daughter in my family. I am a captain in the army, and work in the Military Museum. My parents are both still alive, and grow vegetables in one of the suburbs of Hanoi, selling them by the roadside locally.

In 1972, when I was fourteen, the U.S. bombed Hanoi for ten days, day and night, except for Christmas night. The next night they bombed the populated area in Com Pien Street. At the time I was in the eighth grade of my school, which was seven kilometers away and which I went to daily, except for Sundays, on my bicycle. Because of the bombing I could go to school only on some days, and when I did I had to carry a bag with medicines for first-aid in case I was wounded. Also, I had to wear a straw hat on my head to stop pieces of metal that fell from the sky when the guns fired.

When the bombers came, I and my classmates had to stop our lessons and hide in the shelters around the school, holes in the ground into which a few at a time could go. On nearly all the roads in Hanoi one-man shelters had been dug so that people could take cover when the bombers came. Even when I was sleeping at home I had to run to the shelter. All my family did the same except my father; he seemed not to be afraid, and slept through the raids in spite of the bombs. My mother worried very much for him.

The air-raid warning was given on Radio Hanoi when the bombers were about thirty kilometers from the city, and then we would run to the shelters. My youngest brother was only one year old, but he also had to go to the shelter. My parents thought about going away to the countryside, but we did not like to, we would miss our home, so my family made a shelter under the bamboo, and made it like a home. We put nice pictures in it and even had the oil lamp there. Sometimes we slept there all night because often there were many alerts during one night.

Many people had left the city, but some stayed to do their work or because they were in the self-defense forces, some of them firing anti-aircraft weapons. Many people who left the city were bombed while they were on the roads.

We were very lucky that no bombs were dropped by our place, but we heard the sound of bombs and the loud noise of the artillery near our house. The bombers hit the radio station in Hanoi, and also other targets. Sometimes in daytime we could see the U.S. planes that were bombing, high up, and once I saw a plane fall out of the sky and a pilot wearing a red uniform falling down on a parachute. He was high-ranking, which is why he wore red.

Nobody liked the war, which stopped all our activities and delayed the progress of our society. The consequences are very heavy for the many people who lost their relatives. I and all of my friends know many people who died.

We did not hate the American people. Most of them were our friends, and many of them protested against the war in Vietnam. It was not the people who were to blame, it was the state.

CHAPTER TWENTY-FOUR

THE LAST BATTLES

The bastards have never been bombed like they're going to be bombed this time.

—RICHARD NIXON,
DURING THE EASTER OFFENSIVE

Tet and Khe Sanh had been great watersheds in the war. The Americans no longer believed that they would find a military solution to the conflict; the Vietcong were badly debilitated, and many of the survivors had drifted back to their homes, disheartened because despite years and years of conflict there was no sign of victory. Colonel General Tran Van Tra, at the time commander of the region south of the central highlands, wrote: "Our cadres and men were fatigued. We had not had time to make up for our losses, all units were in disarray, there was a lack of manpower, there were shortages of food and ammunition." To replace the Tet losses Giap rushed between eighty thousand and ninety thousand troops down the Trail, but they were of low quality: only 40 percent of them had more than six months' service and 50 percent of them had less than three months' service—including the time they spent on the journey. It would be years before the PLAF could resume their activities with the same degree of intensity; without their close support the People's Army could not operate in the South in the way it had in the past.

After Tet Giap had come to the conclusion that from a military point of view the war was deadlocked: though he would never be able to match the United States in military strength, the United States would never be able to beat his army because so much of their fighting strength was involved in guarding their gigantic base installations.

In May 1968 Truong Chinh, who had been one of Giap's deputies during the battle of Dien Bien Phu but was now a senior member of the Politburo, set out a plan for a change of strategy. First, he said, Tet had been a mistake because it was assumed the population were ready to revolt, when they were not: COSVN had not built the necessary political base. Second, Tet had altered the correlation of forces in favor of the Americans. In such an adverse situation Lenin had advocated a shift from the offensive to the defensive; to protracted war in order "to gain time, to build up strength, to dishearten the enemy." They should follow his advice. Third, in the North they should concentrate on bettering the economy and let the South get on with their own war.

Le Duan and others in the cabinet opposed Truong Chinh's ideas, saying that they should stay on the offensive, but were overruled. So it was decided to play the long-haul card—the certainty that the United States would not have the will to continue the fight indefinitely. Eventually, the strategy would have to be changed from guerrilla to conventional warfare (as Giap put it, "Great strides would [now] be made only through regular war in which the main forces would fight in a concentrated manner"), but it would be a long time before this could be achieved. Meanwhile, the psychological war against the United States must continue. Giap urged COSVN to continue low-key guerrilla warfare as far as possible. Not that they had given up.

COSVN had organized a mini-Tet at the end of May 1968, but it was snuffed out quickly. Then there was another attempt in August, but that too went off at half cock and was even less successful. Having come to terms with the knowledge that they did not have the strength to do more, for the next four years small-unit guerrilla warfare continued. In response, the Army of the Republic and the diminishing number of Allied troops tried to clear PLAF-dominated areas and "pacify" the rural population—with some success.

Though this new North Vietnamese doctrine was generally a negative one, Giap and his colleagues were able to turn it into grand strategy of the highest order: by prolonging the peace negotiations while at the same time killing American soldiers and airmen wherever and whenever they could, Hanoi eroded American public support for the war more and more. Karl von Clausewitz's most-quoted phrase is that "war is a continuation of diplomacy by other means": Hanoi made the negotiations the continuation of war by other means.

At the peace talks the United States was represented by Henry Kissinger. Kissinger was a German who had come to the United States in 1938, served in the army in Europe during World War II, and then gone to Harvard University, where he gained a Ph.D. A consultant on arms control and foreign policy to Presidents Kennedy and Johnson, he was appointed by Nixon to be his special assistant on national security affairs. The North Vietnamese were represented by that hard man Le Doc Tho, the poet of the "thousand, thousand repressions."

Beginning in August 1969, Kissinger, while the "official" talks were going on in central Paris, held secret talks with Le Doc Tho in a suburb. He proposed a "two-track" solution whereby the United

States and the North Vietnamese would withdraw their troops and leave the South Vietnamese to sort things out with the Vietcong. Hanoi declined, demanding the removal of President Thieu, the South Vietnamese leader. The United States declined to dump him. In 1971 pressure to end the war increased, and in order to exploit strained Russian-Chinese relationships, Kissinger went to Peking to arrange the visit there of President Nixon the next year.

From time to time between December 1965 and May 1968, the United States ordered the cessation of bombing in order to coerce Hanoi into negotiating an acceptable agreement, but it was not until January 1969, when Richard Nixon became president and showed that he was every bit as determined to win the war as his predecessor, thus ending any hopes they had for a change of American attitudes, that the North Vietnamese seriously began to think of trying to find a way to end the war. The crucial factor that finally tipped the balance was President Nixon's visit to Peking, which made the Politburo in Hanoi doubt that China would continue to support them as much as it had in the past.

During 1972 both Washington and Hanoi moderated their positions, and by October an agreement had been thrashed out. President Thieu declined to agree to it. In December, President Nixon ordered the Christmas Bombing, and in January 1973 the formal agreement was signed. North Vietnamese troops would remain in the South, and so would President Thieu.

Throughout the negotiations Kissinger had had no high cards to play: as far as the United States was concerned, the talks were aimed at achieving an undertaking that the South would continue to exist as a separate nation, but he knew that, whatever was promised by Hanoi, after American troops departed Saigon would be vulnerable.

Henry Kissinger and Le Doc Tho were awarded the Nobel Peace Prize for their work in at last achieving a cease-fire. Le Doc Tho declined to accept his.

Another example of Giap's application of grand strategy was that from time to time during the long years of the war he diverted the attention of his opponents by threatening to outflank them in Cambodia and Laos, thus taking their eyes off the ball and making them spread their resources instead of being able to concentrate them in key areas in South Vietnam. Apart from the tens of thousands of men and women he employed to run the Ho Chi Minh Trail, he now and then committed other troops to independent operations, or mounted them in conjunction with the Pathet Lao. Whenever the opposition lowered their guard, he raised the ante again. In Saigon and Washington the western flank could never be forgotten.

In March 1969, in an attempt to stop supplies for Giap's soldiers and the PLAF coming in through the port of Sihanoukville (Kampong Som), and in retaliation for renewed communist activity in South Vietnam, President Nixon ordered the secret bombing of Cambodia in an operation code-named "Menu." Since Cambodia was ostensibly neutral, only the president, Henry Kissinger, and the defense secretary, Melvin Laird, plus a few congressmen, knew about the operation, and elaborate measures had to be taken to keep it secret. Not even the air force chief of staff was told. Considering the number of servicemen and other people involved, it is amazing that secrecy was maintained until the operation was revealed by the *New York Times* in May. Originally, Menu was meant to last only a few weeks, but in May 1970 it was extended to include support for the Cambodian army in their operations against the Khmer Rouge, the anti-government, Chinese-backed force. By the time it ended in August 1973, B-52s had flown 16,527 sorties and dropped nearly four hundred thousand tons of bombs.

In early 1969 Giap had ordered his soldiers to widen the scope of their operations around the border area and encroach further into Cambodia. At about the same time, the United States cut off aid to Cambodia because its leader, Prince Norodom Sihanouk, had aligned himself too closely with the Chinese. This act, plus the looming threat from the PAVN, led the Cambodian cabinet to replace Sihanouk and take strong anticommunist action. They sent the Cambodian army east to try to flush out the PAVN camps; to counter that, in early 1970 Giap sent a force of about fifty thousand men toward Phnom Penh.

In Washington there was concern that Cambodia might fall to

Giap's troops. In retaliation, in April 1970 fifteen thousand Americans crossed into Cambodia, supported by the USAF. The aims of the operation, Freedom Deal, were to relieve pressure on the ragtag Cambodian army, attack Giap's border bases, and if possible capture the COSVN headquarters. Preceded by heavy air attacks the troops forged west and south, only to find that the enemy retreated as they advanced. Farther south, nearly nine thousand men of the ARVN met with some opposition for only two days before that too faded away. However, generally the operations were a success: the American and South Vietnamese troops deflected Giap's attacks, destroyed many communist bases, and captured large quantities of equipment—for example, in total 28,500 weapons and nearly 17 million rounds of small-arms ammunition. They also killed or captured an estimated thirteen thousand enemy troops. However, they failed to eliminate the elusive COSVN—which, it turned out, had gone north across the Mekong on 19 March. On 30 June the ground operations ended and the troops were withdrawn.

Though the Cambodian incursion was justified as being intended to throw Giap off balance and prevent his interfering with American troop withdrawals, it did not have that effect, for he had no intention of interfering. He was quietly restructuring and re-equipping the PAVN and biding his time until there were only a few Americans left in the South. Instead, in the United States, Operation Freedom Deal caused yet another great surge of antiwar feeling, setting off more violent campus demonstrations all over the country, bringing bitter criticism in the media, and putting even more pressure on Nixon's administration. Shocked by its apparent inability to control events, Congress passed legislation prohibiting the use of American troops in Laos or Thailand.

Eight months after the Cambodian operation, in February 1971, ARVN soldiers, again strongly supported by the USAF, invaded Laos in an operation that was, according to Henry Kissinger, "conceived in doubt and assailed by skepticism." Thirty thousand men went to do battle, but with pusillanimous orders from Saigon to cease their activities if they suffered more than three thousand casualties: they did, stopped halfway to their objective, and then withdrew in confusion. Operation Lam Son 719 did nothing at all to choke off the steady flow of supplies down the Ho Chi Minh Trail, but worse still the ARVN had failed lamentably in its first major test unsupported by American ground forces. Yet despite this, on 7 April President Nixon reported to the nation that "Vietnamization" had succeeded. It certainly had not, and the worsening of morale that resulted from this debacle exacerbated tensions in the disintegrating rump of the American forces in the South.

By the spring of 1972 Giap was ready. Leaving only one division in reserve in North Vietnam he committed the majority of the PAVN, including troops withdrawn from Laos, to a massive conventional assault across the demilitarized zone, using a force of some 125,000 men in twenty divisions—a bigger army than General George Patton had commanded in World War II.

At the 19th Plenum, held at the end of 1970, Giap had made an assessment that the American policy of Vietnamization was making progress, that pacification was making gains, and that the Vietcong were demoralized after their drubbing during the Tet Offensive. On the credit side, from his point of view American ground troops would be out of South Vietnam by the end of 1972, and President Nixon was under severe pressure from the antiwar dissenters. The incursion by the ARVN into Laos had clearly been a disaster and indicated that they would offer little resistance to a large-scale assault. He recommended, and the plenum agreed, that there should be a major offensive in the spring of 1972, with a view to inflicting heavy losses on the Americans in what would be an election year, with possibly disastrous consequences for President Nixon.

Operation Nguyen Hue, named after an eighteenth-century national hero, was aimed, Giap said, at "tilting the balance of forces through the use of main-force warfare and political initiative." If a clear-cut victory was not achieved the weight of force used would give strong bargaining power in the peace negotiations.

Giap's plan was based on three simultaneous assaults. The first would be an attack across the demilitarized zone by two divisions plus three infantry regiments toward Quang Tri, while another division drove in from the west toward Hue; as he had done in the 1968

Tet Offensive, he would create a major diversion in the North while at the same time trying to isolate and take over the two northern provinces. A second lunge would strike from the central highlands toward Pleiku and Kontum, with the aim of cutting the country in half. A third offensive, even farther south, would strike down Route 13 toward Saigon. Each of them would have two phases, a secondary thrust by fresh troops after the first had run out of steam.

It was a bold concept but not especially imaginative: given the terrain, the likely worthwhile objectives, and the disposition of forces on both sides, such a three-pronged attack was predictable. In other words, he did not have much choice. The new factor, though, that gave him hope for a major breakthrough this time, was the availability of Russian T-54 and T-72 tanks. For the first time, he would be able to use them in significant numbers; at last, he would be a twentieth-century general in every way, lacking only ground-attack aircraft for the support of his troops.

On the northern front the assault began on 30 March after a heavy artillery barrage. On 2 April most of the ARVN units facing the DMZ fled in panic, but Giap's troops could not break through and on 9 April withdrew to regroup. That done, on 1 May fresh units hooked across and took Quang Tri city.

In the center, the attack began on 1 April. PAVN units pushed steadily forward, and by late April it seemed possible that they would reach the sea and cut the country in half. Between 15 and 25 May the communist troops paused to resupply and replace their battle casualties and then made a strong push toward Kontum. In Washington the progress of Giap's troops was viewed with great alarm, but with the numbers of American troops now much reduced only massive air strikes could give the ARVN the support it needed. Once again the heavy bombers were called in to save the day. The People's Army faltered and pulled back.

In the South, the offensive began on 2 April. Again, as had happened farther north, the soldiers made progress but tac-air and B-52 sorties blunted the edge of their advance. The commanders on the ground were finding it difficult to integrate the movements of tanks and infantry. The tanks got bogged down in a town called An Loc and missed the opportunity to strike out toward Saigon. The capture on 18 April by an ARVN soldier of the plans for the next PAVN attack enabled the defending forces to beat off the assault, and by mid May operations in the South had ground to a halt. They were Giap's last in which American forces were directly involved.

CHAPTER TWENTY-FIVE

PEACE, AT LAST

Yes, we defeated the United States. But now we are plagued by problems. We do not have enough to eat. We are a poor, under-developed nation. Waging war is simple but running a country is very difficult.

—PHAM VAN DONG

In financial terms the cost of the Vietnam war to the United States was colossal, but the cost to the North Vietnamese was minimal, since the Russians and the Chinese picked up most of the bill. At the end the United States was shelling out more than 30 billion dollars a year while Russia and China were spending about 1 billion each.

In 1965 Aleksei Kosygin, prime minister of Russia, had gone to Hanoi and promised rubles worth the equivalent of 1 billion dollars a year in aid, in addition to all the millions that Russia had already given. (He also wanted to persuade the North Vietnamese regime to negotiate peace with the United States, but in that he was unsuccessful.) China too was generous throughout the war years and as well as financial and material aid sent thousands of expert advisers: at one time there were some forty thousand Chinese teachers and technicians in North Vietnam.

In human terms the Vietnam war cost a lot more. About 30,000 Americans had been killed in Vietnam when President Nixon took office; almost 10,000 more died in his first year as president. In the end the officially listed American casualties for the entire war were about 46,000 killed in action (of whom 13,000, or 30 percent, were regular soldiers), plus another 10,000 who lost their lives as a result of aircraft or other accidents. About 300,000 were wounded. In addition, more than 5,200 Allied troops died: 4,407 South Koreans, 469 Australians and New Zealanders, 350 Thais.

The Army of the Republic of Vietnam lost 137,000 killed and about 300,000 wounded. Between 335,000 and 415,000 South Vietnamese civilians died, and nearly three quarters of a million were wounded.

As to communist casualties, the PAVN and the PLAF suffered great numbers of dead and wounded, as did the many North Vietnamese noncombatants who inadvertently got in the way of a bomb or bullet. Giap admitted 600,000 casualties (not all battle casualties; the figure included an estimate of all those who succumbed to fever and disease): Washington claimed 800,000 in the People's Army and 1 million Vietcong. In all, perhaps 2.5 million North and South Vietnamese died, out of a combined population of about 32 million.

The war caused an estimated $400 million dollars worth of damage in the North (though how it could be accurately assessed is difficult to understand): with, in 1972, a gross national product of $1.7 million per annum, the worst in Asia, it was going to take a very long time for Hanoi and its provinces to recover.

By the time of the cease-fire, there were more than half a million refugees in the South. The total expenditure on refugees by the government of the South was less in a year than the United States spent on the war in half a day.

Lyndon Johnson died five days before the Paris agreement to end the Vietnam war was signed on 23 January 1973. It called for:

- A cease-fire in place; that is, wherever the troops were, they stayed.
- The withdrawal of U.S. forces from South Vietnam.
- An exchange of prisoners of war within sixty days.
- No more troops to be sent into South Vietnam by either side.

And it created two commissions to enforce the cease-fire.

In other words the United States, after years of negotiations, had to settle for the shameful minimum—the total withdrawal of its forces in exchange for the return of its prisoners of war. After all its efforts and casualties, it had achieved nothing, while the PAVN remained intact, in theater, and ready to fight on.

On 9 August 1974 President Nixon (re-elected in 1972) resigned in consequence of the Watergate scandal and was replaced by the vice-president, Gerald Ford. It is an interesting footnote to history that the people responsible for the Watergate break-in were part of the same group of government agents who had originally been tasked to try to hide the secret bombing of Cambodia.

The war with the United States might have been over, but Vo Nguyen Giap did not let up. To him, this was just another lap in the marathon that would end only when Vietnam was united.

At the 21st Plenum, held in October 1973, the leaders of the North decided to give priority to a military offensive instead of emphasizing political warfare. The stage was set for the final act—the liberation of the South, as they saw it.

By now Giap had been commander in chief for nearly twenty years, as well as holding political appointments. The armed forces of the North had grown steadily—the army was now the third largest in the world, over eight hundred thousand strong, and the air force and the navy claimed more of his time. He had to shed some of the load and became what might be called the emeritus commander in chief. Though remaining chairman of the Military Committee, Van Tien Dung took over the day-to-day business of running the army. It was Dung who planned the final assault and who led it.

Superficially, there seemed to be good reasons to think that even after the departure of the American forces the South would maintain its independence. There were 450,000 soldiers in the ARVN, and another 100,000 personnel in the air and naval forces, plus over half a million people in what were called the regional and popular forces, a "home-guard" version of Giap's guerrillas. And there were many thousands of South Vietnamese civilians who abhorred the idea of any merger with the North.

One group, obviously, were the past and present members of the South Vietnamese armed forces: should the communists ever arrive they would be the first to see the inside of a prison cell or be executed. Then there were the merchants who had made their pile out of the contracts paid for by the United States: money would not save them when the fingers began to point. And there were the countless civil servants or U.S. employees who in one role or another had helped the Americans to maintain their huge presence in the South: many of them had only been making a living, but that would not excuse them in the eyes of their accusers. And there were the ordinary people who knew that their standard of living would fall if the hard men from the North arrived and bled the South in order to boost the poor economy of the North. With all these interested parties anxious to keep the North at bay, the will to resist the communists should have been strong enough to keep them out. The key was held by the Army of the Republic.

In some respects well-equipped and well-trained, and armed with a military doctrine evolved over years of combat by the U.S. army, they should, in theory, have been up to the task. But less than half of them were in combat units, the rest being in a bloated logistic tail. Furthermore, because of economic difficulties, in 1974 President Thieu had slashed the defense budget drastically: pay, field training, spare parts, training ammunition, were all cut back; even the annual replacement of socks was cut from three pairs to two. And also, and much more significant, the soldiers did not have their heart in it.

The departure of the Americans had done nothing to stop the rampant graft, nepotism, and fraud that had existed for years; indeed, it just took the cork out of the bottle. Morale, efficiency, and discipline went from bad to worse. And, too, the young men who were conscripted came from families that had been divided or had had mixed loyalties all through the long years of war. Sons whose elder brothers had fought with the Vietcong joined the ARVN. Members of the Vietcong joined the ARVN because there was no work for them where they lived. It is not really surprising that when the attack came the ARVN fell apart in a few days. Some units and individuals fought hard, the well-led ones with the greatest conviction or the men who felt they had the most to lose, but they were in the minority.

Van Tien Dung, on 5 February 1975 appointed commander of the Saigon Liberation Campaign Command, led the attack on 8 April 1975 with twenty-two divisions organized in five army corps on five different axes of advance. On 25th March Hue fell to the communists, on 30th Da Nang. (On 7 April Le Duc Tho, veteran of the peace talks, arrived in the South to oversee the final debacle.) On the seventeenth, in an event that was to have awful long-term consequences, Phnom Penh, capital of Cambodia, fell to the forces of the Khmer Rouge led by Pol Pot. On the twenty-ninth, the last Americans left Saigon, and on the thirtieth Colonel Bui Tin took the surrender of the city. It was all over. Thirty years of fighting had ended.

The final campaign had all been too much for Dung's ARVN opponents. As Dung himself puts it, "After defeating the Americans and their puppets, we had captured large quantities of weapons and equipment. We had a sizeable quantity of modern technical equipment, and a strong force with which to take over the South."

And so they did.

Mai The Chinh, a soldier of the People's Army, told the author:

> I married in April 1967 and my wife was very anxious about me. Every half year we could send or receive letters, but I never told my wife just how bad the situation was, about the lack of food and the floods and the hail of bombs that fell all around. But I did tell her that if I died and she was under thirty years old she should marry again.

But I also said that if I died when she was over thirty years old, it was up to her whether she stayed with the children or married again. That is what I wrote to my wife.

I took part in the general offensive on Saigon. Five of our army corps attacked from five different directions. I was in the 3rd Corps attacking from the west toward Saigon. My unit started fighting in the high plateau and then followed Route 17 eastward. Mostly the enemy, the puppet troops, fled, but here and there they fought strongly. Thousands of them were captured. In many places there were piles of uniforms and weapons and helmets along the sides of the roads where they had got rid of them in order to pretend they were civilians.

There was competition to see who would be the first to fly the flag over the palace in Saigon, and everyone tried hard to win that honor. It was men from the 2nd Corps who got there first. We wished it had been us.

After the victory all the families of the soldiers were waiting for their men to come back. At the time my wife was on a course at the University of Hanoi. They told her that if she left the university in order to be able to meet me her course would have to be put back a year, but she left anyway, hoping her husband would return.

When it all ended I went by road for three days and nights from Saigon to Hanoi. I got back on the 1 June and met my wife.

You ask me what I thought of the Americans. We thought the Americans were handsome soldiers but looked as if they were made with flour.

When we made an attack, the cooperation between their infantry and artillery was very good. There was much we could learn from them about that and other things. But it was difficult for them to suffer all the hardships of the Vietnamese battlefront. When we had no water to drink, they had water for showers! We could suffer the hardships much better than they could. That, probably, was the main reason we won.

It took more than a year for the South to merge with the North, a year of appalling confusion and fear. In the United States television pictures of screeching men clinging to a helicopter's skids and falling off as it soared away from the flat roof of the American Embassy in

Saigon were the requiem for a long and disastrous episode for the American people. But for other people it was only another beginning.

A million men, women, and children left South Vietnam after unification, the first of the Boat People. About one hundred thousand of those who stayed behind were sent to "re-education" camps where the brainwashers got to work, trying to expunge capitalist ideas and substitute communist ones. The last of these people were kept in prison until June 1992, during the day cutting bamboo in the jungles, mostly, and in the evenings being taught the error of their ways. But generally things were not as bad as people had anticipated. The lessons of the agricultural reform program of 1956 had not been forgotten, and the aim now was to absorb and convert rather than eliminate. Even so, many died in the camps or while trying to escape from them. The people the communists considered to be capitalists of the most flagrant kind suffered the most.

Soon after the victory Giap and the rest of the Politburo came to Saigon to see the fruits of their victory. But he had not finished, even now.

In Cambodia Pol Pot, who had achieved his takeover with Chinese help, initiated a fearful social restructuring of his country. Most of the people in the towns and cities were forcibly evacuated and put to work on the land. If they protested, they were killed, as had been all educated people, including doctors, scientists, and administrators; they could think and organize and lead, and were therefore a danger to the new regime. The towns withered and died, and so did the crops in the countryside and the starving people who were desperately trying to grow them.

This cold-blooded experiment in political science cost the lives of between 2 and 3 million people; nobody knows, exactly, there were too many skulls to count. The holocaust stopped when soldiers of the PAVN invaded Cambodia in December 1978, an operation Giap masterminded and controlled. (They were to stay there until December 1989.)

The Vietnamese invasion was part of a broad plan to ensure that the whole of Indochina became communist. In August 1975 the Pathet Lao had seized control of Vientiane; after the invasion of Cambodia, a People's Republic was declared there on 7 January 1979. Effectively, Hanoi had achieved its aim. However the invasion of Cambodia was also triggered by fears in Hanoi that China would develop a political and military base there and outflank Vietnam.

China, not surprisingly, took exception to Vietnam's action, and in January 1979 the Chinese army invaded Cao Bang province in the north. After a few months, and the loss of some thirty thousand troops, they withdrew, having intended to teach the Vietnamese a lesson but having got one in return. For another eight years the two sides exchanged artillery fire across the border. The uneasy peace continues. (The last of the Vietnamese prisoners captured by the Chinese in 1979 were released in August 1991.)

At the beginning of the invasion of Cambodia and during the Chinese incursion into Vietnam, Giap had been at the center of decision making—as he had by this time for thirty-five years. In 1980 Van Tien Dung took over from him as minister for defense and commander in chief. He remained a member of the Politburo, however, with special responsibilities for science and technology and other government interests, and for several years was still a deputy chairman of the Council of Ministers.

In July 1991, a month before his eightieth birthday, Vo Nguyen Giap was not re-elected to the Politburo.

CHAPTER TWENTY-SIX

GIAP—
AN ASSESSMENT

We want to live in peace and friendship with all the nations of the world.

—VO NGUYEN GIAP, TO THE AUTHOR

This book has given an account of the life of Vo Nguyen Giap and the People's Army of Vietnam, though it is the people rather than the army who won the war. But then the people were the army: everyone a soldier . . .

Vietnamese men and women were the real victors of the wars—

stoic, determined, disciplined, tough, cheerful. But their military commander in chief was quite exceptional. Though Ho Chi Minh was the figurehead, it was Giap who carved out the victories. If Ho Chi Minh's "constituency" was the Party and Pham Van Dong's was the bureaucracy, Giap's was the army, and it was the people's army that won. To that extent he can claim the largest share of the credit for winning two major wars, for repelling the Chinese, and for securing the unification and independence of his nation. His many victories must place him as one of the great captains of all time. Even so, it is difficult to assess him.

There are four reasons why:

• First, in the nature of the regime he serves, decisions were made in committee; he was first among equals in the military sphere but not the sole arbiter of action.

• Second, for decades Vietnamese politics have dictated that Giap's part in his nation's history should not be too publicly commended lest he should become even more popular and a threat to the collective leadership. Amazingly, no biography of Giap has ever appeared in Vietnam; in the official history of the Vietnam war, his name is mentioned only once, though more often in the history of the Indochina War.

• Third, Vietnam remains a closed society, more open than it was a few years ago but for all that one that does not welcome close investigation of its past by people from the capitalist West. I was able to go to Hanoi because the door was opening, because I am an established author, because I had been a soldier—and was therefore more acceptable to Giap than a writer without a military background—and because I am British, and therefore less likely to be biased than someone from France or the United States.

• Last, Vietnamese are very private people; it is not thought proper to parade personal matters in public—to bare the soul for the benefit of strangers. Details of one's private life, of one's thoughts and feelings, are taboo, so biography in the Western sense is not possible.

However, enough information has been assembled to make an appraisal possible. The facts speak for themselves.

Giap's public life from 1944 until 1975 can be summarized in his battles, offensives, and enterprises. Of the many separately identifiable major initiatives in which he was involved, either as a general or in a ministerial capacity, he failed in four: his term of office as minister of the interior in 1946, the Red River Valley Offensive of 1951, the 1967/68 winter/spring campaign, the Easter Offensive of 1972.

Against these failures can be offset his great successes: the two low-level insurgencies in the Viet Bac in 1944–45 and 1947–48, the campaign on Route Coloniale 4, the battle of Dien Bien Phu, the aid to the PLAF, the creation of two new armed services, the distant coordination of the PAVN and PLAF, the creation of the Ho Chi Minh Trail, the anti-aircraft defense of Hanoi and Haiphong.

Giap was commander in chief of the army for thirty years and was involved in decision making at the highest levels of government for nearly fifty, both unprecedented in history. It is difficult to compare him with other generals because his combination of guerrilla and conventional action on such a scale has not been seen before.

In the main aspects of war, Giap was outstanding. Strategically, he showed depth of vision and grasp of the big issues, putting his opponents off balance through the judicious deployment of his troops in many places: in Laos, Cambodia, the Mekong delta, the central highlands, the coastal plain, around the demilitarized zone.

Tactically, he was a past master of guerrilla warfare—the most successful guerrilla leader of all time. As a conventional-war general he was innovative, as in his use of approach trenches at Dien Bien Phu to literally sap the strength of the defenders, the destruction of each defended position in turn, then the overwhelming of the remainder. He made timing, surprise, camouflage, and deception understood and applied by his soldiers to an amazing degree; for example, his troops hid themselves so well that often the first their opponents knew of their presence was when the point man was blown away by a burst of fire almost from under his feet; in comparison, American trenches in Vietnam, in places such as Khe Sanh, could be seen from space satellites orbiting the earth.

Logistically, he was brilliant throughout the Indochina War: without his mastery of logistics Dien Bien Phu would never have been fought. Likewise, during the Vietnam war the Ho Chi Minh Trail successfully supported his men and the Vietcong for years.

Seldom have great commanders shown such a balanced grasp of all the components of battle. And Giap could delegate, an essential ingredient of successful high command. How else could he have held such responsible positions for such a long time? He advocated leaving "decisions to the man on the spot, who knows the locality, the situation, the best timings for an endeavor."

Asked to comment on Giap's abilities as a soldier, General of the Army Marcelle Bigeard told me that he has great admiration for him. "He learned from his mistakes and did not repeat them." And, "he commanded victoriously for a remarkably long length of time; to do so for thirty years was a unique achievement." However, "to Giap a man's life was nothing."

For the Vietnamese too Bigeard has great respect: "They are courageous, straight, intelligent, hard-working." As he puts it with touching sincerity, "The Viets love us and we, the French, love them. One day we will be married . . ."

For his part General William C. Westmoreland too has great admiration for the Vietnamese. He trusted those he dealt with in the South, but "a big problem was that away from the towns the peasants had no respect for central government: to them it was just an extension, a continuation, of the colonial regime, and it was therefore difficult to get them on our side in the war." Also, "There were so many minorities; it was not a homogeneous society."

Asked to comment on Giap's qualities of leadership, specifically on the characteristics of decision making, resilience, the ability to concentrate the mind—and the intellect to weld all these together—Westmoreland replied that in his view Giap "had them all." He "was very determined, was a great general." But he was "over-optimistic: despite his efforts during the Tet Offensive, there was not one instance of the general uprising that he had expected." (In fact, Giap had consistently doubted the success of a general uprising in 1968. He was overruled.)

With regard to Giap's judgment of men, Westmoreland feels that

Giap "did not have too much talent to choose from." Surprisingly, in view of the fact that Giap was often impulsive, Westmoreland feels that Giap had good self-control: "Any commander at high level must have that quality or he would not last." Giap was bold and determined, was "able to dominate his soldiers because of the mystique that grew about him, a sort of aura of optimism." For all that, "he and his colleagues prolonged the war unnecessarily, and therefore the suffering of the people." Giap "believed his own propaganda; believed the things people told him because they thought they were the things he wanted to hear." Well, it was ever thus with people in high places, politicians or soldiers.

In a deeply felt comment in reply to the question of whether Giap had staying power, General Westmoreland said that for a general that depends on public opinion: "Without the public behind him no commander can prevail, however much personal conviction he may have." As to why the United States did not prevail, "The negative side of the war was given inordinate visibility [by the media], the positive hardly any." "Had the United States employed the massive power of the B-52s in 1968 as they did in 1972, Hanoi would have come to the negotiating table then; the war would have been shortened and thousands of American—and Vietnamese—lives would have been saved." But that reply begs the question of whether public opinion in the United States would have tolerated such action at that time. In 1968 the divisions in the nation were greater than at any time since the Civil War; in 1972 President Nixon could bank on the desperate impatience of the American people for a solution at almost any price.

What indication of the nature of Giap's mind do his published works give?

Often his thoughts when transferred to paper are deadly dull, a monotonous reiteration of jargon of the sort to be found anywhere in communist writings, as, for example, "Marx and Engels regarded the arming of the proletariat as indispensable to smashing the machinery of the state and to the eventual defeat of the bourgeoisie when they betrayed the masses after coming to power." But then suddenly there is a flight of fancy, a lifting up and away from the plebeian: "They for the first time showed the proletariat and oppressed peoples the correct way to create their own organization. Their teachings gave them wings for the revolutionary struggle to overthrow the old world and create a new one; their teachings became the theoretical basis for building the armed forces." But it is when he writes about war that his inspiring personality shines through, as here, referring to the battle of Dien Bien Phu:

> Logistics constantly posed problems as urgent as those posed by the armed struggle, precisely the difficulties that the enemy thought insuperable for us.
>
> The Vietnamese people, under the direct leadership of the committees of supply for the front, gave proof of great heroism and endurance in serving the front. Truck convoys valiantly crossed streams, mountains, and forests. . . . Thousands of bicycles from the towns also carried food and munitions to the front. Hundreds of sampans of all sizes, hundreds of thousands of bamboo rafts, crossed rapids and cascades to supply the front. Convoys of pack horses, from the Meo highlands or the provinces, headed for the front. Day and night hundreds of thousands of porters and young volunteers crossed passes and forded rivers in spite of enemy planes and delayed-action bombs. Never had so many young Vietnamese traveled so far. From the plains to the mountains, on roads and paths, on rivers and streams, everywhere, there was the same animation.

Animation indeed, in that writing.

Giap's communist beliefs had been nurtured since his teens but unfortunately over the years changed very little—unfortunately, because with his intellect he could have contributed new ideas, perhaps seen the flaws and changed the dogma and achieved a better life for his countrymen. But it seems that crouched in the branches of that tree in An Xa he found his bible, and from then on, like a medieval Christian who dreaded the frightful consequences of uttering the slightest heresy, slavishly followed The Word as interpreted by Ho Chi Minh out of Marx and Lenin. When he wrote about communism in later years, he had nothing to add of his own. But then, he was held in the straitjacket of the Politburo.

What, one wonders, does Giap make of the ending of communist rule in the states of Eastern Europe, the disbandment of the Warsaw Pact, the fragmentation of the Soviet Union, the falling apart of the world socialist order for which he had held such hopes?

As to an assessment of Giap's personality, various Western writers have said of Giap that he is vain, arrogant, evasive, surly, ruthless; that he is given to marathon monologues; that he wears expensive uniforms; that for decades he has been ill—with Parkinson's disease, with Hodgkin's disease—that he has had high blood pressure since 1954 and migraines since 1957.

My personal judgment is that he is modest but impatient, friendly but Olympian in his reserve—his past is there in his presence. He is evasive—but typically Vietnamese, it seems, in that respect: never say everything, always keep something in reserve. He is moody, but nevertheless has charm and a sense of humor. He is certainly prone to volubility; once started on a theme he is difficult to stop.

As to being ruthless, yes, no doubt he is, insofar as any successful high commander must have that characteristic in some degree. His personal involvement, in the sense of initiating or conniving at or supporting the atrocities that were perpetrated by the Hanoi regime during the suppression of the VNQDD in 1946 and the land reforms of 1956, will probably never be known. He personally cannot be blamed for the many civil war–type atrocities committed by the Vietcong in the South.

As to expensive uniforms, on the occasions when I met him he was wearing threadbare khaki without ribbons or badges of rank and with only a red patch on the lapels. The collar and cuffs were frayed, and when he came to go his aide helped him on with a sheepskin coat the leather of which was, here and there, worn black and shiny with age.

As to Parkinson's and Hodgkin's diseases and the other alleged maladies, the only sign of any physical abnormality was an occasional tic in his left eye. Other than that he showed no sign of any sickness and for a man of his age was remarkably agile. Until mid

1991 he worked a long day as chief of the Science and Technology Commission, responsible for steering Vietnam into an awareness of modern developments in those fields. He was also president, of all things, of the Vietnam Commission on Demography and Family Planning, a subject he preferred to avoid, presumably because it was a battle he was not winning.

Birth control is one of Vietnam's biggest problems, which is no doubt why he was given that responsibility. At the end of the Vietnam War the population was in excess of 30 million. By the 1970s it had surged to more than 40 million. By 1990 it was 60 million, making it one of the biggest nations in the world in terms of population: comparable to France, Germany, and the United Kingdom. Vietnam had famines when the population was 10 million, 5 million: it is almost certain that they will come again, even though at the moment Vietnam has become a leading rice-exporting country, the third biggest in the world.

In other things too the future looks bleak. Nearly half a million troops have been demobilized since 1987, adding to the number of unemployed, who now comprise more than 20 percent of the working pool. The Russians, with their economy tottering, have stopped giving financial aid to their socialist brethren. With China standing off and with the United States still refusing to give aid, or trade, Vietnam is now more isolated than it has ever been.

EPILOGUE

Most of the men who fought at Dien Bien Phu are dead. De Castries died in 1991, aged eighty-five and full of memories. Langlais made his last jump in 1988—to his death out of a high window, old and ill and forgotten. (When they heard about it his old comrades in Les Paras made sure he had an appropriate send-off.) Bigeard lives: in the shadow of the great medieval cathedral at Toul, aged seventy-five now but still jogging seven kilometers every day and swimming ten lengths of a pool; bright-eyed and forceful as ever, full of honors and much esteemed throughout France.

Thousands and thousands of Vietnam war veterans are alive, but not necessarily well. Smiling Nixon still lives. So does yet another paratrooper, Westmoreland, now seventy-seven but, like the tough old soldier he is, showing great resilience in the face of continuing criticism. (Westmoreland deserved a better deal than the hand he picked up and played skilfully, considering that some of the cards were missing from the pack.) McNamara still lives, silent as the grave. Lyndon B. Johnson went to his in his mid sixties, puzzled, desolate—a man who tried hard but got it wrong.

Giap still lives: ebullient, full of life. Victories are a great tonic for the soul. He got it right in so many ways, but as both Bigeard and

Westmoreland said of him, in almost identical words, in the end he got it wrong: the faith he put his faith in is discredited.

When I was leaving Hanoi, I was asked to send a bottle of whisky to Senior General Vo Nguyen Giap as a parting gift. I found it a very hard thing to do because it seemed insulting to him: did one of the great figures of the twentieth century need trivial handouts from a foreign visitor?

For me, that request epitomized the poverty of Hanoi: the broken electric cables lying on a pavement with children standing around staring at the sparks flying; the chipped paint and grime of the "best hotel," with blue flames coming out of its electricity junction boxes; the rats scurrying around in the restaurants; the paucity of tawdry goods in the shops; the feeling of imminent doom—of epidemics lurking just around the corner waiting to descend on an overburdened medical system in an overcrowded city bulging with people living crammed together in all sorts of shanty dwellings.

On the other side of the coin, the people I met and worked with were friendly, courteous, helpful, cheerful. And everywhere there seemed to be hundreds and hundreds of smiling, bright, chattering, cleanly dressed children. But for me, the effects of decades of war and communism, of the population explosion and unemployment, were all summed up in that request for a bottle of whisky as a paltry gift for an old man full of years and achievement.

This book is full of tragedies. The bones of millions of them, of many nationalities but mostly Vietnamese, lie in the bomb-drenched jungles of Indochina. The names of tens of thousands of them are carved in stone all over France and at the Foreign Legion headquarters in Corsica, and on a long, low, poignant, tapering arc of black shining marble near the Lincoln Memorial in Washington, D.C.

And in the hearts and minds of all those who mourn their passing, wherever they are.

Bristol
England
June 1992

BIBLIOGRAPHY

Barclay, G. *A Very Small Insurance Policy*. Brisbane: Queensland University Press, 1988.

Bibliography of the Vietnam Wars. New York: Burns and Luttenberg, 1977.

Buttinger, J. *A Dragon Defiant*. Newton Abbott: David & Charles, 1973.

Chen, King C. *Vietnam and China, 1938–54*. Princeton: Princeton University Press, 1969.

Cowley, M. C. *Communist Insurgent Infrastructure in South Vietnam; Organization and Strategy*. Washington, D.C.: Department of the Army, 1966.

Dao, Tran Hung. *Vietnamese Studies*, Nos. 2 and 43. Hanoi: Foreign Languages Publishing House, 1983.

Davidson, Lt.-Gen. Phillip B. *Vietnam at War*. Novato: Presidio Press, 1988.

Deans, C., & K. Leitenberg. *The Wars in Vietnam, Cambodia and Laos*. Santa Barbara: ABC-CLIO Information Services, 1984.

Dung, Van Tien. *Military Problems Today*. Hanoi: Foreign Languages Publishing House, 1982.

————. *Our Great Spring Victory*. New York: Monthly Review Press, 1977.

Elliott, D. & M. *Documents of an Elite Vietcong Unit; the Demolition Platoon of 514 Battalion*. Santa Monica: Rand Corporation, 1969.

Eschmann, K. J. *Linebacker*. New York: Ivy Books, 1989.

Fall, Bernard. *Hell in a Very Small Place*. New York: Lippincott, 1967.

————. *Street Without Joy*. London: Pall Mall Press, 1965.

Giap, Vo Nguyen. *Dien Bien Phu*. Hanoi: Foreign Languages Publishing House, 1984.

————. *The Military Art of People's War, Selected Writings*. New York: Monthly Review Press, 1971.

————. *The People's War for the Defense of the Homeland in the New Era*. Hanoi: Foreign Languages Publishing House, 1981.

————. *People's War, People's Army*. Foreword by Roger Hilsman. New York: Praeger, 1962.

————. *To Arm the Revolutionary Masses, to Build the People's Army*. Hanoi: Foreign Languages Publishing House, 1975.

————. *Unforgettable Days*. Hanoi: Foreign Languages Publishing House, 1974.

Grant, Z. *Facing the Phoenix*. New York: Norton, 1991.

Hauser, J. *America's Army in Crisis*. Baltimore: Johns Hopkins University Press, 1973.

Herr, M. *Dispatches*. New York: Avon Books, 1968.

Just, W. *Military Men*. London: Michael Joseph, 1970.

Karnov, S. *Vietnam, A History*. London: Hutchinson, 1983.

Krepinevich, A. F., Jr. *The Army and Vietnam*. Baltimore: Johns Hopkins University Press, 1986.

Maclear, M. *Vietnam: The Ten Thousand Day War*. London: Thames/Methuen, 1981.

Marshall, S. L. A. *Three Battles*. New York: Da Capa Publications, 1982.

McAllister, J. T. *Vietnam: The Origins of Revolution*. New York: Knopf, 1969.

McGarvey, P. J. *Visions of Victory*. Palo Alto: Stanford University Press, 1969.

O'Ballance, Edgar. *The Indochina War, 1945–1954*. London: Faber, 1964.

Oberdorfer, M. *Tet*. New York: Da Capa Publications, 1984.

Parker, F. Charles the IVth. *Strategy for a Stalemate*. Washington D.C.: Washington Institute, 1989.

Pike, Douglas. *History of Vietnamese Communism*. Stanford: Hoover Institute Press, 1978.

———. *The People's Army of Vietnam*. Novato: Presidio Press, 1986.

Pissor, R. *The End of the Line*. New York: Norton, 1982.

Prados, J., & W. Stubbe. *Valley of Decision*. Boston: Houghton Mifflin, 1991.

Rogers, General William D. *Cedar Falls & Junction City*. Washington D.C.: Department of the Army, 1974.

Sinh, Nguyen, and Vu Ky Lan. *Fighting at the 17th Parallel*. Hanoi: Red River Press, 1982.

Summers, Harry G. *On Strategy: A Critical Analysis*. New York: Bantam Doubleday, 1984.

———. *Vietnam War Almanac*. New York: Facts on File Publications, 1985.

Westmoreland, General William C. *A Soldier Reports*. New York: Doubleday, 1978.

Wintle, J. *Romancing Vietnam*. London: Viking, 1991.

———. *The Vietnam Wars*. London: Weidenfeld & Nicholson, 1991.

ANTHOLOGIES:

From the French Reconquest to Dien Bien Phu, Stories and Reportages, 1945–1954. Hanoi: Foreign Languages Publishing House, 1985.

The Ho Chi Minh Trail. Hanoi: Red River Press, 1982.

The Official History of the War Against France. Hanoi: Lich Su Quan Doi Nhan Dan, 1977.

The Official History of the War Against the United States of America. Hanoi: Lich Su Quan Doi Nhan Dan, 1988.

Reportages, 1945–54. Hanoi: Foreign Languages Publishing House, 1985.

The Vietnam Experience, 6 vols. New York: Time-Life Books, 1975–78.

Plus various pamphlets, articles, and reports appertaining to Vietnam and the wars therein of the twentieth century.

Plus fourteen taped interviews with Vietnamese veterans and officials. Also taped interviews with Generals Marcelle Bigeard and William C. Westmoreland.

INDEX